Marketing Strategy

Marketing Strategy

A Customer-Driven Approach

STEVEN P. SCHNAARS
Baruch College, The City University of New York

THE FREE PRESS
A Division of Macmillan, Inc.
NEW YORK

Maxwell Macmillan Canada
TORONTO

Maxwell Macmillan International
NEW YORK   OXFORD   SINGAPORE   SYDNEY

The Free Press
A Division of Macmillan, Inc.
866 Third Avenue, New York, N.Y. 10022

Maxwell Macmillan Canada, Inc.
1200 Eglinton Avenue East
Suite 200
Don Mills, Ontario M3C 3N1

Macmillan, Inc. is part of the Maxwell Communication Group of Companies.

Printed in the United States of America

printing number
3 4 5 6 7 8 9 10

Library of Congress Cataloging-in-Publication Data

Schnaars, Steven P.
   Marketing strategy: a customer-driven approach / Steven P. Schnaars.
      p.   cm.
   Includes bibliographical references.
   ISBN 0–02–927953–4
   1. Marketing—Management.   2. Strategic planning.   3. Competition.
I. Title.
HF5415.13.S345   1991
658.8'02—dc20   90–43633
                                                    CIP

Contents

[v]

Preface

This is a book about strategy from a marketing perspective. It examines marketing's contribution to strategy and strategy's contribution to marketing thought over the past three decades. It argues that today, more than ever before, strategy must be customer driven if it is to be successful.

The material presented in this book is organized around three major themes: (1) strategy's move towards marketing, (2) the move from fixed to flexible planning formulations, and (3) the connections among strategic concepts.

The Move Towards Marketing

This book begins with past strategic planning schemes that stressed competition and ignored consumers. It then moves steadily in the direction of strategic concepts that favor a consumer perspective. By the end of the book, the chapters focus on product quality, long-term consumer satisfaction, and the quick response to changes in consumers' needs.

This book offers an historical treatment of the subject, beginning with the past and ending up in the present. Like strategy itself, the flow of material mirrors the shift in emphasis in strategy from financial analogies to marketing ideas. The discussion begins with the Boston Consulting Group's Growth-Share Matrix, which holds that a firm gains competitive advantage solely through the accumulation of experience effects. The focus of that technique falls squarely on competitors. There is almost no discussion of consumers, their needs, or the products they desire. Competitive advantage is solely a function of production efficiency. It discusses Michael Porter's competitive strategies which are more cogniscent of consumers. As he (1985) notes: "Competitive advantage grows fundamentally out of value a firm is able to create for its buyers that exceeds the firm's cost of creating it" (p. 3).

The book then presents a series of separate chapters on product differentiation, market segmentation, product quality, long-term consumer satisfaction, and speeding new products to market. Each of those chapters stresses a customer-driven approach to marketing strategy.

From the Fixed to the Flexible

The topics covered in this book also flow from single-option, one-approach-is-always-right, views of marketing strategy to views that offer flexible responses and multiple options. Formula planning schemes, for example, offered a "canned" response to what turned out to be fluid strategic problems. In the 1970s, "good" strategy consisted of following a series of mechanical steps. Then, in 1980, Porter portrayed strategy as a choice between three strategic options. More recently, marketing strategy has focused on issues that are more difficult to define, such as customer satisfaction and product quality. As the book progresses, the discussion moves from regimented procedures to contemporary issues in strategy.

Connections in Marketing Strategy

This book traces the historical developments in marketing strategy, beginning with formula planning and ending with a series of current issues in marketing strategy. The intent is not to cover old ideas, but to illustrate how ideas in strategy have progressed over the years. It would be incorrect to conclude that the history of strategy is characterized by a series of fads, which are embraced and discarded with each new decade. Marketing strategy is more than the adoption and rejection of disconnected ideas. The central premise of this book is that over the decades there has been a slow and steady evolution in marketing strategy thought. Clearly, today's ideas are rooted deeply in the past.

The overarching objective of this book is to give the reader a deeper understanding of where marketing strategy came from and to point where it is headed. No magic formula is recommended. Instead, by tracing the flow of ideas over the decades it is hoped that the reader will better understand how consumers and competitors interact with the external environment to create a competitive advantage. In short, this book shows how strategy should be crafted.

Writing this book is the result of more than my individual effort, although I bear full responsibility for its content. The comments from reviewers, some anonymous, some known, have helped guide the content and structure the presentation of the manuscript. I would especially like to thank Wesley J. Johnston of the University of Southern California for his helpful comments and kind remarks. The insights of Professors Leon Schiffman and Gloria Thomas have also been valuable. They used the manuscript in their graduate and undergraduate strategy courses and provided helpful feedback. I am grateful for their assistance. The help of my research assistant Cesar Maloles has also been invaluable. He has been with this project since its inception, and has made a significant contribution. Peter Schneider, a Ph.D. student in marketing at Baruch, helped with the chapter on differentiation. Barry Rosen was extremely helpful with the global marketing chapter. My editor Bob Wallace of The Free Press also deserves mention. He is an exceptional editor who provided precisely the right mix of encouragement and persuasion. It is truly a pleasure and an honor to work with him. Finally, my wife Gail and two sons Paul and John deserve special credit. They provided the stable environment that allowed me to concentrate on writing. To my family I am forever indebted.

Steven P. Schnaars
NEW YORK CITY
September 1, 1990

Chapter *1*

Marketing's Growing Influence on Strategy

B usiness strategy has always relied heavily on marketing ideas. But, in recent years, the influence of marketing on strategic thinking has grown greatly. Today, more than ever, strategy is dominated by ideas that sink their roots deeply into the discipline of marketing. Product differentiation, product positioning, market segmentation, new product planning, innovation, product quality, and long-term consumer satisfaction are among the ideas that influence strategy greatly. They supplement market share, market growth, and myriad other ideas that had previously been mainstays in strategy.

The reasons for this new-found interest in marketing ideas are many. The success of foreign competitors, the recognition that competition is now global, and the failure of financial analogies to produce workable strategies are some of the reasons why marketing's influence has grown greatly in recent years. Most influential has been the groundswell of interest in the study of competition. Strategists now recognize that a focus on products, consumers, and markets is essential to long-term competitive success.

While strategists have long been interested in marketing, marketers have only recently become interested in strategy. Ten years ago, while strategy grew at the hands of management scholars, marketers farmed in other fields, especially consumer behavior. In the 1970s, the study of consumer behavior dominated marketing. Marketers focused on discovering the characteristics and behaviors of individual consumers. The influence of psychology was strong and dominant. Marketers learned much about individual consumers, but they learned little about strategy.

In corporations, marketing played a limited role as well. Mostly, marketing's function was to provide information to management, and implement plans set at higher levels. Marketers concentrated on specifics while management dealt with the broader issues affecting the future of the firm.

Beginning in 1980 priorities began to change. As strategists renewed their interest in marketing ideas, marketing scholars shifted their attention to strategy. Marketers began to emphasize the study of aggregated markets over individual consumers. They began to study groups of consumers and, as well, sought to discover how individual consumers decided which products to purchase. Competition joined consumer behavior as a primary area of marketing interest.

Interest in marketing strategy increased the influence of economics on the field of marketing and lessened the influence of psychology. Marketing returned to its historical roots as a subspecialization of economics, from which it had emerged decades earlier.

Marketing's expanded role in strategic thinking has revolutionized the discipline. Marketers now routinely consider issues once reserved strictly for business strategists. It is important to remember that marketers have not changed disciplines, nor have they expanded into the domain of others. Instead, business strategists have come to recognize that basic marketing ideas are essential to successful strategy. In a sense, there has been a meeting of the minds: strategy has moved closer to marketing at the same time as marketing has moved closer to strategy. The result has been a growing influence of marketing on strategic thinking.

Why Marketing Has Become More Important

The growing influence of marketing on business strategy has occurred for a number of important reasons.

GROWING INTEREST IN COMPETITION

In recent years, competition has emerged as the central focus of strategy. The success of lower-cost Asian competitors and higher-status European imports has led to claims that American firms are uncompetitive in today's global markets. Criticisms have centered on poor product quality, dissatisfied customers, a failure to respond to market changes, and a host of other competitive shortcomings. Many of these criticisms speak directly of an inattention to basic marketing principles.

FINANCIAL ANALOGIES PROVED INCORRECT

Throughout the 1970s strategic planning relied heavily on concepts borrowed directly from financial management. It was widely believed that a diversified business could be managed in much the same way as a portfolio of stocks and bonds. Some even argued that it was not necessary to know the business. It was management by the numbers, and it turned out to be mistaken.

The growing influence of marketing on strategy has come at the expense of financial concepts. Compiling unrelated portfolios of businesses, calculating declining cost projections, and managing solely for cash flow are ideas whose time has passed. They simply did not work out as they were supposed to. Knowing your business, your markets, your customers, and your products are the new strategic bywords. It is clear today that a firm without quality products offered at good value to satisfied customers has little chance of long-term competitive success. Managing a diversified business has proved to be a much different exercise than managing investments.

FOCUS ON MARKETS AND PRODUCTS

The focus of marketing has always been on products and markets. The focus of strategy has historically been on other concepts, such as declining cost curves and prices.

Limits of Declining Costs

In the past, much strategic planning ignored consumers totally. Successful strategy consisted solely of keeping costs declining. Some schemes even held that it did not matter what you sold, as long as your position in the business was acceptable. Today, such notions seem ridiculous.

Strategy and Marketing Ideas

Historically, strategists' treatment of basic marketing ideas has been superficial, and limited to a few key variables—such as market share and market growth. In some cases, for example, the growth of a market alone was used to judge the attractiveness of that market. Firms were advised to enter high-growth markets at all costs. Declining markets were to be uniformly de-emphasized.

Role of Price in Strategy

In past years, there was a fundamental disagreement between marketers and strategists on the role of price in strategy. Traditionally, price had always played an important role. Lowering costs (and prices) to survive the shakeout was a dominant theme in the 1970s. Unfortunately, price competition often proved ruinous for competitors that strove to lower costs faster than one another. Furthermore, lower-cost foreign producers excelled at price competition.

In contrast, avoiding price competition has been a central tenet of marketing. Marketers have long held that competition is best shifted to nonmarketing variables through product differentiation and other forms of non-price competition. Business strategists now agree with marketers on the issue of price competition. Today, most strategists recognize the importance of avoiding price competition in marketing strategy.

Strategy and the Marketing Mix

In the past, strategy emphasized price but ignored the other components of the marketing mix. Distribution, promotion, and often the product itself were viewed as incidentals to be tinkered with at lower levels. The emphasis on price proved misplaced. In many cases, marketing mix variables turned out to be the sources of strong competitive advantages rather than incidental factors.

Consider the importance of distribution (place) in the high-growth personal computer market of the early 1980s. Many entrants failed because they could not get distribution for their innovative products. Instead of an incidental, distribution turned out to be a key competitive weapon. Radio Shack, for example, with thousands of existing retail outlets possessed a key advantage in personal computers, even though its product carried a tarnished image of low quality with consumers.

Early in the 1980s stressing costs at the expense of real product differences hurt General Motors. The firm cut costs by producing the same car for each of its five nameplates—Chevrolet, Pontiac, Oldsmobile, Buick, Cadillac. Cadillac would change some trim and sell the same car as Chevrolet. Production efficiencies were increased. It was no longer necessary to bother with so many different models. Financial gains looked impressive on paper, but consumers were confused and disappointed. They had trouble telling the difference between a Cadillac and a Chevrolet. More important, they were reluctant to spend more money for a Cadillac that looked like a Chevrolet. Marketing's contribution to strategy is largely driven by the natural interest of the discipline in all of the marketing mix variables, of which price is only one component.

ORIENTATION TOWARD THE EXTERNAL ENVIRONMENT

The natural orientation of marketing is outwards, toward markets and customers. Sales, advertising, new product introductions, and just about every other marketing function require that close attention be paid to the world that exists outside the company's gates. Marketing is a boundary-spanning function. The outward perspective of marketing is unique. Management, finance, accounting, research and development, data processing and most other company functions face inward towards events that occur within the firm.

Power of External Events

Marketers see strategy as driven by external events rather than by internal actions. Consider the technological substitution of videocassette recorders for 8mm home movie cameras and projectors that occurred in the late 1970s. This is an extreme case, but one that illustrates the power of external events. No matter what the price, or how persuasive the salespeople, the makers of movie cameras were doomed. Change came quickly and it came from the outside. And, it changed the character of the industry forever. What had once been a viable product was made obsolete by a technological development in another industry.

Also consider the case of Coleco, the Connecticut toymaker. The original name of the firm was the Connecticut Leather Company, which aptly described the products it produced. In the early 1980s the company targeted the burgeoning computer market with its entry, the Adam computer. Adam bit the biblical apple and was cast out of the market. Instead, a doll that had been turned down by myriad other manufacturers, Cabbage Patch Kids, proved to be a winner. The firm was unable to follow up, however, and went bankrupt in 1988. A leather company making a hit with a doll while focusing on personal computers highlights the vagaries of external forces. It is difficult to develop long-range plans in such a devilish environment.

A Fit with the External Environment

Marketing's external focus offers a better opportunity to cope with disruptive change than does a orientation that faces inward toward the firm's own capabilities.

In the past, many formal planning procedures implied a world characterized by a sense of order and precision that just was not there. The growing influence of marketing on strategy seeks to remedy this deficiency.

BIAS TOWARD ACTION VERSUS ANALYSIS PARALYSIS

The predilection of marketing is toward action over analysis, which contrasts greatly with the emphasis of strategy in the 1970s when planners pondered strategy and avoided action. Armies of professionals produced elaborate plans to guide firms into the future—plans that worshiped calculation and abhorred action. In fact, the goal of planning shifted from creating workable plans to the process of drawing up the plans themselves. Vision was replaced with a false sense of precision. The result was that planning became more and more removed from the real world. Planners became paralyzed by the actual process of planning. They were afflicted by analysis paralysis. Firms avoided risk, but they avoided opportunities as well.

Operational personnel, those who ran the day-to-day operations of the firm, came to view planning as an arcane art with little practical value. They were correct in their assessment. Consequently, many elegant plans ended up in file cabinets, read by no one but those who drew them up; and by the early 1980s many firms had disbanded or drastically cut back their strategic planning departments. Today, strategy values action over analysis. Moving quickly has replaced long, careful study. The change bodes well for marketing.

The popular business press has recognized marketing's bias toward action and called for an expanded role for marketing. A prominent *Business Week* (1983) cover story noted that firms want managers who can develop and implement product strategies. They do not want "bean counters" who will foster further study and promote analysis paralysis. Is it any wonder that marketing's contribution to strategy has grown greatly in recent years?

Strategic Orientations Toward the Marketplace

Over the past two decades marketers and business strategists have looked at the world in very different ways. These disparate world views roughly match the four orientations toward markets typically found in marketing textbooks. Specifically, they mirror: (1) the marketing concept, (2) the selling concept, (3) the product concept, and (4) the production concept. In addition, a fifth orientation is examined, an orientation toward competitors, which has been a mainstay of business strategists. This section looks at these different orientations and tries to reconcile the divergent views held by marketers and business strategists.

THE MARKETING CONCEPT

Marketing has a long history of placing customers at the center of all marketing actions. Typical of this orientation is the series of concentric

Exhibit 1.1 *Customer Orientation*

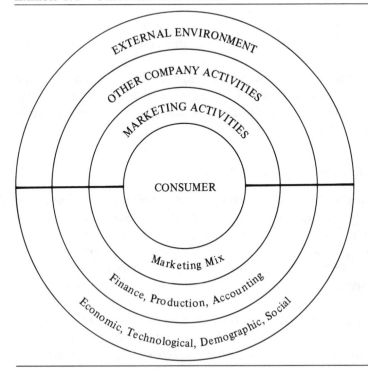

circles shown in Exhibit 1.1. As this exhibit illustrates, "good" marketing consists of orienting all of the firm's actions toward serving consumer needs, wants, and desires. At the heart of this orientation is the marketing concept, which is the most fundamental precept in the discipline of marketing. It holds that a firm should try to discover what consumers want and make products to satisfy those wants. It is based on the "market-pull" model of marketing, a commonsensical notion that consumers will demand products that meet their needs. When a firm implements this concept correctly, it will not have to rely on hard sell campaigns to persuade consumers to buy the goods it produces. At the extreme, the marketing concept can be defined as that condition where selling is unnecessary.

Origin of the Marketing Concept

The origin of the marketing concept lies with three prominent authors in the 1950s: (1) Peter Drucker in his landmark book *The Practice of Management,* (2) John B. McKitterick of General Electric (a firm that also developed many strategic planning techniques), and (3) Ted Levitt, the noted Harvard professor, and author of the seminal article ''Marketing Myopia.'' All three agree that the purpose of business is to create satisfied customers. Most important, the marketing concept was conceived as, and remains, a long-term business orientation rather than a short-term fix.

The marketing concept held sway throughout the 1950s and 1960s, a time when American business dominated world markets. By the 1970s, however, times had changed. Finance dominated strategic thinking. Consumer satisfaction clearly came second.

Marketing's Contribution to Strategy

The marketing concept is marketing's most important contribution to strategy. It infuses strategy with a focus on customers, a dimension sorely lacking from strategic planning formulations. It reinforces the idea that customers for the firm's products ultimately determine whether a strategy was brilliantly conceived or blindly concocted. It is based on a simple proposition: a firm without satisfied customers has little chance of long-term success.

In examining the contributions of marketing to strategic management, Biggadike (1981) lists the marketing concept as key. Segmentation, positioning, and the product life cycle are listed as other valuable contributions.

As an example of the successful implementation of the marketing concept, consider the case of Honda automobiles, cars that sell themselves. Other automakers rely on rebates, deep discounts, discount financing, and the aggressive actions of ''happy-gladhanders'' (salespersons) garbed in brightly colored sport coats to vigorously persuade consumers of the merits of their products. Honda has correctly implemented the marketing concept. Less savvy competitors must still rely heavily on the selling concept to move their products off the showroom floor.

Limits of the Selling Concept

Some marketers mistakenly rely on the selling concept, the second strategic orientation. The selling concept holds that a firm should produce what it wants and then expend a great effort convincing consumers that they should buy those products. The selling concept goes hand-in-hand with high-pressure selling. Antithetical to the marketing concept, it is an example of the ''sales-push'' model of marketing, where marketers push unwanted products through the channel of distribution.

The strategic ramifications of the selling concept are many. Firms focus on sales volume, the higher the better. The quality of sales is unimportant. Small customers are pursued with the same vigor as large customers. Any order is welcome, even if those orders are not worth the effort the sale requires. The goal is to sell more goods this month. It is a short-term strategy that emphasizes short-term goals.

The selling concept constitutes bad strategy, although it may serve other purposes. It may be acceptable to meet short-term sales goals or help the firm over temporary hard times. But, as a long-term strategic orientation it is unacceptable. It is one that is likely to fail when pitted against strategies that serve consumers with products that they really want.

CRITICISMS OF THE MARKETING CONCEPT

The marketing concept is not without its critics. Some critics have argued that it has hurt rather than helped American business. Bennett and Cooper (1979, 1981) have proved to be two of the most vocal critics. In two strongly worded articles, they argue that the marketing concept has diverted attention away from a long-term emphasis on product development and quality manufacturing to a short-term emphasis on superfluous advertising, selling, and promotion. As a result, product value has suffered.

As evidence, they point to the automobile and television industries, where American firms once dominated, but which are now dominated by imports. They blame the marketing concept for the industries' problems. While American firms stressed short-term promotions, these authors argue, foreign firms offered superior product value. The marketing concept is flawed, they contend, because of its reliance on the "market-pull" model, whereby marketing research is used to discover what consumers want. According to this model, marketing tells R&D which products to develop.

Consumers can only speak in terms of the familiar. They cannot express a need for radically new innovations with which they have no experience. Imagine consumers trying to tell a market researcher about their need for a compact disk player or a microwave oven before those products were introduced. It would be very unlikely. As a result, firms that rely on the "market-pull" model miss truly innovative products. Instead, they focus on products that are "new and improved" but are really nothing more than minor product modifications. They are then forced to rely on heavy promotion to compete against firms with truly innovative products, which is the tragedy of the marketing concept, according to these authors.

The "technology-push" model is an alternative. It relies on the creativity and insight of scientists and engineers to discover radically new products, which are then either accepted or rejected by consumers. According to this model, technology pushes the process rather than it being pulled by consumer demand. Bennett and Cooper argue that the "technology-push" model leads to truly new products of superior quality and higher product value.

Hayes and Abernathy (1980) hold similar opinions. They contend that three trends have combined to decimate the competitiveness of American business: (1) an overreliance on financial controls (management by the numbers), (2) portfolio management (managing a business like a portfolio of stocks), and (3) the marketing concept. They too belittle the "market-pull" model, which has given us new-fangled potato chips, deodorants, and pet rocks, but missed the truly creative innovations of our time, such as lasers, instant photography, xerography and the transistor. In short, with the marketing concept, we managed our way to economic decline.

CALL FOR THE PRODUCT CONCEPT

Criticisms of the marketing concept are often a call to replace it with a third strategic orientation—the product concept. This concept holds that consumers will demand products of the highest quality, and is predicated on the "technology-push" model of innovation. Products are designed by engineers and scientists, who then present consumers with the fruits of their research. It begins with the ingenuity and inventiveness of scientists rather than the needs and wants of consumers. The product concept has led to the discovery of many stunning innovations, including the videocassette recorder, the microwave oven, and the compact disk player.

IN DEFENSE OF THE MARKETING CONCEPT

Marketers argue that it is not the marketing concept that is flawed but the misapplication of it by a handful of short-sighted firms that are actually following the selling concept. Some firms have mistakenly translated the marketing concept into a call for short-term promotional expenditures at the expense of long-term consumer satisfaction. Critics and proponents alike agree that problems have occurred. They disagree, however, in attributing blame. Marketers argue that it is the implementation of the marketing concept that is to blame, not the concept itself.

More recently, McGee and Spiro (1988) note that criticisms of the marketing concept do not contradict the basic tenets of the concept itself. In fact, they contend that the marketing concept and the product concept are actually quite consistent with one another. The product concept is really just "synonymous with customer satisfaction as described by the marketing philosophy" (p. 44).

These authors contend that the product concept is but one implementation of the marketing concept. In many product categories, consumers do favor high-quality products, and are willing to pay a premium price for them. But, not all products require technological excellence, or should be positioned as premium goods.

The two concepts are consistent because the product concept must ultimately be subservient to the marketing concept for a product to be successful. Without consideration of the marketing concept, the "technology-push" model of innovation often leads to product failure. Scientists and engineers may well be the source of new ideas, but they are also the proponents of products that end up serving no market at all. DuPont's Corfam, the Nimslo three-dimensional camera, and AT&T's picturephone are among the many examples of products that followed the product concept but failed the marketing concept. Each of these firms offered consumers high-quality products that were unwanted.

CONTROVERSY OVER THE PRODUCTION CONCEPT

The fourth strategic orientation is the production concept, which holds that firms should focus on low-cost, efficient manufacturing, and seek to obtain widespread distribution for their products. The emphasis is on keeping costs low. The production concept hypothesizes that consumers will desire products that are priced low.

Throughout the 1970s, strategy embraced the production concept. The Boston Consulting Group's growth-share matrix is little more than a variation of the production concept. Experience curve analysis, the central premise of the matrix, is that firms should strive to keep costs falling by expanding cumulative production. Historically, marketers have ridiculed this concept as an old-fashioned perspective that best describes how business was conducted in the late 1800s. In the eyes of marketers, the production concept shows how times have changed over the past century. The contrasting views of the production concept by marketing and business strategists illustrate how differently the two disciplines have looked at strategy in the past. Marketers abhorred what strategists have embraced.

In retrospect, both views proved extreme. Marketers' dismissal of the production concept was presumptuous. In many markets, consumers do favor products that are widely available at lower cost. In nearly every sector of the economy there are firms that excel by employing the production concept. Toys 'R' Us in retailing, for example, is a superb marketer that has grown rapidly using such a production orientation. Service is low, but so are prices.

Similarly, foreign firms with lower-cost structures have excelled with the production concept. Hyundai, in automobiles, and Goldstar, Sharp, and Sanyo, in electronics, are examples of successful implementers. Each has done well by doing precisely what marketers would advise against. Clearly, the production concept has a place in today's markets.

Likewise, the strategist's view of the production concept as the only path to business success has been oversold. It is but a single orientation. Focusing too intently on production while ignoring customers is as faulty an orientation as focusing too intently on consumers while ignoring production efficiencies. Like the product concept, the production concept does not really contradict the marketing concept. Efficient production of 8mm movie projectors in the age of VCRs would surely fail. The emphasis still must be placed on consumers before the product is made. Only then can companies strive to gain efficient production.

COMPETITOR ORIENTATION

The greatest chasm between marketers and business strategists exists in terms of the last orientation—the one towards competitors. Historically, strategy has focused on competition. Almost every popular strategic planning formulation of the past few decades has explicitly considered competitive effects. It is often their reason for being.

That orientation contrasts with traditional paradigms in marketing, which have given little consideration to competitive forces. Marketers have traditionally focused on consumers and ignored the effects of competition.

Strategy's Contribution to Marketing

The key contribution of business strategists to the development of marketing strategy has been the focus on competitive effects. Paying attention to your competitors has proved to be at least as important as paying attention to your customers. Since the publication in 1980 of Michael Porter's landmark book, *Competitive Strategy*, competition has moved even further to the forefront of strategic thinking. Firms now seek to develop competitive strategies in search of competitive advantages to earn higher-than-average profits. Marketing, too, has jumped on the competition bandwagon.

Balancing Consumer and Competitor Orientations

Marketing strategy requires a balance between two separate groups—consumers and competitors. Historically, marketers and business strategists have focused on only a single orientation. Marketers have long favored an orientation that places consumers at the center of all actions. In the process they have ignored competitors. Strategists, on the other hand, have focused on competitors. In the process they have ignored consumers. It is now clear that focusing solely on consumers or competitors is insufficient; it is necessary to merge the two orientations into a complete view of marketing strategy. Exhibit 1.2 illustrates the balance required.

ADDED FOCUS ON COMPETITION

The marketing concept, by itself, has proved to be an incomplete view of business. By ignoring competition, it has painted only part of the picture. While marketers have sought to satisfy consumers' needs, competitors have outmaneuvered them in the marketplace. Often, innovative products developed by American firms are copied by overseas competitors

Exhibit 1.2 *Consumer Versus Competitor Orientations*

Consumer Orientation	←——→	Consumer/ Competition Balance	←——→	Competitor Orientation
Examples:				
Marketing and Consumer Behavior		Competitive Marketing Strategy		Corporate Strategy

who make them more cheaply, and of higher quality. In many instances, American marketers have won the battle of discovering consumer needs only to lose the competitive war to keep the markets they pioneered. It is important to understand what consumers want. It is equally important to protect your discoveries from competitive response. The marketing concept needs to be empowered with a sense of competition, maybe even warfare, that is otherwise missing from an orientation that focuses solely on consumer needs.

Consider the case of distribution arrangements viewed from a "strategic" perspective. Distribution can be viewed as a weapon, as a means not only of serving consumers but protecting markets from threatening competitors.

Coke and Pepsi, for example, serve consumers with a wide product line, which ties up valuable supermarket shelf space with their products, forcing others to find alternative means of serving consumers. The practice is common. It is also strategic. Producers of other products routinely employ methods to preclude entry into their markets by competitors. A strategic orientation is aimed at stopping your enemy and advancing your own troops.

Contractual marketing agreements, a controversial topic in the late 1980s, accomplish the same task. Coke and Pepsi offer retailers large discounts if the retailer agrees to feature promotions only for their brand. Pepsi might tie up a particular retailer for six months. Coke would then tie up the same retailer for the other six months. The agreements have the effect of excluding smaller bottlers from the competition. The agreements are controversial. They are also strategic.

Oxenfeldt and Moore (1978) have argued forcefully that marketers should switch from a traditional customer-oriented approach to a stance that stresses competition. A focus on competitors allows firms to exploit competitors' vulnerabilities and defend their own flanks against attack.

Day and Wensley (1983) have gone even further. They contend that a "paradigm shift" is underway in marketing. Marketing has moved away from its traditional focus on consumer decision making. In the authors' own words: "Another set of priorities has emerged, with the emphasis on the development of sustainable competitive positions in product-markets" (p. 88).

Consider the interplay between consumer and competitor orientations in the light beer market that emerged in the mid-1970s.

In the mid-1960s Rheingold, a local New York brewer, introduced a "diet" beer named Gablinger's. It failed badly. Rheingold's entry strategy misunderstood the consumers it sought to serve. Men, the primary market for beer, do not drink diet beer. To ask for it in a tavern is to invite ridicule, or, at least, subtle intimidation.

In the early 1970s, Meister Brau, a small midwest brewer introduced its version of light beer. It was promoted by Miss Meister Brau, a bikini-clad model holding a can of the product. Men liked the model but hated the beer. The strategy was muddled from the start. Miller bought Meister Brau, stripped off the label, reformulated the product, and advertised it squarely to men. Its Lite beer did not fill you up; it was not a "diet" beer. The burly sports figures featured in advertisements reinforced the "manliness" of Lite. Consumers felt comfortable asking for it. Miller felt comfortable with its successful new product, which held a large share of a fast growing market. Miller had used its orientation towards consumers to dominate larger rivals. The competitive orientation of Anheuser-Busch, the market leader, torpedoed Miller's consumer focus. Anheuser-Busch had missed the trend towards light beer. Its initial entry, Natural Light, failed and was withdrawn. Bud Light, with a relentless advertising campaign, has kept up the pressure, along with the fight for market share, for years now. Miller Lite has steadily lost market share. It has also faced extreme pressure on profits due to the huge promotional expenditures necessary to defend its declining share of the market.

Most important, subsequent competitors must surely ask whether a market-share battle against Anheuser-Busch is worth the effort. Anheuser-Busch serves customers a fine product. But it also serves notice on competitors of its intention to fight back at any cost. It is focusing on consumers and competitors.

RENEWED CONCENTRATION ON CONSUMERS

While marketers discover the importance of competition, strategists are moving towards a consumer orientation. One noted marketing scholar contends that the marketing concept is being rediscovered by corporate America after being rejected during the strategic planning boom of the 1970s. Attitudes are swinging back to marketing's point of view. The scholar lists myriad firms that are "coming back to the basic marketing concept articulated in the mid-1950s" (Webster 1988, p. 37). A focus on consumers is, once again, an important element in business success.

Many marketers believe that management has spent too much time on strategic planning and too little time on marketing. The focus on finance was misplaced. Webster also notes: "Financial goals are seen as results and rewards, not the fundamental purpose of the business. The purpose is customer satisfaction, and the reward is profit, as noted by Peter Drucker in the original statement of the marketing concept'' (p. 38). We are in the midst of a marketing renaissance, Webster contends.

Gluck (1986), an expert on strategic planning, agrees with Webster's assessment. He concludes that newer strategic planning techniques are aimed at better understanding customers. The shift is long overdue. He notes: "The same kind of diligent information gathering some managers reserve for their competition should be focused on getting closer to their customers" (p. 33). Strategy is reaffirming the marketing concept after a bout of philandering in the 1970s.

Longs Drug Stores Inc., a $1.8 billion chain with 234 stores in six western states, has excelled by discarding the usual retail drug store formula. Store managers are treated and compensated as entrepreneurs. They are given broad powers to tailor their individual stores to the community. In a retirement area, a Longs store stocks may aspirins and laxatives but few diapers. Small package sizes dominate. In a community that contains many professionals and families, the local Longs store stocks stereos and cameras. As the CEO of Longs was recently quoted: "They [the managers] literally customize their stores to the customers they serve" (Paris 1988, p. 62). The focus on customers has worked. Longs holds 20 percent of an intensely competitive market.

Clearly, a focus on consumers must be joined with a focus on competitors. Today, marketing strategy is based on that premise.

References

Bennett, Roger C., and Robert G. Cooper. "Beyond the Marketing Concept." *Business Horizons,* June 1979, pp. 76–83.

Bennett, Roger C., and Robert G. Cooper. "The Misuse of Marketing: An American Tragedy." *Business Horizons,* November–December 1981, pp. 51–60.

Biggadike, E. Ralph. "The Contributions of Marketing to Strategic Management." *Academy of Management Review,* vol. 6, no. 4 (1981), pp. 621–632.

Day, George S., and Robin Wensley, "Marketing Theory with a Strategic Orientation." *Journal of Marketing,* Fall 1983, pp. 79–89.

Gluck, Fredrick W. "Strategic Planning in a New Key." *McKinsey Quarterly,* Winter 1986, pp. 18–41.

Hayes, Robert H., and William J. Abernathy. "Managing Our Way to Economic Decline." *Harvard Business Review,* July–August 1980, pp. 67–78.

Levitt, Theodore. "Marketing Myopia." *Harvard Business Review,* July–August 1960, pp. 24–47.

"Marketing: The New Priority," *Business Week,* November 21, 1983, pp. 96–106.

McGee, Lynn W., and Rosann L. Spiro. "The Marketing Concept in Perspective." *Business Horizons.* May–June 1988, pp. 40–45.

Oxenfeldt, Alfred R., and William L. Moore. "Customer or Competitor: Which Guideline for Marketing?" *Management Review,* August 1978, pp. 43–48.

Paris, Ellen. "Managers as Entrepreneurs." *Forbes,* October 31, 1988, p. 62.

Porter, Michael. *Competitive Strategy.* New York: Free Press, 1980.

Webster, Fredrick E. Jr., "The Rediscovery of the Marketing Concept." *Business Horizons,* May–June 1988, pp. 29–39.

Chapter 2

A Brief History
of Marketing Strategy

Marketing strategy is both unique and commonplace. That might sound like a contradiction of terms but it is not. The term "strategy" is widely used to describe a seemingly endless number of marketing activities. Today, everything in marketing seems to be "strategic." There is strategic pricing, strategic market entry, strategic advertising, and maybe even strategic strategy. The glut of competition has focused more attention on performing traditional marketing actions strategically, with an eye towards beating the competition. In that sense, marketing strategy is commonplace. In recent years it seems to have been appended to nearly every marketing action.

But, marketing strategy is also unique. There is not one unified definition upon which marketers agree. Instead, there are nearly as many definitions of it as there are uses of the term. Clearly, marketing strategy is a commonly used term, but no one is really sure what it means.

Boyd and Larreche (1978), for example, reviewed the history of marketing strategy. They found tremendous confusion over just what strategy is. The term "strategy," as used in marketing, has been applied to at least three types of issues, each at a different level of aggregation.

At the most macro level, there are *Marketing Strategies,* which focus on manipulations of the marketing mix variables—product, price, place, and promotion. According to that definition, setting a strategy for a product consists of selecting a price for a product, designing an advertising campaign, then deciding on a plan of distribution.

There are also *Marketing Element Strategies,* a more narrow concept that applies only to one element of the marketing mix—a "push-versus-pull" promotional strategy, an "intensive, selective, or exclusive" distribution strategy, or a "skimming versus penetration" pricing strategy. All qualify as marketing strategies using that definition.

Finally, there are *Product-Market Entry Strategies,* which include strategies that look at specific marketing decisions. Strategies that call for a firm to build market share, harvest profits (and share), or defend market share from competitors.

The scope of marketing strategy has shown even greater variability over the past few decades. One definition that has been prominent in the marketing literature focuses on two elements: (1) picking a target market, and (2) selecting a marketing mix to serve that market. Notice the emphasis on consumers, not competitors.

Another widely used definition of strategy in marketing emphasizes the broader perspective of strategy in management. That definition views strategic market planning as a four-step process: (1) defining the business, (2) setting a mission, (3) selecting functional plans for marketing, production, and other areas, and (4) budgeting for those plans (Abell and Hammond 1979). In that sense, marketing strategy is more akin to corporate strategy.

Marketing's confusion over strategy is not unique. The content and scope of corporate strategy has proved equally elusive. Bracker (1980) reviewed seventeen sources and found myriad definitions of strategic management. He did, however, find three recurring themes throughout most discussions of strategy. Most definitions agree that corporate strategy has to do with *environmental analysis,* an analysis of the markets the firm must compete in. Most definitions also focus on the *firm's resources,* or special competences. A prominent theme in strategic management is that a firm must fit its resources to the environment it faces. Finally, most definitions consider the setting of *objectives and goals,* which the firm seeks to satisfy. The firm's resources are deployed with the intent of achieving those goals. Marketing strategy, like its counterpart in management, also tends to embrace those recurring themes.

In marketing, Gardner and Thomas (1985) traced marketing strategy back to Leverett S. Lyon, who, in 1926, provided a very modern-sounding discussion of strategy. Lyon talked explicitly about the ever-changing environment, and how marketers had to re-arrange their product offerings to fit that environment. Said Lyon: "Marketing management . . . may be conceived of as the continuous task of re-planning the marketing activities of a business to meet the constantly changing conditions both within and without the enterprise (Gardner and Thomas 1985, p. 19). That definition holds up pretty well after more than sixty years.

Strategic management holds a similar definition, but pegs its origins more than twenty years later. One study traced the history of strategy in management back to Von Neumann and Morgenstern, who in 1947 developed the first "strategic management concept" (Bracker 1980). They, like Leverette Lyon before them in marketing, viewed strategy as a series of actions taken by a firm to deal with the environment they had to compete in. Clearly, there are consistent themes in strategy.

But, marketing strategy is not static. It has changed greatly over the years, each step building on that which went before. This chapter is about those changes. It traces the roots of modern marketing strategy, shows what trends it has followed, and examines issues that are currently popular.

Historical Trends in Marketing Strategy

The ancient Greeks were the first to formally discuss the concept of strategy, but their interest was in military rather than marketing applications. Business and marketing strategy came centuries later. Most reviews of formal strategic planning trace its origins to the period beginning just after World War II. Since that time, strategy has gone through at least four distinct phases, each phase corresponding roughly to one of the decades in that forty-year period: (1) budgeting and the search for overall strategy in the 1950s, (2) long-range planning in the 1960s, (3) formula planning in the 1970s, and (4) the trend towards strategic thinking that began in the 1980s and continues to the present time. Each phase is described below, and is illustrated in Exhibit 2.1.

ORIGINS OF MODERN STRATEGY

Modern strategy began with two trends that emerged right after World War II. Those trends were: (1) the growth and sophistication of budgeting techniques, and (2) the search for a way to create an overall corporate strategy.

Budgeting

Budgeting is the financial and accounting practice of allocating funds within a particular firm. In the 1950s, strategy was little more than a "gussied-up" form of budgeting. There really was no explicit strategy. Instead, there were annual budgets that allocated funds to different projects within the organization. The emphasis was on control rather than strategic intent. Budgeting, which allowed the firm to control its operations, is sometimes called basic financial planning. In essence, budgeting gradually grew into strategy as the 1950s grew into the 1960s.

Exhibit 2.1   *Historical Trends in Strategy*

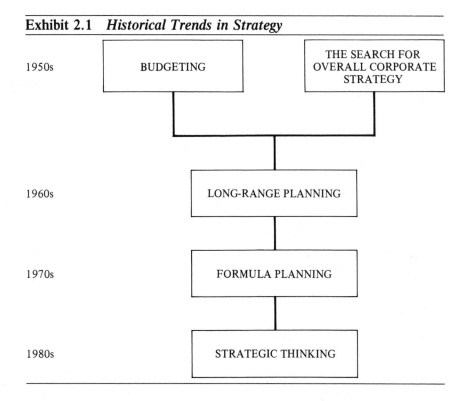

1950s	BUDGETING

THE SEARCH FOR OVERALL CORPORATE STRATEGY

1960s — LONG-RANGE PLANNING

1970s — FORMULA PLANNING

1980s — STRATEGIC THINKING

Search for Overall Strategy

Strategy grew out of another trend as well. It emerged from attempts to create an overall, explicit corporate strategy. Before the 1950s, most business disciplines focused on their own subject matter. Business theories progressed on a discipline-by-discipline basis. Marketing was concerned solely with marketing topics, production with production issues, finance with financial issues. Each discipline moved ahead on its own, without regard for the other. In the 1950s, as strategy emerged, there was an interest in integrating those functions to achieve objectives that benefit the entire company, not just the individual functions. That interest in overall corporate strategy had a great influence on the rise of long-range planning.

EMERGENCE OF LONG-RANGE PLANNING

The 1960s was the decade of long-range planning. Slowly but surely, budgeting evolved into long-range planning.

Motivation for Long-Range Planning

The move from budgeting to long-range planning was motivated by four key factors.

Long-Term Budgeting Consequences

First, it became apparent that annual budgeting decisions had consequences far beyond one year. If a firm funded a new product-development project, for example, it expected the payoff from that product to be realized many years later. That led to five-year plans, based on five-year forecasts of sales, profits, market share, and market growth. Annual budgeting became longer-term planning.

Interest in Objectives and Goals

Second, the interest in creating an overall strategy for the firm focused on setting explicit objectives and goals for the firm. Firms set goals and sought to achieve them. Simple budgeting was pushed to respond to an overall corporate purpose.

Trend Towards Conglomeration

Third, there was a trend towards conglomeration in the 1960s, which made it difficult to allocate resources within a firm. Firms competed in so many different types of businesses that top management was unfamiliar with the specifics and potential of each business.

Resource Allocation

Fourth, and as a result of conglomeration, it was unclear which businesses should be funded heavily and which should be funded lightly. Not all opportunities could be funded. The supply of capital was less than that for investment opportunities that presented themselves in the booming 1960s. The economy roared ahead for most of the decade. A more systematic approach to planning was necessary as firms became more diversified and their operations became more complex. Hence the rise of long-range planning.

Key Characteristics

Long-range planning had the following two key characteristics:

Objectives and Goals

A central feature of long-range planning was the setting of missions, objectives, and goals. Objectives would be set by top management and communicated to others in the organization. Strategies were then designed to achieve those objectives. Long-range planning laid the foundation for objectives-driven strategies. Those goals and objectives has been one of the primary contributions of long-range planning.

Long-Range Forecasting

Long-range planning in the 1960s was based squarely on long-range forecasting. In fact, it is often called "forecast-based planning" (Gluck, Kaufman and Walleck 1980). Forecasts were made, and plans were then set in light of those forecasts. As Steiner (1969), in one of the most prominent books on the topic, noted: "The forecast is the basic premise upon which planning proceeds" (p. 17). The very essence of long-range planning was captured by Steiner as he said: "Planning is concerned with making current decisions in light of their futurity" (p. 18).

At the time it was believed that the ability to accurately predict future markets and long-term trends was increasing rapidly. Steiner observed: "The theory of forecasting is growing stronger" (p. 718). At the time great strides were being made in quantitative model building, but, unfortunately, accuracy stumbled. Consequently, plans predicated on those forecasts turned out to be mistaken.

Long-range planning grew rapidly during the 1960s. The profession of long-range planning also grew rapidly. Top management established objectives and goals, then professional planners provided ever-thicker plans that looked ever-further into the future. An atmosphere of science and precision permeated planning. By the end of the decade, the results came in.

DECLINE OF LONG-RANGE PLANNING

By the mid-1970s, long-range planning had fallen out of favor. There were two key reasons for its demise.

Trouble with Forecasts

Long-range forecasts proved less accurate than anticipated. Five-year forecasts were obsolete after one year. Consequently, five-year plans were worthless. The longer time horizon did not materialize. Long-range planning degenerated into one-year planning.

Problems with Resource Allocation

The "go-go" years of the late 1960s, when conglomeration was popular, produced widely flung businesses. Top management did not know the specifics of each business. They needed something that would allow them to allocate resources among those businesses. The promise of long-range planning proved deficient in that regard.

Management faced an abundance of investment opportunities with little means of selecting which to fund and which to deplete. There was no formal theory to follow. At the end of every year, when budgets were allocated, it was difficult for managers to tell which opportunities were most promising, and which were merely the result of the best presentations for funds. That dilemma led to seemingly scientific schemes for making strategic decisions.

Magic Bullets: The Rise of Formula Planning

If the 1960s were the decade of long-range planning, then the 1970s were surely the decade of what has been come to be known as "formula" planning. Formula planning proposed a consistent, and easily understood, conceptual scheme for allocating resources in a diversified organization. There were many versions of formula planning, each promoted by a prestigious consulting firm. What they all had in common was a simple, but powerful, set of strategic concepts that allowed management to guide their firm into the future. It was all very persuasive. Consultants thrived as firms rushed to have their businesses plotted strategically.

The most popular version of portfolio planning was the Boston Consulting Group's Growth-Share Matrix, which is covered in detail in the next chapter. It was one of many offered. The genre was called "portfolio" planning because those plans proposed that managing a widely diversified business was like managing a stock portfolio. You did not need to know the business itself, the consultants advised. You merely managed the parts of the portfolio for the overall good of the company. Top management embraced portfolio planning with enthusiasm. Formula planning sounded like science at work in management.

It was during the 1970s that planning grew fastest. The rise of professional strategic planners at corporate headquarters and the growth of strategic consulting firms accelerated. In many instances, planners gained control of companies. As planning staffs grew, plans grew too. The power of operating managers waned as the power of strategic planners grew. Operating managers were required to fill out forms aplenty. The plans were drawn by people who were strong on theory but weak on actual business experience. The two groups were hostile to one another. The end was near for formula planning.

DECLINE OF FORMULA PLANNING

By the 1980s formula planning had fallen out of favor. It seemed to be attacked from every angle. Criticism abounded.

Theoretical but Impractical

First, was the problem of implementation. Plans were constructed by professional planners at corporate headquarters. To be successful the plans had to be implemented by those who actually made and sold the firm's products. Since those groups were not involved in writing the plans, they viewed them as a burden rather than a guide. More often than not, elaborate and elegant plans got filed away. They were beautifully written but never implemented. As one Westinghouse Electric executive noted: "The notion that an effective strategy can be constructed by someone in an ivory tower is totally bankrupt" (*Business Week,* Sept. 17, 1984, p. 64).

Ritualistic Rather than Useful

The criticism of implementation resulted from what happened to the planning process itself. Planning became ritualistic and mechanistic. It desensitized people. It became routine. Strategic planners ended up pursuing form over substance. Formula planning moved further and further away from customers and competition. It relied on data rather than marketing instincts. Plans were written in isolation from those who would have to implement them, as well as from those who would eventually buy the products. By 1980, the errors of those ways were apparent.

More Problems with Forecasting

The third, and final, criticism of formula planning is that it never really overcame the problems of forecasting that led to the demise of long-range planning. It often held unrealistic assumptions. Forecasts of market growth, sales, and profits were often based on "hockey-stick" financial projections (they looked like a hockey stick). Needless to say, those projections often proved inaccurate. Some critics even referred to the genre as the "sea gull" method of strategy. Consults flew in, left a mess, then flew away.

More than twenty years ago, George Steiner (1969) recognized the pitfalls that would destroy planning. His insights proved remarkably prescient. He argued that planning would fail if the following occurred:

"Extrapolating rather than thinking,

Developing such a reverence for numbers that irreverence for intuitive and value judgments predominate,

Seeking precision in numbers,

Developing a rigid structure,

Top management's assumption that it can delegate the planning function to a planner" (pp. 720–721).

In spite of Steiner's advice, many of the popular planning formulations of the 1970s committed those very errors. In hindsight, formula planning offered a magic bullet that promised an easy way to win the game of business. Beginning in the early 1980s, strategy departments began to shrink or be disbanded. Strategy fell on hard times.

RISE OF STRATEGIC THINKING

In the 1980s strategic thinking gained favor. Porter (1987) has argued forcefully for this idea. Many other authors have espoused similar ideas to describe changes in strategy during the 1980s but this section subsumes those ideas under Porter's term "strategic thinking." Strategic thinking is different than strategic planning. Those differences overcome many of the criticisms that led to the downfall of formula planning in the previous decade. Strategic thinking is an alternative to those who argued that strategic planning is obsolete, and should be discarded.

Strategic thinking captures many of the current trends in marketing strategy. Among those trends are:

From Forecasting to Competitive Advantage

Whereas past strategic planning formulations relied heavily on forecasting, strategic thinking relies heavily on the concept of competitive advantage, which is discussed in the next section. Competitive advantage is not a new idea, but one that is newly emphasized in marketing. Unlike strategic planning techniques, competitive advantage will never become obsolete. If anything, it is more important today than ever before.

From Elitism to Egalitarianism

Strategic thinking is not conducted solely by an elite group of professional planners. Instead, *it is a way of thinking about consumers, competitors, and competitive advantage that is inculcated into every member of the organization.* It is not strategy that was deficient in previous decades, but the way in which it was pursued.

Strategic thinking holds that an operations manager is his own best planner. Planners must be subservient to managers, not the other way around. Strategic thinking has the participation of lower-level employees—a practice that aids implementation. Those who are doing the planning are actually implementing their own plans. It also allows for learning by those in the field, who are actually serving customers. Strategic thinking goes hand in hand with the basic tenets of participatory management. Ideally, every member of the organization thinks strategically about consumers' needs, competitors, and competitive advantage.

From Competitors to Competitors and Consumers

Historically, strategy has stressed competition and minimized the importance of consumers. Today, the emphasis is more balanced. Strategic thinking offers a more balanced view of customers and competitors as sources of competitive advantage. As Porter (1987) notes: "The questions that good planning seeks to answer—the future direction of competition, the needs of the customer, the likely behaviour of competitors, how to gain competitive advantage—will never lose their relevance" (p. 18). Clearly, as was detailed in the first chapter, consumers, competitors, and competitive advantage are the bywords of strategic thinking.

From Calculation to Creativity

Marketing problems are usually ill-structured. In recent years, that has led to the recognition that applying deterministic formulations to such problems are likely to lead to failure. Those techniques will end up focusing only on those issues that can be quantified and manipulated mathematically.

The formula planning approaches of the past focused too intently on measurable, quantitative factors. In the process they ignored the important qualitative aspects of marketing problems. Like marketing itself, strategy is more likely to be viewed as an art than a science.

Furthermore, marketing strategy problems are constantly changing. They rarely remain static. Consequently, the application of static planning formulations—if they ever held promise—are surely deficient now. As Mintzberg (1987) notes: "Smart strategists appreciate that they cannot always be smart enough to think through everything in advance" (p. 69). The environment in which firms operate is different than that presupposed by formula planning tools.

Many authors have recognized that the strategy formulation process itself is usually ill-structured. Rarely are strategies formed with the precision proposed by the planning approaches of the past. Quinn (1978) argues that the strategy process is not the rational-analytic process found in most textbooks. Instead, it is a fragmented, intuitive, and evolutionary process, where initial decisions and external events flow together.

Mintzberg (1987) also calls for a more qualitative perspective. He contends that strategies should be "crafted" rather than calculated. The image of an artisan shaping a pot is a more appropriate analogy to the construction of marketing strategy than is the image of a engineer making calculations. Strategy relies more on the senses than it does on analyses. It is less of a deliberate process that foresees the orderly flow of events than it is a process where one idea leads to another until a pattern appears. In short, marketing strategy proceeds with the imprecision of an art rather than the exactitude of a science. You craft strategy: you do not calculate it.

Porter's (1987) views on strategic thinking make similar arguments. He argues that problems with strategic planning techniques should not be confused with the merits of strategic thinking. Strategic issues are still important. It is the techniques once used to tackle them that have clearly proved faulty.

Haspeslagh (1982) concurs. He found that portfolio planning techniques were widely used and had "deeply affected" corporate planning. He surveyed the Fortune 1000 and found that 36 percent of the Fortune 1000 and 45 percent of the Fortune 500 had adopted the approach by the late 1970s. He is troubled that those theories are "divorced from the real world . . . and view business in depersonalized, economic terms." He believes: "The exceptions and discontinuity with which managers are all too familiar may be more important in planning the future of a business than impersonal forces or established industry structures" (p. 58). He, too, seems to be arguing for a greater input from creativity.

That is not to say that creativity should replace control. Shank, Niblock, and Sandalls (1973) argued persuasively that firms should balance those two important aspects of planning. More recently, Ramanujam and Venka-traman (1987) surveyed 207 large American firms and found that high-performing companies felt that they successfully balanced both creativity and control.

From Rigid to Flexible

It is the rigidity of previous strategic planning that deserves the most criticism. Setting strategies for five years in advance precluded learning and adaptation. Likewise, the formula-planning grids of the 1970s offered a single approach to business success. There was little room for flexibility.

Strategic thinking is more flexible. There are fewer guidelines to follow, and no rituals to perform. As Mintzberg (1987) notes, it merges thoughts and actions, balances control and learning, and manages stability and change. It recognizes that ''strategies can form as well as be formulated'' (p. 68).

Strategic thinking embraces strategies that are adaptive and flexible to changes in market conditions. Quick response has replaced long-range forecasts as the preferred approach to dealing with an uncertain environment. It is an approach that is more in sync with the times in which we live.

Concept of Competitive Advantage

Most strategic planning formulations have a common thread running throughout—the search for competitive advantage. Be it implied or explicit, strategies proposed over the past few decades have almost always offered a means whereby a firm can outperform its competitors and earn higher-than-average profits. In fact, the connection between strategy and competitive advantage is so strong, and so direct, that strategy is often defined as the search for competitive advantage.

Ansoff (1965) is usually considered the first to develop the idea of competitive advantage, arguing that it results from the search for ''unique opportunities . . . which will give the firm a strong competitive position'' (p. 110).

Over the years, numerous competitive advantages have been proposed and studied. Some schemes have argued for price advantages based on lower costs of production. Others have proposed erecting barriers to entry to keep competitors out of markets. More recently, marketers have focused on improving product quality, and building long-term relationships with customers as the desired path to competitive advantage. This section looks at the connections between marketing strategy and competitive advantage.

WHAT IS COMPETITIVE ADVANTAGE?

Competitive advantage is something that allows a firm to earn higher-than-average profits. The connection between competitive advantage and profits is direct and well known. A stronger advantage leads to higher profits; a weaker advantage, or worse yet, a competitive disadvantage, leads to lower profits.

Competitive advantage has the following five characteristics:

Special Competence

A competitive advantage is something special that a firm does, or possesses, that gives it an edge against competitors. Some firms have established brand names that connote premium quality in a particular product category. IBM, with those three powerful blue letters, leads in computers, McDonald's dominates in hamburgers, Heinz "owns" the ketchup business, and Coca-Cola leads in soft drinks. In each instance, consumers happily pay extra for the quality and service implied by those brands. That price premium goes directly to higher profits.

Other firms dominate distribution channels. Soft drinks, for example, are sold through fast-food chains—fountain sales—and in supermarkets—retail sales. Coke and Pepsi dominate both channels. McDonald's sells Coke exclusively. Pepsi, which owns Taco Bell and Pizza Hut, sells its soft drinks through those captive establishments. Second-tier soft drink sellers have little chance of penetrating those outlets. The competitive advantage in distribution is held by the market leaders. A similar pattern exists in supermarket sales. As the leaders offer more brands, the followers are pushed from the shelves.

A special competence can also be negative. A competitive *dis*advantage arises from something that the firm lacks or does poorly. The firm may not have a salesforce of its own. Or, it might be forced to distribute through middlemen, whose loyalties lie elsewhere. The firm may lack brand recognition, have higher costs, or lack the capital to match the level of advertising. If it is a large firm, it may lack the ability to respond rapidly to changes in the environment or competitors' moves. It may take years to bring new products to market. Those disadvantages, and many others, offer opportunities for other firms to gain competitive advantage.

Creating Imperfect Competition

In essence, competitive advantage is gained by creating imperfect competition. By definition, there is no competitive advantage in perfectly competitive markets. All firms produce similar products. There is no market leader. And, firms can enter and leave the market at will. It makes for very average profits for all competitors.

Marketers seek to gain competitive advantage by moving away from the economist's model of perfect competition. Strong brand recognition, for example, and product differentiation, destroys the assumption that all products are the same. Likewise, advantages in distribution mean firms cannot enter the market at will. The concept of competitive advantage runs contrary to the economic model of perfect competition.

Sustainability

To be successful a competitive advantage must be sustainable, not transitory. A true competitive advantage cannot be easily copied by competitors. A firm must be able to hold on to it over the long term. A competitive advantage that cannot be sustained is fleeting and ineffectual.

Sustainability is a controversial issue. Some strategists argue that most competitive advantages are not sustainable, but are easily imitated. A firm that develops a technological innovation, for example, often gains an initial advantage. But almost immediately competitors reverse engineer the product, and introduce variations of it to the market. The competitive advantage is quickly lost. Critics contend that the search for a sustainable competitive advantage is a search for the will-o-the-wisp. It is a search for something elusive, something that is desirable but cannot be obtained. Other strategists argue that many advantages are sustainable. They are not as easily copied as critics suggest. A leading brand name, for example, often leads for decades.

To be successful, a competitive advantage must minimize the opportunity for competitive response. Clearly, the focus must be on thwarting competitors' responses. Consider the competitive advantage claimed by some American textile producers, who compete in an industry battered by lower-cost imports. American producers have a clear competitive disadvantage in cost, but they are located close to the markets they serve. Therein lies their opportunity to gain a competitive advantage. American manufacturers are using sophisticated electronic communications to link retailers with producers to create "quick-response" delivery systems, akin to the "just-in-time" inventory methods in other industries. Manufacturers deliver quickly in much smaller lots, keeping retail inventories lean and flexible to unexpected changes. Markdowns are minimized. Most important, imports cannot respond. They require longer lead times and larger orders. A competitive advantage of speed is pitted against an advantage in cost. The strategy of American producers is an attempt to pit their strengths against competitors' weaknesses.

Competitive advantage is about strengths and weaknesses. Specifically, it is about aligning your strengths against a competitor's weaknesses. it is about stacking the deck in your favor. To use a military analogy, it is about attacking their cavalry with your tanks.

A Fit with the External Environment

The environment also affects competitive advantage. Some advantages are gained by better matching market needs. A competitive advantage must look not only at competitors' weaknesses, but market conditions as well. The external environment poses opportunities and threats to all competing firms. By design or serendipity, market changes enhance the strengths of some firms and exacerbate the weaknesses of others. What the firm does well, relative to competitors, can turn out to be either an advantage or disadvantage depending on the demands of the external environment.

One of the oldest formulations in strategy is known by the acronym SWOT (*s*trengths, *w*eaknesses, *o*pportunities, and *t*hreats). It proposes that the essence of strategy is to match: (1) strengths against competitors' weaknesses and (2) strengths against market opportunities. Exhibit 2.2 illustrates the SWOT format, showing the dual orientations towards markets as well as competitors. SWOT is as important to strategy today as it was when it was first introduced decades ago.

Path to Higher-Than-Average Profits

Finally, the ultimate goal of competitive advantage is to earn higher-than-average profits. By moving away from the model of perfect competition, by focusing strengths against competitors' weaknesses, and by better fitting the needs of the external environment, a firm is able to exercise

Exhibit 2.2   *SWOT*

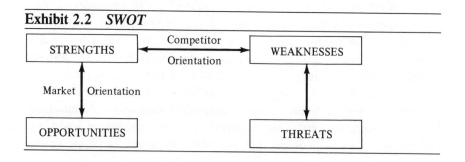

Exhibit 2.3   *Two Sources of Competitive Advantage*

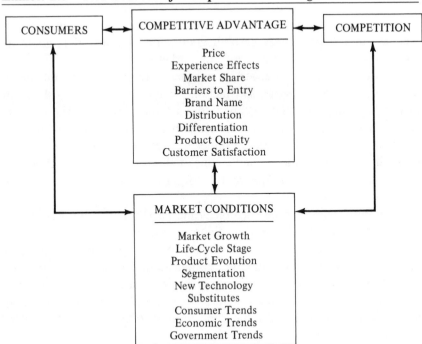

some degree of influence over the market in which it competes. As Porter (1985) notes in his landmark book *Competitive Advantage:* "Competitive strategy aims to establish a profitable and sustainable position against the forces that determine industry competition" (p. 1).

SOURCES OF COMPETITIVE ADVANTAGE

Competitive advantage arises from two separate sources—better serving consumers or outfoxing competitors. Exhibit 2.3 illustrates that basic pattern.

Better Serving Customers

Marketers' interest in consumers does not arise solely from altruism, but primarily as a search for competitive advantage. Marketers have long known that better serving customers leads to numerous business benefits. Satisfied consumers are more likely to return for subsequent purchases, and are more likely to remain brand loyal than customers who have been treated poorly. Dissatisfied customers are likely to seek out other vendors. It is true in industrial and consumer markets, as well as for the purchasers of both goods and services. It is about as close as you can come to a "law" in marketing.

Throughout the past decade, a dominant trend has been the move towards long-term customer satisfaction. That trend often takes the form of building enduring relationships with customers. In industrial markets representatives visit customer factories to better understand how the customer uses their product. In consumer markets it entails better service, more liberal return policies, and a concerted effort to make the customer happy. In each instance, the goal is to gain competitive advantage by better serving customers.

Long-term consumer satisfaction is intimately tied to the new-found interest in product quality. Selling higher-quality products promotes long-term consumer satisfaction. L. L. Bean, for example, the upscale mail order seller of quality merchandise, has had a fundamental policy towards customers for decades: if a consumer is dissatisfied with a product—for whatever reason—it simply returns it for a full refund. No questions asked. In more recent years, the trend in marketing has been for sellers to copy that strategy.

Long-term consumer satisfaction is a new and more stringent implementation of the marketing concept as first espoused in the 1950s. It is a return, even a magnification, of the decades-old observation that to be successful a firm must favor a long-term focus on the customers it seeks to serve. What is new is the extent to which firms will go to make customers happy. The reason for such extraordinary efforts is twofold: first, many consumers today demand higher-quality products. Second, the demand for higher-quality products is driven, in part, by the sheer number of competitors that make their wares available to customers.

Customer-based approaches to competitive advantage succeed by better tracking customer needs. Not all needs are for high-priced, premium goods. Consider the sorry case of Cuisinart Inc., the pioneer of home food processors. The company filed for bankruptcy in August 1989 after failing to follow the customers it once understood so well. The firm failed to respond to the needs of low-end customers who wanted a lighter, less expensive machine with easily understood features. Black and Decker, Sunbeam, Hamilton Beach, and Presto entered the market to serve that need. In 1985, Sunbeam sold 700,000 of its $60 machines. In contrast, Cuisinart's models averaged $225. Its strategic response: introduction of a heavy-duty, $600, feature-laden model for the well-heeled, chef of the future. Unfortunately, customers wanted convenience rather than gourmet delight. Cuisinart lost what its competitors gained—a competitive advantage earned by better responding to the changing needs of modern consumers (Hannon 1989).

Outfoxing Competitors

Competitive advantage also arises from outmaneuvering competitors. Many of the specific advantages listed in Exhibit 2.3 succeed by thwarting competitors' moves in the marketplace. Focusing on competitors rather than customers, they are more analogous to military strategies than to advantages based on better serving customers. Erecting barriers to entry and creating distribution strangleholds are but two examples of competitive advantage that arise from the perspective of military strategy rather than attempting to serve customers better.

Formal strategic planning theories from the 1970s embraced the competitor focus. Military analogies in marketing exhibit a similar emphasis. Ries and Trout (1986), for example, in a book titled *Marketing Warfare*, argue that the strategies of famous military generals can be directly applied to marketing. They contend that marketing is warfare. Their analogy is controversial, but it points up the importance and ferocity of competition in today's markets.

Even the word "strategy" conveys the military bias. It is derived from the same source as the current Greek word *stratigiki*, which means "art of the general." Like their military counterparts, marketing strategists must marshal their forces to fight the enemy.

Balance of Consumer and Competitor-Based Advantages

The best competitive advantage usually combines both the consumer and competitor orientations. Neither approach, by itself, is sufficient. As Jack Trout was quoted in *Business Week:* "Knowing what the customer wants isn't too helpful if a dozen other companies are already serving the customer's wants" (Oct. 7, 1985, p. 55).

Likewise, outfoxing competitors is not possible without products that consumers want and will purchase. Consider the experience of Texas Instruments. In the 1970s, Texas Instruments gained a clear competitive advantage in the low-cost production of home computers and digital watches. It had "slid down" the experience curve faster than competitors, but unfortunately, consumers did not want the products of its efforts. Texas Instruments had beat its competitors at the production of unwanted goods. When it comes to competitive advantage, it is balance that is important.

Most of the specific competitive advantages listed in Exhibit 2.3 are a mixture of consumer and competitor perspectives. Lower prices, for example, can be used to beat back competitors, but entice consumers to the firm's products. The lower prices can serve as a barrier to entry. They can also provide consumers with product "value." Likewise, product quality serves consumers, by offering them superior products. But, product quality also keeps competitors at bay. It renders competitors' products as inferior. Clearly, the two sources of competitive advantage are not mutually exclusive. Specific advantages merely tend to favor one source over the other.

Market Conditions

Marketing strategy is not constructed in isolation, but in light of prevailing market conditions. Like the earlier discussion of SWOT, the state of those conditions has a tremendous influence on the nature of competitive advantage, such an advantage based on serving consumers better requires attention be paid to the external environment, which includes monitoring consumer trends, economic issues, and government policies.

The external environment changes constantly, with many of the changes beyond the control of individual firms. Firms must react to, or anticipate, market changes. Overall, changing market conditions create opportunities for some firms and poses threats to others.

Some firms, for example, have found themselves in a favorable environment. General Mills gained share in the cereal market in the late 1980s when the rage for oat bran began. At that time 40 percent of its cereals happened to be made with oats. Cheerios gained a whooping 3.1 percent share in just one year. An unhappy Kellogg's spokesman claimed its competitors just got lucky. A General Mill's executive claims that superior product quality was the reason for success. Whatever the real cause, General Mills clearly faced a favorable external environment with a product that was clearly in sync with the continuing trend towards healthful living rather than indulgent behavior. Kellogg's product, in contrast, was out of sync with the times (Mitchell 1989). The stakes were high. Kellogg's president lost his job in late 1989 over the market-share loss. Kellogg's had not found a way to deal with changed market conditions.

Scotch whiskey has also been affected by changing market conditions. Throughout the 1980s, distilleries in Scotland closed in unprecedented numbers. Marketing strategy helped stem the decline, but not reverse it. In the United States the long-term trend has been clearly downward—volume was down 10 percent in 1988 alone. Due to diligent marketing efforts, however, dollar sales volume fell only 1 percent. Scotch marketers decided to make up for volume declines by moving towards the high end of the market. Premium scotch, that carries a premium price, is now emphasized. Lower-margin, high-volume brands have been de-emphasized. It is an attempt to gain competitive advantage under unfavorable market conditions (Whitney 1989).

Miller Beer's "Matilda Bay" wine cooler faced a similar fate. Miller entered the market late, figuring it would muscle its way into the market with superior marketing and distribution expertise. After spending $30 million on promotion it made it to fourth place. Then sales of wine coolers began to cool. Matilda Bay was especially hard hit. Sales fell 50 percent in the first eight months of 1988. Miller pulled the plug quickly and focused its attention on its more successful Genuine Draft Beer. Changes in consumer demand conspired to defeat Miller (Siler 1989).

Likewise the Edsel, one of marketing's most famous failures, failed, in part, because it was introduced in 1958 at the beginning of a recession. Consumers faced with the dire economic prospect of losing their jobs were likely to postpone the purchase of a new and expensive car. In contrast, CD players were introduced in the early 1980s right at the beginning of the longest-running period of economic growth in postwar history. The product was a major success.

A later chapter on the evolution of markets looks at how products evolve, and how market conditions play an important role in that evolution.

A competitive advantage that arises from a focus on competitors is also affected by market conditions. Relative market shares held by competitors, the market-growth rate, the extent of segmentation in the market, and the opportunity for future segmentation all affect the strengths and weaknesses of the players involved. A new entrant into a high-growth market, where no firm holds a dominant position, has a greater chance to gain competitive advantage over rivals than a new entrant into a low-growth market, which has been dominated for decades by a strong market leader.

References

Abell, Derek, and John Hammond. *Strategic Market Planning*. Englewood Cliffs, NJ: Prentice-Hall, 1979.

Ansoff, Igor. *Corporate Strategy*. New York: McGraw-Hill, 1965.

Boyd, Harper, and Jean-Claude Larreche. "The Foundations of Marketing Strategy." In *Review of Marketing,* Gerald Zaltman and Thomas Bonoma (eds.). Chicago: American Marketing Association, 1978, pp. 4–72.

Bracker, Jeffrey. "The Historical Development of the Strategic Management Concept." *Academy of Management Review,* vol. 5, no. 2 (1980), pp. 219–224.

"Forget Satisfying the Consumer—Just Outfox the Competition." *Business Week,* October 7, 1985, pp. 55–58.

Gardner, David, and Howard Thomas. "Strategic Marketing: History, Issues, and Emergent Themes." In *Strategic Marketing and Management,* H. Thomas and D. Gardner (eds.). London: John Wiley & Sons, 1985.

Gluck, Fredrick, Stephen Kaufman, and Steven Walleck. "Strategic Management for Competitive Advantage." *Harvard Business Review,* July–August 1980, pp. 154–160.

Hannon, Kerry. "Diced and Sliced." *Forbes,* October 2, 1989, p. 68.

Haspeslagh, Philippe. "Portfolio Planning: Uses and Limits." *Harvard Business Review,* January–February 1982, pp. 58–73.

Mintzberg, Henry. "Crafting Strategy." *Harvard Business Review,* July–August 1987, pp. 66–75.

Mitchell, Russell. "Big G Is Growing Fat on Oat Cuisine." *Business Week,* September 18, 1989, p. 29.

"The New Breed of Strategic Planner." *Business Week,* September 17, 1984, pp. 62–68.

Porter, Michael. *Competitive Advantage*. New York: Free Press, 1985.

Porter, Michael. "The State of Strategic Thinking." *The Economist,* May 23, 1987, pp. 17–22.

Ramanujam, V., and N. Venkatraman. "Planning and Performance: A New Look at an Old Question." *Business Horizons,* May–June 1987, pp. 19–25.

Ries, Al, and Jack Trout. *Marketing Warfare*. New York: McGraw-Hill, 1986.

Quinn, James Brian. "Strategic Change: Logical Incrementalism." *Sloan Management Review,* Fall 1978, pp. 7–21.

Shank, John, Edward Niblock, and William Sandalls Jr. "Balance Creativity and Practicality in Formal Planning." *Harvard Business Review,* January–February 1973, pp. 87–95.

Siler, Julia Flynn. "How Miller Got Dunked in Matilda Bay." *Business Week,* September 25, 1989, p. 54.

Steiner, George. *Top Management Planning*. New York: Macmillan, 1969.

Whitney, Craig. "Scotch's New International Status." *New York Times,* September 17, 1989, p. F6.

Chapter 3

The Boston Consulting Group

Experience Effects and the Growth-Share Matrix

The name Bruce Henderson is synonymous with the Boston Consulting Group's growth-share matrix. In the mid-1960s, when Henderson was a purchasing agent at Westinghouse, the company wanted to know why per-unit costs declined when the firm gained experience manufacturing products. Henderson adapted the experience curve, a derivative of the learning curve, which had been known about for decades, to answer the question. Henderson deduced the strategic implications of the experience curve, founded the Boston Consulting Group (BCG), and offered the findings to other companies in the form of the growth-share matrix. The matrix took the world of planning by storm. The ideas of the BCG ruled thinking in strategy during the 1970s.

Henderson popularized the idea that strategy could be made universal. Diversified firms could diversify risk and optimize the performance of the entire organization by managing the parts of their business as they would a portfolio of investments. It was management for modern times, and the idea caught on.

In recent years, the matrix has taken a beating however. Many of the ideas it proposed have been severely criticized. But, some of its contributions are as important today as when they were first presented more than twenty years ago. In many respects, the BCG efforts laid the foundation for today's ideas about marketing strategy. This chapter reviews and evaluates the theoretical underpinnings of the Boston Consulting Group's efforts. The next chapter examines the marketing strategies that arise out of the matrix method of formulating marketing strategy.

It is important to note that the BCG matrix was only one of many matrix approaches to marketing strategy that became popular in the 1970s. There was the General Electric/McKinsey market attractiveness/business position matrix, which is best described by Abell and Hammond (1979), the life-cycle portfolio matrix (Patel and Younger 1978), and the directional policy matrix (Robinson, Hichen and Wade 1978), to name but a few of the more popular entries. Together those approaches fell under the rubric of "formula planning," "portfolio planning," or "matrix planning." They differed in some important respects but the similarities were striking. Each one reduced strategy to a series of boxes that prescribed the best strategy for a particular situation.

Only the BCG matrix, and its theoretical underpinnings, are covered here. The similarity of the matrix approaches, and the fact that they dominated strategy more than ten years ago, suggests that once is enough. Besides, the similarity of the approaches means that their contributions and criticisms are also similar. What applies to the BCG approach also applies to the other matrix approaches as well.

There are three major components to the BCG's observations: (1) strategic business units (SBUs), (2) experience effects, and (3) the growth-share matrix.

Strategic Business Units

Strategic business units (SBUs), which represent a major contribution of the BCG matrix to marketing strategy, are a way of organizing a diversified business so that each individual part resembles a free-standing enterprise. SBUs were originally developed by McKinsey and Company, the management consulting firm, in conjunction with General Electric in the late 1960s. As a method of organizing American businesses, they caught on quickly. SBUs are an integral part of the Boston Consulting Group scheme, even though they were developed elsewhere. (For a detailed discussion of SBUs, see the article by William Hall listed at the end of the chapter.)

CHARACTERISTICS

Organizing by SBUs allows large diversified firms to compete as though they were a collection of much smaller independent firms. Strategic business units can be defined as:

A way of organizing a business so that each unit sells an identifiable set of *products* to an identifiable *set of customers* in competition with an identifiable set of *competitors*. SBUs are *managed independently*, with their own set of *objectives. Resources, costs, and profits* are attributed to each unit separately.

External Focus

SBUs are organized around markets and customers, both external factors. Each SBU serves a clearly defined market with an identifiable set of products. Products might be placed in different SBUs even though they share the same production facilities. Consistent with the marketing concept, it is the market that matters not internal production similarities. An SBU organized around breakfast foods, for example, might include products manufactured by very different processes. It might include instant breakfast drink mixes, muffins, and egg substitutes.

Identifiable Competitors

SBUs are also designed so that competitors can be more easily identified. The breakfast foods SBU, for example, would be designed so that the firm could compete against other firms selling breakfast foods.

Autonomous Profit Centers

SBUs operate like independent businesses. Each unit has its own managers and also its own objectives. One unit may be slated for market-share gains, another might be targeted for divestment.

Distinct Marketing Strategies

SBUs also have their own marketing strategies, and follow their own paths. Strategies are restricted only in that they must be consistent with the overarching objectives of the firm. If a firm wants to be number one in automotive parts, for example, it is unlikely that breakfast foods will be slated for high growth. Divestment is a more likely prospect.

Separate Accounting

To compete as an independent unit, each SBU must be able to tabulate its profits and costs. It must also have separate accounting of the resources at its disposal.

DEFINITIONAL PROBLEMS

In theory, the concept of SBUs is clear and admirable. In practice, it is neither. It is difficult to implement all aspects of the SBU definition. In keeping with the subjective and creative nature of strategy some combination of the factors listed above is usually sufficient to define a business as a SBU. More precise definitions are left to the physical sciences where more precise physical laws operate.

Entangled Businesses

One particularly vexing problem with SBUs has been the separate accounting required for autonomous operation. Large diversified firms are usually highly interrelated. Individual products assigned to different SBUs share the same production lines, market research, and other functions. It makes for an accountant's nightmare. In theory, each SBU should have its own production facilities, marketing research, R&D, and distribution. In practice, however, individual facilities are impractical. Shared facilities are more likely. Accountants then try to sort the details of who pays for what.

In a vertically integrated business, where one unit of the firm buys the output of another unit, it is difficult to decide what price should be paid. Should the captive seller sell at cost? Or, should he try to charge the highest price possible to maximize the profits of his particular business unit? A high price helps the "seller" SBU but hurts the "buyer" SBU. A low price does the opposite. Autonomy for SBUs often rubs up against overall corporate policy.

Aggregation Issues

There is also the problem of aggregation. Some SBUs are defined very narrowly—instant breakfast foods—while others are defined broadly—the consumer foods division. A division is usually too large to use in portfolio planning. Besides, in practice, divisions are often drawn around parameters important to the firm rather than customers. When it comes to SBUs, there is great variability in definitions.

Marketers favor the more narrow definition of "product markets." In fact, marketers often apply the BCG matrix to individual products rather than SBUs. Marketers, for example, might plot cereals on the matrix, rather than all breakfast foods. The BCG matrix is applicable to both products and SBUs.

Experience Effects

Experience effects constitute the central theoretical basis of the Boston Consulting Group's growth-share matrix. They hold that there is an opportunity to lower costs as a firm gains experience producing a product. Experience is gained by increasing sales volume over time, and the more experience gained the lower the costs to produce each unit.

The concept of experience effects is not new. As early as the 1920s, military manufacturers noticed that the more planes they produced, the more efficiently—and more economically—they were able to produce each one. Simply put, they learned how to do the job better. Planes produced later in the process were less expensive to manufacture than planes made earlier.

Experience effects were first promoted for business use by Andress (1954). He argued that lower costs could be achieved as a firm gained experience making a product. Ten years later, Hirschmann (1964) expanded the value of the concept. He argued that experience effects were more pervasive than previously thought. They applied to all businesses, not just aircraft manufacturers. Henderson ran further with the ball, elaborating on those early observations.

According to experience effects, costs do not decline automatically. In fact, costs are more likely to rise than fall. The tendency is for staffs to expand, product lines to proliferate, and workers to earn higher wages as a business grows. The pressure is for costs to climb over time, not decline.

Anyone familiar with the "wheel of retailing" hypothesis in marketing is familiar with the tendency for costs to rise over time. The theory holds that low-cost discount stores inexorably evolve into higher-cost, more upscale retailers. They are then replaced by newer, lower-cost entrants. Retailers find higher costs with greater experience.

Experience effects hold that there is an opportunity to lower costs in business, but there is no guarantee. Cost declines arise from a strict adherence to productivity goals, the adoption of new technologies to increase productivity, and a constant effort to cut unnecessary expenditures. Each of these opportunities requires the active attention of management, as experience effects do not occur by themselves.

It is the resourcefulness and ingenuity of those working at the firm that results in experience effects; in other words, they are due to the clever application of new procedures and methods. Hirschmann summed it up nicely a generation ago with three simple words: "Practice makes perfect" (p. 125).

EXPERIENCE EFFECTS VERSUS ECONOMIES OF SCALE

Experience effects are due to something other than the sheer size of the operation. Cost declines due to size arise from scale effects or economies of scale. Size effects are something much different from experience effects. As well, experience effects accrue over time. The time dimension is what makes them different. Scale effects arise from the size of the operation. Time is not a factor.

Consider the cost of building a power plant to generate electricity for public consumption. To double the capacity of that plant does not require twice the investment. The same is true for other types of plant and equipment. Larger operations often realize economies of scale. Bigger size often leads to lower costs per unit.

Economies of scale are not restricted to large factories, but exist in marketing-related activities as well. A salesforce that sells two product lines, for example, does not have to be twice the size of a salesforce that sells a single product line.

EXPERIENCE EFFECTS VERSUS LEARNING EFFECTS

Experience effects are more encompassing than the learning curve, a popular concept in psychology. The learning curve captures the notion that productivity improvements are gained as a worker learns how to perform a task better (and faster), but the learning curve focuses only on worker productivity. If you have ever observed the speed with which a bookkeeper's fingers manipulate the keys of a calculator, you have observed the learning curve in action. If you plotted the number of calculations made by that bookkeeper from the first day hired to the end of that employee's first year on the job, you would be plotting the learning curve. The curve would decline as the bookkeeper mastered the task of repetitive calculation. The bookkeeper's fingers would learn to move faster. Yelle (1979) provides a detailed review of the history of the learning curve and experience effects.

The learning curve is part of experience effects, but they capture other sources of improvement as well. The bookkeeper, for example, might figure out a better system for making the required calculations, by calculating groups of numbers rather than one number at a time. Better calculators, with multiple memories, might be invented to make the job easier. A specific computer program might be applied to speed the calculations. Or the job might be redesigned to require fewer calculations. In every instance, experience effects would be at work improving the efficiency of the operation over time.

SOURCES OF EXPERIENCE EFFECTS

Experience effects arise from the following six sources:

The Learning Curve

The learning curve plays an important part, but not the only part, in experience effects. The learning curve captures gains in worker productivity. The workers learn to do the job more efficiently.

Specialization of Labor

Specialization (or division) of labor also improves the efficiency of an operation over time. When a radically new product is first manufactured, volume is small, and workers are likely to perform many tasks. Often each piece is custom-made. As more items are sold, and experience accumulates, however, the opportunities for specialization increase. Workers tend to perform only a few tasks. Efficiencies increase as experience is gained. With his use of assembly line techniques, Henry Ford dominated his contemporaries. His was not the first car, nor the most sophisticated. It was the first car to gain experience effects through worker specialization.

Process Innovations

Process innovations are inventions and improvements in the machinery and procedures used to produce products in an industry. Radically new products are often made on radically new, custom-made machines. Often, those machines are crude and inefficient. As experience accumulates, machine design improves. Through their ingenuity and creativity machine manufacturers find ways to increase the efficiency of production machinery. Manufacturers also find better ways to structure the production process. More efficient machines used in more efficient configurations leads to experience effects.

Consider the case of disposable diapers, a difficult product to manufacture. In the 1950s disposable diapers were extremely expensive to produce. Consequently, few people bought them. By the mid-1960s, Procter and Gamble had perfected the production process. Reduced costs expanded the market for Pampers. Disposable diapers still require a block-long production process, but experience effects have been gained from process innovations.

New Materials

New materials also help lower costs. As an industry increases its experience with the manufacture of a product, new materials are invented that replace the old. In autos, for example, plastics are now used to make parts once made exclusively of steel. Plastic is lighter and often more durable. Truly successful new materials have higher performance and lower costs than the existing materials they replace.

Product Standardization

Product standardization occurs when an industry agrees on what form the product will take. In the early days of cars, for example, there were different types of engines, radically different designs, and completely unique systems of production and sales. As the market grew, the industry settled on a more standardized product and process of producing it. Many other products have also been standardized. Stereo equipment, televisions, CD players, VCRs, and a host of other products are standardized on a single design. The moves from multiple models of the same product, different systems of production, and competing and incompatible technologies to standardization allow suppliers to increase their efficiency, and lower per-unit costs.

Product Redesign

Product redesign occurs when a firm designs its products for efficient manufacture. As time progresses, a firm discovers more efficient ways to design products. In auto production, for example, the dashboard is designed to bolt quickly into place.

The Experience Curve

Experience effects are plotted on experience curves. A typical curve (shown in Exhibit 3.1) depicts how much it costs an individual firm to produce each unit according to the total number of units the firm has produced to date. This exhibit captures two important properties of experi-

Exhibit 3.1 *Idealized Experience Curve*

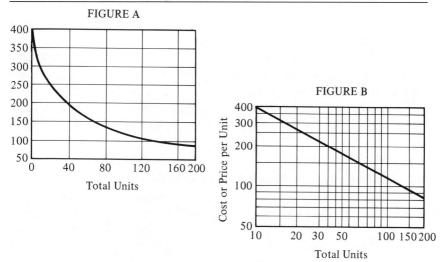

FIGURE A

FIGURE B

Cost or Price per Unit

Total Units

Total Units

When prices or costs are plotted against cumulative volume, the resulting graph characteristically takes the form of a curve on a linear scale (Figure A). Although the smoothness of the curve suggests the regularity of the relationship, some of the particular aspects are obscured. As a result, it is more useful to plot C/V or P/V slopes on double logarithmic scales (Figure B).

Plots on a log-log scale have the unique property of showing percentage change as a constant distance, along either axis at any position on the grid. A straight line on log-log paper means, then, that a given percentage change in one factor results in a corresponding percentage change in the other, the nature of that relationship corresponding to the slope of the line, which can be read right off a log-log grid.

In the case of cost-volume or price-volume slopes, the plotting of observed data about costs or prices and accumulated experience for a product on log-log paper has always produced straight lines reflecting a consistent relationship between experience and prices and experience and costs.

SOURCE: *Perspectives on Experience,* The Boston Consulting Group, 1968, p. 13. Reprinted by permission from The Boston Consulting Group, Inc., Boston, Mass. © Copyright 1968.

ence effects. First, the curve slopes downward, showing that costs per unit decline as experience accumulates. Second, it shows that costs decline more slowly as experience accumulates. As a product category matures, substantial cost declines become more difficult to realize. It is harder to double sales of a mature product than it is to double sales of a vibrantly growing new product. Hence, it is harder to realize significant experience effects later in the life of a product than it is at the beginning. Substantial declines in the cost of manufacturing refrigerators, for example, have already been realized.

Experience curves are often plotted on a "log-log" grid to ease interpretation. The relationship between costs and units produced remains the same. The graph simply becomes easier to read. Exhibit 3.1 also includes an experience curve plotted on a log-log grid.

Typically experience curves decline at a rate of 10 to 30 percent each time production doubles. An 80 percent experience curve is considered average, and is interpreted as follows: as experience doubles costs per unit fall to 80 percent of their original value. As sales rise from 1,000 to 2,000 units, for example, costs per unit decline from $100 to $80.

Experience curves are usually described in terms of percentages. Lower percentage experience curves mean costs are falling faster. A 70 percent curve indicates that costs fall to 70 percent of their present level each time volume doubles. That is, costs decline by 30 percent. Higher percentage curves mean costs are falling more slowly. A 90 percent curve indicates that costs fall to 90 percent of current levels each time volume doubles. Costs decline by only 10 percent.

Exhibit 3.2 shows an experience curve for Japanese beer, a branded consumer product. It has roughly a 90 percent slope. That is, every time sales (and hence production) double, costs decline by 10 percent. In Exhibit 3.3 an experience curve for integrated curcuits, an electronics product, shows that costs have fallen faster. This is roughly a 70 percent curve. Each time sales of integrated curcuits doubles costs, and eventually prices, fall by 30 percent.

Cost-Price Patterns

Experience curves plot costs to the firm, not prices to the consumer. The relationship between costs and prices determines not only the firm's profits, but whether it will be able to survive in the marketplace. The relationship between costs and prices is a central feature of the BCG's observations. Sometimes prices move in tandem with costs as the product moves from introduction to maturity. Often, they do not. The following two patterns are typical in stable and unstable competitive environments.

STABLE COMPETITION

Exhibit 3.4 shows the relationship between prices and costs when the two move in tandem. Price cuts follow cost reductions as the market expands, whereas profit margins remain constant.

Exhibit 3.2   *Experience Curve for Japanese Beer*

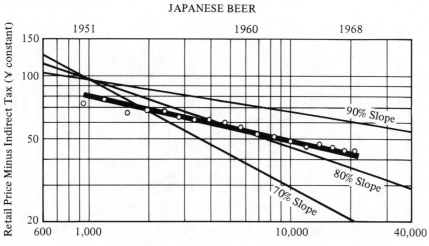

YEAR	INDUSTRY TOTAL ACCUMULATED VOLUME (MILLION TONS)	RETAIL PRICE MINUS INDIRECT TAX (¥ CONSTANT)
1951	930	72.34
1952	1,206	76.44
1953	1,578	65.60
1954	1,968	67.53
1955	2,371	66.42
1956	2,823	63.00
1957	3,375	60.33
1958	3,991	60.83
1959	4,736	58.96
1960	5,655	55.73
1961	6,888	51.97
1962	8,371	50.41
1963	10,058	48.14
1964	12,051	45.97
1965	14,044	46.86
1966	16,167	44.76
1967	18,578	43.03
1968	21,046	43.17

Source: The Boston Consulting Group K.K.

Exhibit 3.3 *Experience Curve for Integrated Circuits*

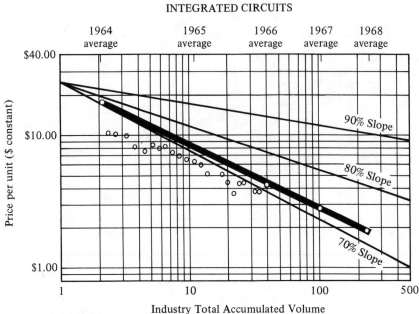

INTEGRATED CIRCUITS

	INDUSTRY TOTAL ACCUMULATED VOLUME (MILLION UNITS)	PRICE PER UNIT ($ CONSTANT)	MONTH/YEAR	INDUSTRY TOTAL ACCUMULATED VOLUME (MILLION UNITS)	PRICE PER UNIT ($ CONSTANT)
MONTH/YEAR					
End 1964	2.05	16.91 (annual average)	February	14.41	4.94
January 1965	2.42	9.78	March	16.40	5.81
February	2.80	9.82	April	18.34	4.92
March	3.33	9.47	May	20.40	4.30
April	3.90	7.84	June	23.01	3.66
May	4.62	7.35	July	25.05	4.27
June	5.30	8.12	August	27.53	4.35
July	5.99	7.72	September	30.47	4.06
August	6.72	7.88	October	33.44	3.74
September	7.61	7.21	November	36.38	3.71
October	8.66	6.79	December	40.39	4.10 (annual average
November	9.91	6.37	End 1967	108.50	2.76 = $4.92)
December	11.41	6.11 (annual average	End 1968	241.70	1.87
January 1966	12.71	5.77 = $7.20)			

Source: Derived from published data of Electronics Industry Association
            Boston Consulting Group estimates

SOURCE: *Perspectives on Experience,* The Boston Consulting Group, 1968, p. 75. Reprinted by permission from The Boston Consulting Group, Inc., Boston, Mass. © Copyright 1968.

UNSTABLE COMPETITION

Exhibit 3.5 illustrates how prices track costs in an unstable competitive environment. There are four distinct stages.

Exhibit 3.4   *Cost/Price Trends in a Stable Environment*

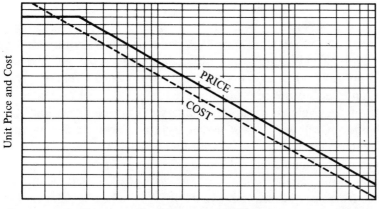

Total Accumulated Volume

SOURCE: *Perspectives on Experience,* The Boston Consulting Group, 1968, p. 19. Reprinted by permission from The Boston Consulting Group, Inc., Boston, Mass. © Copyright 1968.

Introduction

In the first stage, Introduction, prices are lower than costs, and the firm looses money on each item sold. Volume is low. Inefficiencies are high. Experience effects have not yet been realized.

Exhibit 3.5   *Cost/Price Trends in an Unstable Environment*

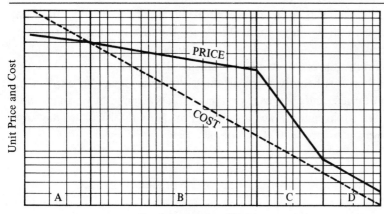

Total Accumulated Volume

SOURCE: *Perspectives on Experience,* The Boston Consulting Group, 1968, p. 22. Reprinted by permission from The Boston Consulting Group, Inc., Boston, Mass. © Copyright 1968.

Market Leadership

In the Growth stage (labeled price umbrella by the BCG) demand is growing rapidly. In fact, demand for the product exceeds supply. Experience effects accumulate rapidly as sales volume doubles easily. Costs decline rapidly. There is little competition during this stage. As a result, prices do not fall as fast as costs. There is no reason for sellers to cut prices. Profit margins are high. In theory, life is easy and profitable at this stage of the cycle. But, all good things must come to an end. So too with the growth stage. No market grows forever. It is with the coming of hard times that the benefits of experience effects manifest themselves most magnificently.

According to experience curve analysis, as a market matures one of two things happens: (1) one firm eventually cuts prices to gain market share so that it too can gain experience, or (2) the higher margins being earned by those already in the industry attract new entrants who add new capacity to produce the product. Those new entrants cut prices to fill that capacity and gain market share.

Shakeout

In either instance a shakeout is inevitable, and when it is over only two or three major players remain. All others are shaken out of the market; they are forced to withdraw or face mounting losses.

Return to Stability

When the shakeout is over prices stabilize at somewhere above the costs of the lowest cost producer in the industry—the firm that has accumulated the most experience—and below the price at which other firms are attracted. From that point on, prices run parallel to costs. It is clear that the BCG borrows heavily from product life cycle theory to explain the behavior of prices and costs as experience effects accumulate in an unstable competitive environment. The arguments made by the BCG are the same as those made by product life cycle advocates.

Strategic Implications of Experience Effects

The strategic implications of experience effects are clear—a firm must gain experience with the market leader if it is to survive the shakeout. Costs must be kept falling. The firm must accumulate experience—by increasing sales volume—at least as fast as other firms in the industry. If it does not, it will not survive. Its cost will be higher than the industry price.

MERITS OF BUILDING MARKET SHARE

The likelihood that individual firms will survive the shakeout depends on where they are on the experience curve when the shakeout occurs. Exhibit 3.6 illustrates that dilemma. Firm "A" has managed to increase its sales, and hence its production, faster than competitors. It is the market leader. Firm "A" has gained experience and lowered costs to a point that is below the average industry price. In fact, it can exert great influence over the industry price. Firm "A" will earn a profit after the shakeout. It will survive and prosper.

Firm "B" is less fortunate however. It has not managed to increase sales volume fast enough to realize experience effects. Since its costs are higher than the prevailing market price, it will lose money. Firm "B" will eventually be shaken out of the industry. It will not survive.

MERITS OF HIGH MARKET GROWTH

Accumulating experience is easiest in the early stages of a product's evolution. It is more likely that sales and production volume can be doubled when a market is growing quickly. Doubling volume is difficult,

Exhibit 3.6 *Merits of Market Share*

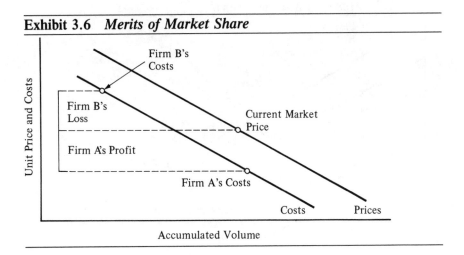

if not impossible, in a mature market. The reasons are obvious. In a high-growth market, sales are growing rapidly throughout the industry. It is easier for individual firms to increase their sales. Furthermore, market shares are unsettled in a high-growth market. The market is new and evolving, and no one competitor yet dominates. Brand switching, lower consumer loyalties, and other market changes are more likely to be found in the early stages of market growth.

In a low-growth market, any gains in market share must come at the expense of entrenched competitors who are likely to fight vigorously to defend their turf. One firm's gain is another firm's loss.

Exhibit 3.7 illustrates the merits of high-market growth. Firm "A" competes in a market growing by 20 percent per year. It is easier to accumulate experience and lower costs. Costs fall rapidly as sales volume expands. Firm "B," by contrast, competes in a mature market growing by a bit over 4 percent per year. It is harder to accumulate experience. Gains are slow, and cost deadlines are harder to come by. The only way to increase sales volume greatly is to steal market share from entrenched competitors, a more difficult proposition than increasing sales in a growth market.

BATTLES FOR SHARE IN HIGH MARKET GROWTH

At its heart, the Boston Consulting Group scheme argues for the following sequence of events: (1) high market growth leads to (2) market-share

Exhibit 3.7 *Merits of Market Growth*

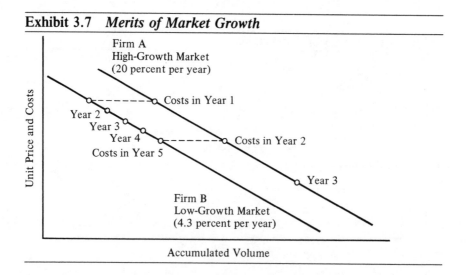

Exhibit 3.8 *Logic of BCG Strategy*

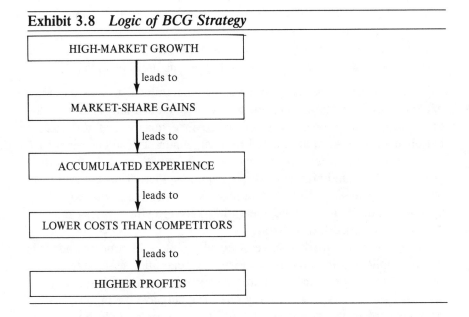

gains, which gives the firm (3) accumulated experience, which leads to (4) lower costs than competitors, which leads to (5) higher profits. Exhibit 3.8 illustrates the progression of events more lucidly.

The strategic implications of this sequence are simple: a firm should target its fight for market share to high-growth markets. The BCG matrix is a theoretical model for deciding where to fight for market share and where to retreat. It is also about how to fund such battles. The matrix illustrates how money can be taken from areas of a diversified business where opportunities are less and used to fund entries into areas where opportunities are likely to lead to success.

The Growth-Share Matrix

The growth-share matrix has its roots in 1969 when the Boston Consulting Group examined the businesses in which the Mead Corporation competed. The result was the predecessor of the four-cell matrix that exists today. The growth-share matrix goes by many aliases. It is alternatively referred to as portfolio planning, cash-flow analysis, or the planning grid. Whatever the appellation, the purpose of the matrix is to help diversified firms decide how to allocate scarce resources among the businesses they compete in. Specifically, the objectives of portfolio analysis are:

1. to optimize the performance of the *entire* portfolio of businesses in which the firm competes, and
2. to balance the cash flow among those businesses, designating some products as sources of funds and others as users of funds.

The growth-share matrix itself, presented in Exhibit 3.9, cross-classifies market share and market growth to yield four quadrants. Each of the firm's products (or businesses) is placed in a quadrant of the matrix. Different strategies are designated for each quadrant. The cutpoints used in the cross-classification to distinguish high-growth markets from low-growth markets, and high-share firms from low-share firms are arbitrary, but not controversial. High-growth markets are defined as those growing by more than 10 percent per year. Markets growing by less than 10 percent are deemed low growth.

The cutpoint for market share is equally simple in concept, but it is more complicated in calculation. Firms are classified as having a high share if they hold the largest share of their market. Otherwise, they are classified as low-share firms. Only one firm can have the highest market share (except in the rare case of ties). Consequently, only one firm is classified as a high-share firm. All other firms are classified as having a low share.

The matrix relies on the concept of relative market share, which calculates the ratio of unit sales for one firm with unit sales for the largest share firm. If firm "A," for example, has a 10 percent share of the market, and the largest share firm has a share of 20 percent, then it has a relative market share of 0.5 (10/20). It has a low share—the ratio is less than 1.0. If firm "B" has a 20 percent share, the largest

---

Exhibit 3.9 *Growth-Share Matrix*

		MARKET SHARE	
		High	Low
MARKET GROWTH	High	STAR	QUESTION MARK
	Low	CASH COW	DOG

Exhibit 3.10   *Growth-Share Matrix with Market Size*

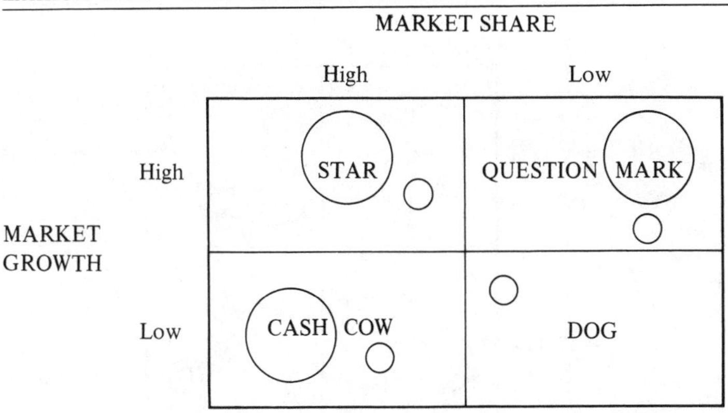

MARKET SHARE

	High	Low
High	STAR ○	QUESTION MARK ○
Low	CASH COW ○	○ DOG

MARKET GROWTH

---

share in the market, then firm "B" has a relative market share of 1.0. It has a high share.

The growth-share matrix often incorporates a third dimension as well— the size of the market. With bubbles of different sizes, Exhibit 3.10 illustrates how market size is incorporated into the growth-share matrix. Larger bubbles represent larger markets. The size of the bubbles can represent either the dollar sales volume of the entire market, or the sales contribution of that market to the firm's profits. In either case, larger markets are more important than smaller markets.

Finally, the growth-share matrix can be used to show how positions on the matrix will change in the years ahead. In Exhibit 3.11 Day (1977) illustrates the use of the matrix for dynamic, rather than static, analysis. Instead of merely plotting the position of products for today, the matrix can be used to show: (1) what changes can be expected in the markets themselves, usually vertical movements on the graph, and (2) what will be the results of changes in strategy, usually horizontal movements. By forecasting the movement of the markets, and results of strategic choices for each of those markets, a firm can assess where it is headed in the future. The following section discusses those changes in greater detail.

BALANCING CASH FLOW

The logic of the cross-classification is based on balancing the flow of cash among the firm's businesses based on the opportunities they offer. There are sources of funds and uses of funds specified by the matrix.

Exhibit 3.11   *Changes over Time in the Growth-Share Matrix*

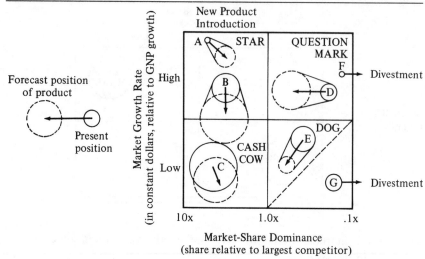

Diameter of circle is proportional to product's contribution to total company sales volume.

SOURCE: Day, George, "Diagnosing the Product Portfolio," *Journal of Marketing,* April 1977, p. 34. Reprinted from *Journal of Marketing,* published by the American Marketing Association.

Walter Kiechel III (1981) sums it up most vividly. He notes that the purpose of the growth-share matrix is "to show which businesses would throw off cash and which would wolf it up" (p. 149).

Sources of Funds

Products that have a high share of their market usually earn more money for firms than products that have a low-share position. According to the BCG, the reason is simple and straightforward. High-share firms have gained more experience, and have higher sales volume and lower costs than lower-share firms. Consequently, their profit margins are higher. Higher margins lead to greater cash flow. High-share firms also have strong cash flow. Low-share firms have weak cash flow. Overall, market share is indicative of the supply of funds available to the firm.

Uses of Funds

The chances of gaining a higher share of the market are greatest in high-growth markets. Consequently, the BCG matrix advises firms to

Exhibit 3.12 *Sources and Needs for Funds*

	Source of Funds	Need for Funds	Cash Balance
Question Mark	low	high	− in need
Star	high	high	0 in balance
Cash Cow	high	low	+ in excess
Dog	low	low	0 in balance

use funds from some businesses to "buy" market share in businesses where the chances of success are greatest. Market growth is indicative of the sources and needs for funds in the firm.

Cash Balance

Exhibit 3.12 summarizes the cash balances that result from the cross-classification of market share and market growth. Two quadrants of the matrix are in cash balance—they generate about as much cash as they need. The two other quadrants are off balance; each in the opposite direction. One generates more cash than it needs to maintain operations, the other needs more cash than it generates. The specific situation for each types of business is detailed below.

FOUR TYPES OF BUSINESSES

The growth-share matrix gives cute, but descriptive names to the four quadrants it creates, and the products in each quadrant have a distinct set of characteristics.

Cash Cows

Cash Cows are off balance as they hold a large share of a low-growth market. Market shares tend to be stabilized in such markets. Drastic changes in market share, including significant share gains by competitors, are unlikely. Cash cows generate a lot of excess cash, since they have a high market share. Their need for cash is low; they compete in a low-growth market. On balance, they generate more dollars than they need to sustain their market position. As such, they are a source of funds for the firm. As Exhibit 3.12 illustrates, they are the only category with a strong positive cash flow.

Question Marks

Question Marks are the opposite of cash cows. They have a small share of a desirable high-growth market. Their chances of gaining market share are typically good since the market has not yet settled. Competitors are not entrenched in high-share positions. The market is fluid. Question marks are off balance. They need a great deal of cash to gain market share, but generate very little cash, since they possess only a small share of the market. Question marks are a product or business where the firm might use excess funds. They are also referred to as Problem Children or Wildcats, names which all mean the same thing. As Exhibit 3.12 illustrates, they have a strongly negative cash flow.

Stars

Stars have a high share of a high-growth market. Stars generate cash because of their high market share, but require about as much cash as they earn to fend off firms trying to gain share in their high-growth market. Relative shares are still unsettled in a high-growth market. The firm must fight hard to maintain its position. On average, stars make about as much as they need. They are said to be in cash balance.

Dogs

Dogs occupy the least desirable position in the growth-share matrix. Their current position is poor and their future outlook is bleak. Dogs have a low share of a low-growth market. Dogs are sometimes called "cash traps," a label that indicates their intrinsic value to the firm. But, dogs can be controversial. They are in cash balance. They generate little cash. But they need little cash to maintain their position. Not all dogs are mangy mutts. Some can be a faithful friend for many years.

Strategic Implications of the Growth-Share Matrix

No market grows forever. High-growth markets inexorably degenerate into low-growth markets as the market matures and demand levels off. Mostly, market growth is beyond the control of individual firms. It is an external event. Try doubling the number of toasters sold next year and you will get an idea of the power of market maturation.

Market share is more controllable however. Gains in share can be "bought" by spending heavily on advertising and promotion. Share is

Exhibit 3.13   *Path to Success*

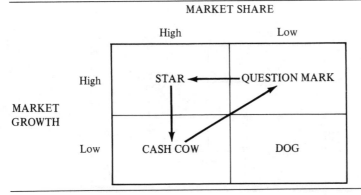

MARKET SHARE

most easily gained in growing markets. As a result, the BCG's growth-share matrix is really a battle for market share in high-growth markets.

PATH TO SUCCESS

The primary objective of the BCG matrix is to continuously generate future cash cows. That objective is accomplished by following the path to success illustrated in Exhibit 3.13. Money earned by a cash cow is not reinvested in that part of the business. Instead, it is invested in a question mark with the intent to gain share. The firm hopes to turn that question mark into a star. As the market matures, and competition lessens, that star will degenerate into a cash cow and the process will be repeated. With a new cash cow the firm has a steady source of funds to pursue future avenues of growth.

THREE PATHS TO FAILURE

Success is not assured, and disaster awaits the firm that does not follow the path to success outlined above. Exhibit 3.14 illustrates the three paths to failure outlined by the matrix. First, many firms mistakenly overinvest in cash cows and underinvest in question marks. They focus on past successes and ignore future opportunities for growth. As a result, their question marks become dogs rather than stars. Eventually, their current cash cows become obsolete and the firm is left with few funds to finance future ventures. These firms have traded future opportunities for present cash flow. That is the first path to failure.

Exhibit 3.14   *Three Paths to Failure*

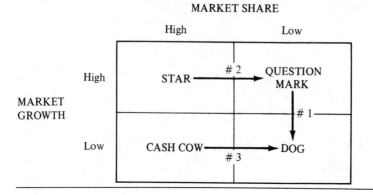

Similarly, some firms drop their guard and allow competitors to gain share in a high-growth market. They underinvest in their stars. Those stars then become question marks, which degenerate into dogs. The firm has followed the second path to failure. Adidas, for example, allowed Nike to gain share in the high-growth market for running shoes that emerged in the 1970s. It never regained the loss of share.

The final path to failure occurs when a firm milks its cash cow too hard and the cow dies, or degenerates into a dog. Xerox milked its copier business too hard in the late 1970s and early 1980s to fund entry into the wild world of personal computers. The Japanese entered the market for copiers at the low end and Xerox never gained a dominant position in personal computers. It followed the final path to failure.

References

Abell, Derek, and John Hammond. *Strategic Market Planning*. Englewood Cliffs, NJ: Prentice-Hall, 1979.

Andress, Frank J. "The Learning Curve as a Production Tool." *Harvard Business Review*, January–February 1954, pp. 87–97.

Day, George. "Diagnosing the Product Portfolio." *Journal of Marketing*, April 1977, pp. 29–38.

Hall, William K. "SBUs: Hot, New Topic in the Management of Diversification." *Business Horizons*, February 1978, pp. 17–25.

Hirschmann, Winfred B. "Profit from the Learning Curve." *Harvard Business Review*, January–February 1964, pp. 125–139.

Kiechel, Walter. "Oh Where, Oh Where Has My Little Dog Gone? Or My Cash Cow? Or My Star." *Fortune,* November 2, 1981, p. 139–150.

Patel, P., and M. Younger. "A Frame of Reference for Strategy Development." *Long-Range Planning,* April 1978, pp. 6–12.

Robinson, S., R. Hichen, and D. Wade. "The Directional Policy Matrix— Tool for Strategic Planning." *Long-Range Planning,* June 1978, pp. 8–15.

Yelle, Louis E. "The Learning Curve: Historical Review, and Comprehensive Survey." *Decision Sciences,* April 1979, pp. 302–328.

Chapter 4

Market-Share Strategies

O ver the years, more attention has been paid to market share than to any other strategic marketing variable. Nowhere is that more true than with the BCG scheme. In fact, market share is the central feature of the four strategies that arise from the growth matrix: (1) gaining share, (2) holding or maintaining share, (3) harvesting, and (4) divestment. As Figure 4.1 illustrates, each of those strategies implies a declining level of commitment to the product or service. This chapter is about those strategies.

Market-share strategies are an integral part of the growth-share matrix, but they are not unique to it. Share strategies have been discussed extensively in the broader strategy literature. The Boston Consulting Group (BCG) view is merely one view of the role of market share in strategy.

This chapter takes the broader view. It examines market-share strategies using the framework and terminology of the growth-share matrix. But it covers those strategies in the context of the broader body of marketing literature on the topic. It concludes with some of the criticisms that have been leveled against the growth-share matrix and its theoretical underpinnings.

Gaining Market Share

Gaining or building market share is an offensive or attack strategy aimed at trying to increase market position at the expense of competitors. A firm builds market share by stealing it from others. The sense of a battle is conspicuous. Discussions of market-share strategies are surfeit with military analogy.

Exhibit 4.1 *Market-Share Strategies*

GAINING   HOLDING
  SHARE ⟶ SHARE ⟶ HARVESTING ⟶ DIVESTMENT

High   Low
Commitment ⟶ Commitment

WHEN TO GAIN SHARE

Gaining market share is an expensive and risky proposition that takes more than desire on the part of the firm wishing to do so. The overwhelming conclusion of research on the topic is that it is not always possible nor advisable to gain share. A firm should seek share gains only when the situation is right. Numerous instances have been proposed as ideal for gaining share.

In Growth Markets

The central premise of the growth-share matrix is that building share is easiest when a market is new and competitors have not had a chance to establish an impenetrable position. Competition is less severe in growth markets. Competitors are less likely to fight hard in a market that is expanding, as there is less impetus for them to do so. Their own sales are growing. There are fewer reasons to start a price war. Those observations are consistent with those made over the years by advocates of the product life cycle.

According to the growth-share matrix, share gains are targeted mostly to question marks. The goal is to turn question marks into stars. A firm may also wish to gain share in a growth market when a star has lost share at the hands of an aggressive competitor (a question mark).

When a New Product Shows Potential

Initial success with a major new product also presents an opportunity to claim share from competitors (Fogg 1974). That new product may offer consumers better performance or lower costs. As such, it represents a competitive advantage, with which the firm may seek to gain share.

When an Acquisition Is Underperforming

An acquisition that has the potential to perform better under the auspices of new management also represents an opportunity to gain share from competitors (Fogg 1974). Consistent with the portfolio approach to strategy, a firm with marketing expertise in consumer products, for example, may be able to transform a small product entry into a larger market opportunity. The acquisition of Gatorade by Quaker Oats transformed a small beverage aimed at athletes into a strong contender in soft drinks. Sales have grown tremendously under Quaker Oats' tutelage.

When a Competitor Is Unwilling to Fight Back

In many situations, a market leader may be unwilling to defend the share sought by the attacking firm. The reasons for that unwillingness are many. First, the leader may not be willing to sacrifice profit margins to defend share. The defender may be targeting opportunities in other industries. Or, the defender may have a short-term orientation. The share leader may be willing to cede market position rather than spend the funds necessary to defend that share.

Consider the case of how Sorrell Ridge, a small jam seller, gained share on Smucker's, the market leader with a 38 percent share. Sorrell Ridge sweetens its jams with 100 percent fruit, a more expensive but higher-quality approach. Smucker's uses sugar cane and corn sweeteners, which costs less than half as much as pure fruit. Jams and jellies sweetened with fruit are the fastest-growing segment. They have natural appeal. Smucker's dilemma is as follows: Does it match Sorrell Ridge, and raise its costs and lower profits greatly? Or, does it ignore the attack? In 1989 it introduced a knock-off, made with all fruit, but would prefer that consumers simply continue to buy the traditional Smucker's product. With a name like that it has to be good (Levine 1989).

Second, in some industries there may be no history of vigorous competition. In fact, competition may be viewed as a "gentleman's game," where retaliations are considered undignified (Porter 1985). Twenty years ago, in the wine industry, for example, there was little advertising, few promotions, and meager competition in comparison to soft drinks, beer, and other beverage markets. That all changed when Coca-Cola entered the market, trying to gain share in a gentleman's market. Lawyers, doctors, dentists, and other professionals still battle over whether competition for business is beneath the dignity of their professions.

When a Competitor Is Unable to Fight Back

In some situations a competitor may have the desire to defend its share but lacks the strength to compete with the attacker. There are many reasons why a firm may be unable to fight back.

First, the firm may lack funds. The rash of takeovers and leveraged buyouts that occurred in the 1980s left many firms starved for cash. They could not respond to increases in advertising and promotion foisted on them by less-leveraged competitors seeking to gain share. Those market leaders had to concentrate on paying the banks, and could not afford to pay attention to their competitors' actions. Many lost share.

Second, small firms in large markets often cannot match the marketing muscle of larger firms. They cannot fight back. It is as if a small country, such as Grenada, went to war with a large superpower such as the United States.

The small-firm/large-firm battle frequently occurs in growth markets. Small firms often pioneer growth markets. Equally as often, however, those firms lose share to larger competitors who enter the market later with greater resources.

It is important to note that for either the attacking firm or the defender, share gains come at the expense of short-term profits. A firm wishing to gain a dominant position in an industry must be willing to accept short-term losses, often for years. A firm wishing to protect the share it has already gained must also be willing to forfeit short-term profits.

Avoid Share Battles Against Entrenched Competitors

There are numerous situations in which a firm should not try to gain share. Gaining share in a low-growth market, where powerful competitors are entrenched in high-share positions is a difficult, if not impossible task. The odds are against success. The market leaders possess most of the competitive advantages. They have myriad resources. And, growth is slow, meaning that share gains by the attacker must come directly from the leader's share. In the language of the BCG matrix, turning dogs into cash cows is an unlikely proposition.

Avoid Share Battles in Commodity Markets

It is well known in marketing that attempting to gain share against a larger competitor when there is no difference between products is likely to lead to failure. In such instances the firm has no competitive advantage and is unlikely to succeed. It is well known in marketing that a firm—especially a smaller firm—should never attack head-on with the same product. A successful attack requires something more than competition among commodities, which are defined as products that are identical.

Most marketers advise against attempting to gain share in a commodity market, where price is the only difference between products (Fogg 1974). That advice contradicts the central premise of the growth-share matrix, however. Recall that the BCG assumes that all products are commodities that compete only by offering lower prices, gained through experience effects. BCG makes no allowance for product differentiation.

Marketers find that aspect of BCG market-share strategies most controversial. Most marketers believe that building share is difficult in the absence of real or imagined product differences. It is a recipe for disaster.

Avoid Price Competition

The reason why gaining share is destructive when there is no real or imagined difference between products is that in such situations competition quickly degenerates into pure price competition. Competitors cut price to gain share, those cuts are easily matched, and profits fall for the entire industry. Most marketers would argue that pure price competition, in the absence of product differentiation, results not in market-share gains but lower profits for all players in the market.

How to Gain Share

Gaining share can be accomplished in a number of ways. Some of those ways are presented below.

Lowering Prices

The BCG position on building share is simple: gaining share is accomplished with lower prices. A firm gains share by earning a lower-cost position than its competitors, and eventually passing those lower costs along to customers in the form of lower prices. Texas Instruments, for example, cut prices on products in the 1970s in anticipation of future production efficiencies. Marketers usually advise against the use of price as a competitive weapon. In that regard, there is a fundamental disagreement between most marketers and the growth-share matrix as to how share should be gained.

Increasing Promotion

Most marketers favor gaining share with nonprice variables. The most obvious tactic is to increase promotional expenditures vis-à-vis competitors. There are two variations on that theme. The first is a strategy of pure spending, which entails huge promotional expenditures to overcome the advantage of the incumbent. Bud Light, for example, has used pure spending to buy share of the light beer market. A variation on pure spending is to identify markets where promotion has been ignored. Coke's foray into wines, for example, increased spending in an underspent market.

New Product Introductions

It has long been observed that firms that introduce many new products tend to gain share, which has led to the current interest in speeding new products to market. That topic is the subject of a later chapter.

Improving Product Quality

Recently, attention has turned to quality improvements as a means of gaining share. An entire chapter is dedicated to product quality later in this book. Suffice it to say, selling higher-quality products often leads to gains in market share. A variation of this concept is improving the level of service. Fogg (1974) advises that increasing service can also lead to market-share gains.

There is empirical support for the value of quality improvements. One landmark study found that increasing quality led to higher market share and higher profits (Phillips, Chang and Buzzell 1983). There is also anecdotal evidence for the value of product quality in attacking a market leader as the case of Smucker's versus Sorrell Ridge illustrated.

There is also empirical support for the value of many of the other nonprice variables as well. An earlier study using the PIMS database found that share gains were related to new product activity, quality improvements, and an increase in marketing expenditures (Buzzell and Wiersema 1981). Most often, a combination of those factors was responsible for the gain in market share. Interestingly, that study found no relationship between price cutting and share gains. Price gains, it surmised, are too easy to match.

Still, the results of that study cannot be used to argue against the merits of cutting price to gain share. The study actually found few examples of aggressive price cutting, that is, because of the nature of the

PIMS database. Most businesses in the PIMS database compete in mature markets. The growth-share matrix argues that going for gains in market share in a mature market is foolhardy.

Changing the Market

A final way to gain share on a competitor is to change the market in some way that negates the market leader's advantage. Abell (1978) and Porter (1985) discuss means whereby a firm can change a market to their advantage.

Doing so, however, can entail pioneering a new channel of distribution, as Timex did in low-end watches, or eliminating middlemen, as YKK did in zippers. It can also entail changing the product through increased performance or a new low-cost design. In each of these ways the firm can build share.

Whatever the means, gaining market share is an expensive proposition with high risks. Building share requires special competencies, of which lower prices is but one possibility.

Moves Up-Market

A more general strategy for gaining share is to move "up-market" from a beachhead established at the lower end. Many competitors, especially foreign competitors with lower costs, establish a solid position at the bottom of a market. First, they build a reputation for producing inexpensive goods that provide good value to consumers. Then, once that position is firmly established, low-end firms look for growth by moving towards the higher, and more profitable, end of the market. They seek to gain share in the more broadly defined market.

Consider the case of Japanese automobiles. Throughout the 1960s, the Japanese built a solid reputation for producing low-priced econoboxes that served utilitarian needs. Once that position was firmly established, those firms introduced more expensive models that carried higher margins. By the late 1980s, entire new divisions of Japanese firms such as Acura (Honda), Lexus (Toyota), and Infiniti (Nissan) were created to compete at the high end of the market. From a beginning at the bottom of the market, Japanese automakers now compete over the entire spectrum of the auto market—from the low end to the high end. They successfully gained share by moving up-market.

The primary barrier to moving up-market is that consumers will not pay premium prices for goods that are perceived to have a pedestrian image. Hyundai's Sonata, for example, is a move up-market that has less success than its low-priced Excel model. Consumers are reluctant to pay high prices for a Hyundai.

Moves Down-Market

Moves "down-market" are equally common. Firms that have established a position of providing consumers with premium quality goods seek to gain share by moving down to the mass market. Often, those firms attempt to trade their coveted cachet or image for gains in market share. There are many successes and many failures, as the following cases illustrate.

The American Express card is not for everyone, or so the company would like you to think. It sells exclusivity. But it has gained share by broadening the definition of exclusivity to include a very large share of the market. Its platinum, gold, and green cards serve a broad spectrum of 33 million exclusive customers. Amex has moved from the premium end towards the mass market. Interestingly, as Amex moved down-market competitors Visa and Mastercard move up-market. Both firms now offer gold cards, which attempt to convey the prestige, and profits, of the Amex gold card.

Many hotel chains have also followed a move down-market. Marriot, a high-end chain, expanded its product line in the late 1980s to include Fairfield Inns, which serve lower-end customers, albeit without the Marriot nameplate. Before that, Holiday Inn opened Hampton Inns to serve the same low-end customers. Even the brewers have moved down-market to gain share. Miller Brewing brought out Meister Brau and Milwaukee's Best, two low-end beers aimed at the high-volume segment of the market.

The primary risk of moving down-market is that the firm will tarnish its high-end image. Amex, for example, has gained share but risks diluting its exclusive image for which consumers are still willing to pay a premium. It is a risky strategy. Tiffany & Co., the upscale jeweler, almost did lose its coveted image. When Tiffany's was owned by Avon in the mid-1980s, it began to broaden its market appeal by selling less expensive items. Consumers avoided the entire line.

Holding Share

Holding or maintaining market share is a defensive strategy that seeks to protect what has already been gained. It is a strategy that reacts to an attacker's challenge. The advantage in holding share belongs to the defender. According to the BCG scheme, market leaders have stronger experience effects than lower-share firms. They also have more money to wager on marketing battles. In low-growth markets, the defender's advantages are even more pronounced.

WHEN TO HOLD SHARE

Holding market share is usually a strategy for a firm that has dominant position in the market and wishes to defend that position. The defense can be in either growth or mature markets. According to the BCG matrix, holding share is aimed at cash cows or stars, products that are likely to be under attack by competitors seeking share gains. Of course, it is easier to defend cash cows than stars since cash cows compete in low-growth markets.

HOW TO HOLD SHARE

There are many ways to defend share from competitive attacks, most of them similar to those used to gain share. The choice of a specific action is based on whether the defender or the attacker holds the competitive advantage. Consider the following choices:

COST AND PRICE CUTTING

The BCG's position is that the advantage in cutting costs and prices lies clearly with the market leader. In the unfortunate event of an all-out price war, the greater experience of the share leader means that ruthless cost and price cutting can be used to fend off competitors. Smaller competitors, with less experience, cannot retaliate because they have higher cost structures. They will be shaken from the market.

Selective Price Cuts

An alternative to blanket price cuts is selective price reductions that target the attacking product. By targeting the price cuts to only part of the market, or to only a few products in the line, the defending firm exposes only part of its sales to lower prices. It is an especially effective strategy when competitors have a smaller scope of operations and cannot retaliate across a broad front.

Hershey Foods Corp., for example, tried to enter the cake frosting business with the intent to gain share. Its luscious chocolate entry should have been a strong contender; instead, it failed badly. Market leaders cut prices on their cake frostings and raised prices on their cake mixes. Hershey could not retaliate, since it had no cake mix. The defense was successful, and Hershey gained no share.

Price Cutting in the Attacker's Home Market

A variation of selective price cutting is to cut prices in the attacker's home market. That counterattack has the effect of sapping the attacker's source of funds. Porter (1985) refers to this strategy as a "cross-parry."

Consider the case of a small airline expanding into the profitable route of a larger carrier. The small airline is funding its entry from profitable routes it already runs. A cross-parry by the larger airline would entail expanding into the profitable routes of the smaller airline and cutting prices. The goal of that strategy is to sap the financial strength of the weaker opponent.

Heavy Promotional Spending

Nonprice competition can also be used defensively. Heavy spending on advertising and promotion also favors the share leader. The defender has a larger volume over which to spread promotional expenditures. In an all-out war, the advantage in promotional spending lies with the market leader.

Perpetual Innovation

A strategy of perpetual innovation can also be used defensively. By staying one step ahead of aggressive competitors, the leader allows no room for competitors to leapfrog current products. One result of perpetual innovation is to proliferate product lines. Those new products can leave no room for competitors to enter with new and improved products, or products that serve special segments. Product proliferation has been used successfully by soft drink bottlers and soap suds manufacturers.

Vigorous Later Entry

Often, a market leader misses a major new product opportunity in its home market when it allows an attacking firm to gain a beachhead in its primary market. The attacker wins share with a strategy of innovation. The market leader looses share by either not innovating, or innovating the wrong products. But all is not lost. The defender can frequently regain the share lost through vigorous later entry. Entering a market after the attacker, with a competitive advantage, can often serve as the best defense against an attacker's offensive use of innovation (Schnaars 1986).

Exhibit 4.2 lists some of the cases in which market leaders have regained the share they initially lost. Exhibit 4.3 lists some of the cases in which the pioneer held on to an early lead. In each case, the largest share went to the firm that possessed the most potent competitive advantage.

Market leaders can defend their markets and regain the share lost through imitation and improvement. The leaders can introduce a superior product, and enter "second but better." To do so, the defender must have an advantage in brand name, reputation for quality, or distribution.

If improvements are not possible, or not the source of competitive advantage, the market leader can respond with an imitation coupled with heavy promotional expenditures. Large market leaders, like Coke and Pepsi, for example, possess an unmatchable competitive advantage in terms of promotional expenditures over smaller rivals such as Royal Crown Cola, and entrepreneurial upstarts such as Soho Cola and Snapple (when they were independent). The smaller firms cannot hope to compete on the basis of promotion with these powerful market leaders. The lack of patent protection, and the importance of promotion, ensures that later entries by these giants will usually result in their dominating those markets as well.

Blocking Access to Distribution

The rapid introduction of new products can be used to tie up limited distribution space and preclude competitors from entry. Blocking access to distribution is an excellent defensive maneuver. Without distribution, a competitor is at a severe disadvantage. Distribution can be blocked with exclusive agreements, backwards integration, and other defensive measures.

Signaling Commitment

Firms looking to gain share will look for opportunities where competitors will not fight back. Competitors will be reluctant to attack committed competitors. There are numerous ways to show commitment.

Attacking new products in test markets can serve as an effective signal of the impending ferocity of competitive retaliation if the attack enter the larger market. It is common for defending firms to offer two-for-one coupons or blanket a test market area with free samples of their own product while a competitor's test market is in progress.

More insidious, defending firms sometimes buy up large quantities of the test marketed product, which they analyze and reverse engineer. As a result, the firm running the test market might mistakenly conclude that it has a winner on its hands when the product is really a dog.

Fighting brands—or peripheral brands used to fend off attacks on the mother brand—can also be used defensively. Pick a fight with the mother brand and the defending firm will counter with the fighting brand.

Commitment is the key to market-share maintenance. If competitors think that the defender is not interested, and that they can enter unopposed, they will do so.

Harvesting

Harvesting, a compromise between holding and divesting, extracts cash from products that face imminent decline or possess few opportunities for future growth. It is a recognition that a business can still generate income, but that future prospects for the business do not justify reinvestment. Harvesting is, in essence, a tax on products that face a bleak future (Kotler 1978). The receipts of that tax are spent on more promising opportunities. A euphemism for harvesting is "managing for cash flow."

When to Harvest

The decision to harvest is a delicate one, and depends on the answers to three key questions:

1. *What are the future prospects for the product or service?* Generally, harvesting is an option when a product or service competes in a declining market. If there is no potential for future growth, profits are poor; and if there is a better use for the money elsewhere, then harvesting should be considered. It is especially important if the firm has a low share of the market. In the language of the growth-share matrix, harvesting is a strategy best suited to dogs and some cash cows.

2. *Does the product or service face imminent or slow decline?* The second consideration in selecting a harvesting strategy has to do with the speed with which sales of the product or service will decline. Will the market decline slowly, or remain stagnant for years? Or will it disap-

Exhibit 4.2   Successful Later Entry

Market	Pioneers	Early Entrants	Later Entrants	Outcome
Videocassette Recorders	CBS/Motorola (1968–71) Avco's Cartridge TV (1972) Sony's Betamax (1975) —Zenith —Sanyo	Matsushita VHS (1988) —Panasonic —Quasar —JVC —RCA —GE —Magnavox —Sylvania —Sharp		Sony gained dominant share through its extensive marketing expenditures but then lost it to the superior design and lower cost of Matsushita.
Diet Soft Drinks	Cott (1950s) Kirsch's No-Cal (1950s) Royal Crown Diet Rite Cola (1962)	Coke's Tab (1963) Pepsi's Patio Cola (1963) Diet Pepsi (1964)		Tab and Diet Pepsi quickly dominated the market with massive advertising expenditures.

Market-Share Strategies

Personal Computers	Apple (1977) Tandy TRS-80 (1977)		IBM-PC (1981) Osborne (1981)	IBM quickly dominated the business market, using marketing clout and product innovation.
Hand-Held Calculators	Bowmar Brain (1971) Canon Pocketronic (1970)	Texas Instruments (1972)	Foreign producers	TI moved into first place in 1973 with a strategy based on low-cost production.
Digital Watches	Hamilton Watch Co.'s Pulsar (1971–77) Intel's Microma (1972–77)	National Semiconductor (1974) Texas Instruments Litronix Fairchild (all 1975)	Timex (1977) Very low-cost Japanese producers	Pulsar lost out to low-cost producer TI, who lost out to still lower-cost foreign manufacturers.

SOURCE Reprinted from Steven P. Schnaars, "When Entering Growth Markets, Are Pioneers Better than Poachers?," *Business Horizons* (March–April 1986) p. 30. Copyright 1986 by the Foundation for the School of Business at Indiana University. Used with permission.

Exhibit 4.3	Successful Pioneering			
Market	Pioneers	Early Entrants	Later Entrants	Outcome
Low-Calorie Beer	Rheingold's Gablingers (1960s) Meister Brau Lite (1960s) Miller Lite (1975)	Schlitz Light (1976)	Anheuser-Busch's Natural Light (1977) Michelob Light (1978) Bud Light (1981)	Miller Lite holds 60 percent of the market, due primarily to massive advertising support.
Disposable Diapers	P&G's Pampers (1961–66) Borden's White Lamb (1965) Scott Paper Baby Scotts (1966)	K-C's Kimbies (1971) Scott's Raggedy Ann & Andy (1971) Curity (1971)	P&G's Luvs (1976) Scott's Tots (1976) K-C's Huggies (1977) J&J (1978)	Pampers holds the largest share, but it is losing share to Luvs and Huggies as the market moves upscale.
Personal Stereos	Sony Walkman (1979)	Panasonic Toshiba Sanyo (1980–82)	Aiwa (1982)	Sony still holds about 50 percent of the market.
Microwave Ovens	Raytheon's Amana Radarange (early 1960s) Litton (1964)	Sharp (1973) Sanyo (1973)	Sunbeam (1977) Samsung Lucky-Goldstar (1980s) —K Mart —J. C. Penney —Magic Chef	Amana and Litton split more than half of the market, but imports are gaining share in the growing lower end.

Smoke Detectors	GE (1972) GE Home Sentry (1975) Emhart 911 (1975) Pyrotronic (1974)	Pittway's First Alert Norelco's Smokey Gillette's Capt. Kelly Teledyne (all 1976)	GE held the dominant position until the late 1970s, when its growth ebbed and First Alert moved into first place.
Bottled Waters	Perrier (1977)	Previous market leaders were Arrowhead and Sparkletts	Perrier pioneered snob appeal rather than the pollution solution. Market growth is now shifting back to still water.
Running Shoes	Nike	Brooks Etonic New Balance	Previous market leaders were Adidas and Puma	Nike quickly surpassed Adidas and Puma as the market grew. Early entrants could not surpass Nike. The battle has now shifted to apparel and overseas markets, where Adidas still dominates.

SOURCE: Steven P. Schnaars, "When Entering Growth Markets, Are Pioneers Better than Poachers?," *Business Horizons* (March–April 1986) p. 29. Copyright 1986 by the Foundation for the School of Business at Indiana University. Used with permission.

pear virtually overnight? The rate of market decline does not affect the choice to harvest or not, but which kind of harvesting to select.

3. *What will happen if investment in the product or business is reduced? Will sales plummet or petrify?* Amazingly, many products do not decline rapidly when promotion is withdrawn, or slashed drastically. Instead, market share and sales often fall only slightly. In the parlance of harvesting, sales petrify. Cashmere Bouquet soap is an example of petrified sales. Almost everyone has heard of the brand, even though substantial advertising support has been lacking for years. Lifebouy soap, by Lever Brothers, is another product that continues to sell even though it receives very little promotion.

TWO TYPES OF HARVESTING STRATEGIES

There are two very different types of harvesting: (1) extracting a moderate amount of cash over a long period of time with the intention of staying in the business for years to come, and (2) extracting a large amount of cash over the short-term before the bottom falls out of the market. Consider each in turn.

Short-Term Harvesting

If a product faces imminent decline the choice is severe, short-term harvesting. The firm's goal is to withdraw as much cash from the business as possible before the market disappears.

The reasons a product might face imminent decline are many. A technological innovation may be coming to market shortly, which will soon make the existing product obsolete. Compact discs, for example, have greatly affected the future prospects, and company support, for cassette tapes, which have been the most popular medium for music sales. Similarly, a model change may be in the works. Or, the market might simply be disappearing. In each instance, severe harvesting is the best choice.

Long-Term Harvesting

In other instances, the product faces less dire prospects. Demand for the product may simply be stagnant, with few opportunities to increase demand. The market may be saturated. The firm might have a dominant share of a no-growth market. In such situations, there is little need to plow large sums of money back into the business. Opportunities lie elsewhere. The guiding principle for long-term harvesting is to extract cash without destroying the product that provides that cash. Moderation is the key.

Petrified sales is the goal of long-term harvesting. The intention is to reduce costs drastically while reducing sales and market share only slightly. Often the goal is attainable.

How to Harvest

Both long- and short-term harvesting are accomplished using the same basic set of marketing tools, and differ only in the degree to which they use these tools. Severe short-term harvesting applies them vigorously. Long-term harvesting applies them in moderation. The essence of harvesting is to cut costs to the bone. These costs can come from many aspects of the business, as shown in the following (Kotler 1978):

Cut Marketing Expenditures

First, and most important, is to cut marketing expenditures. Firms routinely spend 3 to 6 percent of sales (depending on the product category) on advertising. Cutting these expenditures goes directly to the "bottom line."

Reduce Service

Service is expensive. Service cuts can be made in the amount and selection of inventory carried, delivery schedules, and the size and quality of the salesforces. Short-term harvesting makes more severe cuts than long-term maintenance.

Drop Small Customers

Small customers often take a disproportionate amount of the service effort. By dropping them, a business can cut the costs of service with only a small loss in volume.

Trim Product Line

Carrying many products in each product line increases costs unnecessarily in a declining market. If customers have few other options they are forced to choose from a more limited menu.

Cut Research and Development

Another harvesting tool is to cut research and development expenditures. R&D costs typically run between 3 and 6 percent of sales. Those cuts also go directly to the bottom line. On products and services with a future, cutting advertising and R&D is a short-sighted tactic. It trades long-term potential for quick profits. But, when the future is bleak, a short-term perspective offers the only opportunity to obtain profits that would otherwise be lost. Long-term harvesting makes more moderate cuts.

Reduce Plant and Equipment

Harvesting also calls for reduction in plant and equipment expenditures. In long-term harvesting, it is unnecessary to spend anywhere near as much as the product generates. In severe harvesting, few investments are made at all. Broken windows are fixed but not much else.

Substitute Cheaper Materials

In severe short-term harvesting, it might be possible to reduce costs by substituting cheaper materials. But, it is a dangerous strategy in long-term harvesting where the product could be killed prematurely.

Raise Prices

Finally, in a declining market it is sometimes possible to generate additional income by raising prices. Remaining customers with ties to the declining product may be forced to pay more to gain supplies.

Feign Commitment

Tools for harvesting are dangerous and must be carefully assessed on a case-by-case basis. Even stagnant markets are competitive. Competitors who face an equally bleak future may wish to gain share on a firm that seems uninterested in the product it sells. Similarly, suppliers will be reluctant to stock products that are not supported. For those reasons, the following actions are recommended:

Splash Advertising

Kotler (1978) advises that firms provide "splash advertising" to give the appearance of being interested. Offering deals to suppliers also helps gain continued distribution. It is important not to signal competitors that you are not interested in the business.

Maintaining Employee Morale

Employees must also be considered, as their morale will be low if severe harvesting is under way. Management careers are rarely built by presiding over declines. It is often desirable to bring in management that is experienced in harvesting.

Maintain Consumer Support

It is also important not to signal customers that a harvesting strategy is under way. When harvesting, a firm is essentially existing on the past good will of consumers. Abusing that good will can quickly boomerang. Harvesting is a fascinating but dangerous strategy that sometimes deserves consideration.

Divestment

Divestment is the ultimate choice in a lack of commitment to a product or service. The firm seeks to sell or abandon the business.

WHEN TO DIVEST

There are two primary reasons why a firm would wish to divest a product or service: (1) a poor market position or (2) a poor fit for the company.

Poor Market Position

According to the growth-share matrix, divestment is a strategy targeted primarily towards dogs. It entails selling the dog to someone else, and luckily dogs are not difficult to give away. In fact, some firms will pay handsomely for what seems like a mangy mutt. What may be a dog for one firm may fit nicely into the portfolio of another.

Divestment is also sometimes targeted to question marks. A question mark has to "get up or get out." That is, it must gain share and become a star or opt out of the competition. A firm with limited funds for market-share battles, or too many opportunities to pursue simultaneously may opt for divestment of their weakest question mark.

A Poor Fit with the Firm's Other Products

Divestment is also a good strategic choice when the product or service is a poor match for the company. Today, firms want to be able to say what business they are in. Divesting far-flung, unrelated businesses compiled during a bygone era that valued conglomeration makes sense in our time. It allows the firm to concentrate, and build a competitive advantage, in one area of business. Usually, that is an area of business that the firm knows a great deal about.

Related to the issue of concentrating on one area of business is the need to build critical mass. Firms often need to build a "critical mass" of market share to make a market worthwhile. If a firm has decided what business it is in, it will want to build a dominant position in that business. A firm that already competes in a market, but without a critical mass, may welcome the dog into its portfolio if the dog builds critical mass. The dog may make the firm an effective competitor.

SHOULD DOGS BE DIVESTED?

In theory, the growth-share matrix argues that dogs should be divested. In practice, such doings would be disastrous. A few simple calculations indicate why.

Using acceptable definitions, dogs are not a rare breed. Only one firm can have the largest share of any market. If we assume that the average market has five competitors (a generous estimate in favor of the growth-share matrix), then only 20 percent of the businesses in the United States are market leaders. Eighty percent hold a lesser position.

Likewise, most U.S. markets are growing by less than 10 percent per year. If we assume that 20 percent of the markets are growing by more than 10 percent, another optimistic estimate in favor of the growth-share matrix, fully 80 percent of the markets are low growth. Combining these estimates leads to the conclusion that almost two-thirds of all products and services in the United States are classified as dogs using the "cutpoints" specified by the BCG!

Does it make sense to write off two-thirds of American business? Unlikely. Nor does it make sense to de-emphasize or ignore such a large chunk of business. No wonder U.S. firms have proved uncompetitive against foreign competitors who treat their dogs with affection rather than neglect. While American firms routinely put their dogs to sleep, more supportive foreign competitors nurture their dogs back to health and vigor.

One empirical study examined the performance of 418 dogs contained in the PIMS database (Hambrick and MacMillan 1982). It found that: "Dogs are not all mangy cash losers. In fact, some of them are handsome cash generators" (p. 89). Successful dogs followed narrow product lines, avoided price competition with market leaders, and stressed product quality. Many dogs, it seems, are really man's best friend.

Another study barked up the same tree (Christensen, Cooper, and DeKluyver 1982). It argued persuasively that some dogs "might be viewed as bonds traditionally have been in a security portfolio, providing modest but relatively certain returns" (p. 15). As a result, the study concludes that divesting dogs is often a mistake. Dogs can yield a steady, if small, return if managed correctly.

Critics contend that a strategy that stresses the rejuvenation of dogs is often superior, and less risky, than a strategy that seeks to enter uncertain growth markets. It is but one of the many criticisms that has been leveled against the BCG scheme.

Criticisms of the Growth-Share Matrix

During the 1970s, the BCG's growth-share matrix was immensely popular. In more recent years, however, it has attracted considerable criticism, much of which also applies to problems that have been observed with attempts to gain market share. The major criticisms are presented below.

SUCCESS OF LOW-SHARE FIRMS

In the 1970s, the essence of market-share strategy was to become the market leader. The "iron rule" of the growth-share matrix was that high share leads inexorably to higher profits. But, from the very beginning, there was contradictory evidence.

Many low-share firms have proved to be very profitable. One study examined forty low-share firms and found that successful firms focused on higher quality and lower costs (Woo and Cooper 1982). Those firms also tended to compete in low-growth markets, where few product changes were necessary. For the most part, they made frequently purchased items and sold industrial components or supplies. The implication is that gaining the highest share is not the only path to business success. It is but a single path.

An earlier article also argued against the advice that low-share firms should either fight for higher share or withdraw from the competition (Hammermesh, Anderson, and Harris 1978). Four characteristics of successful low-share firms were identified.

First, low-share firms focus on market segments. They avoid toe-to-toe competition with larger competitors. Second, low-share firms use R&D efficiently, focusing on a few innovations rather than battling on a broad front. Third, they purposely think small. Successful firms limit sales growth and diversify cautiously; they stress the quality of sales over sheer quantity. Finally, low-share firms are usually led by a ubiquitous chief executive, like Lee Iaccoca, who inculcates the entire firm with his vision and personality.

FUTILITY OF MARKET-SHARE GAINS

Another criticism of going for the highest market share is that it often fails and devastates the firms involved in the battle. It is not a recent observation. As early as 1972, studies found that firms that spent heavily to gain the number one position often ended up worse off than when they started (Fruhan 1972). It is an argument that gaining share is not always the best strategy. Share gains require special competencies. Most important, market-share wars are often won by no one, but frequently leave the entire industry worse off than it had been originally.

SUCCESS OF LOW-GROWTH MARKETS

High-growth markets are not the panacea they once seemed. High growth is difficult to identify, dissipates quickly, and often attracts heavy competition. The presumption that high-growth markets are inherently more attractive than low-growth markets is not always true. Aaker and Day (1986) questioned six particularly shaky assumptions about growth markets, and argued the following points:

Gaining share is not necessarily easier or less costly in growth markets. Share gains in growth markets are not necessarily more valuable than share gains in mature markets. As a market expands it is likely to splinter into segments, or change in other ways, leaving the rewards to others rather than the first firm into the market. It is competitive advantage that maintains share not early entry.

Share gains in growth markets do not necessarily give firms a head start down the experience curve.

The pressure to lower prices is not necessarily less in growth markets. The many firms battling for position can make competition as vigorous in growth markets as in mature ones.

Early entrants do not necessarily gain access to new technology, which is unavailable to later entrants.

Early entrants do not necessarily outperform later entrants.

Additional support comes from Fierman (1985) who studied seven successful companies that competed in stagnant or declining markets, and, as a result, generated handsome profits. They did not milk their bread-and-butter products. Instead, they avoided battles for market share, emphasized quality, treated employees like family, used low-technology means to lower costs, and moved cautiously when it came to strategy. They succeeded without market growth.

Destruction of Bread-and-Butter Products

Many firms fund entry into unproven markets at the expense of bread-and-butter products. The result is often disaster rather than success. Leading products in less glamorous industries have been decimated to finance opportunities in exotic markets that turned out to be no such thing.

More than ten years ago, for example, the food companies spent heavily to diversify out of the food industry into new and exotic areas. Food products were almost universally considered to be undesirable low-growth markets. Most diversifications failed badly. Instead, in more recent years, the food companies found growth in, of all places, the food industry they had tried so hard to leave. After searching opportunity in glamorous markets, they found growth in their own backyards.

Wholesale attacks on personal computers, information technologies and a host of other areas have led to similar results.

One particularly telling tale is that of Addressograph–Multigraph, a company that changed its name to AM International in the late 1970s. The company decimated its primary product, mechanical offset duplicators, to pursue a host of exotic information technologies, none of which panned out. Subsequent management divested the exotic technologies and focused on the mainstay business. But it was too late. *Business Week* (1982) quoted an executive of the firm, referring to the core business, as saying: "We're now No. 2 and we have two Japanese companies breathing down our necks" (p. 68). AM International filed for bankruptcy shortly after. Harvesting hurt it dearly.

IMPORTANCE OF KNOWING THE BUSINESS

A basic assumption of the BCG matrix is that it is not necessary to know the business in which the firm competes. The matrix itself derives from finance where portfolios of stocks and bonds are routinely managed to diversify risk. But, diversifications into unknown businesses proved less successful than expected. Managing products turned out to be a much different exercise than managing stocks and bonds.

PROBLEMS WITH EXPERIENCE EFFECTS

Experience effects often progress differently than theory said they would. Since at least the mid-1970s, the limits of the learning curve have been recognized (Abernathy and Wayne 1974).

Consider the more recent case of the Anchor Glass Company, a glass bottle manufacturer, described by *Business Week* (1988). In 1987 Anchor became the market leader by acquiring Diamond-Bathurst Inc., another bottlemaker. In response, Owens-Illinois Corp., the previous share leader, acquired glassmaker Brockway Inc., which returned it to the number one position. Share gains turned into industry consolidation. Instead of experience effects, the industry experienced competition among debt-ridden giants.

Then, customers for bottles reacted. The food and soda companies sensed trouble and demanded long-term contracts at cut-rate prices. They got what they wanted. The bottlemakers had to keep production humming to pay down the costs of their acquisitions. The food and soda companies also consolidated. More powerful suppliers faced more powerful buyers. The reactions of competitors and suppliers negated the market share gained by Anchor. Anchor's losses mounted with market share.

Overoptimistic Estimates

Wide variability in the slopes of experience curves has been observed from one industry to the next. Strategies predicated on the assumption of steep cost declines have failed when cost declines proved more meager than expected.

Costs, Capacity, and Sales

Expanding production to gain experience faster than competitors did not consider that products had to be sold as well as manufactured. The focus on production led to overcapacity and destructive price competition. Drastic reductions in prices were necessary to move merchandise, and the gains in experience led to accumulating losses.

Confounding Effects of Shared Experience

Shared experience is gained when a firm has experience making similar products, and already knows part of the process. A firm that makes wine, for example, enters the competition for wine coolers further down the experience curve than a firm in an unrelated line of business. Problems and opportunities in shared experiences often negated early leads in experience. Firms were cutting ahead on the experience-curve slide. Calculating shared experience proved even more nettlesome.

MISTAKEN ASSUMPTION OF COMMODITY MARKETS

Experience effects have also been criticized because they assume that all products are commodities that compete on price alone. It is an unrealistic assumption. Few products are pure commodities (milk, beef, and eggs, for example). Marketers have been adept at transforming commodities into differentiated goods so that consumers will shop on a basis other than price.

Differentiated products negate the advantage presupposed for experience effects. The cheapest chicken is often passed by in favor of Perdue's more expensive alternative.

OVEREMPHASIS ON PRODUCTION COSTS

At its root, the BCG matrix is a low-cost producer's game. You win by perpetually lowering production costs. There is no other path to success. But many firms that are not the lowest-cost producers have been extremely successful. Furthermore, American firms have proved to be particularly poor at cost competitiveness in international markets. As such, the BCG matrix forced firms to focus on their weaknesses rather than their strengths. It violated one of the central precepts of marketing strategy—competitive advantage.

Reemergence of Cost Competitiveness

Ironically, what the BCG scheme failed to achieve—an emphasis on lower costs—current practice deems of great importance. Today, more than ever, American business embraces the desire to be "lean and mean." Ruthless cutting of staff and stripping away layers of middle management are now widely used ways to cut costs. Criticisms of the BCG technique notwithstanding, the very premise of it has been wholeheartedly adopted. Lowering costs is considered more important than ever. But, restructuring, and other competitive realignments, not the BCG matrix, have caused these changes.

In contrast, during the heyday of the BCG matrix in the 1970s, inflation soared pushing costs upward. While the matrix reached its zenith costs spiraled upwards.

Creative Response Stifled

A final criticism of the BCG matrix is that it stifles creativity by offering a canned response to strategic opportunities. It is essentially a mechanical procedure that replaces creative solutions to unique situations with a predetermined sequence of events. Such rigidity ensured that the matrix would fail when it was widely applied to many industries. Furthermore, the BCG matrix offered only a single strategy to every firm in every industry. It offered one answer to many questions. It was the Johnny-one-note of strategy. As a result, it was a recipe for disaster. There is no one way to succeed at marketing strategy.

In hindsight, it proved clear that there are many roads to business success. A strategy based on lower costs is an acceptable orientation towards markets but it is not the only way to win the game of business. A strategy formulation was needed that expanded the paths a firm could take. That is the topic of the next chapter.

References

Aaker, David, and George Day. "The Perils of High-Growth Markets." *Strategic Management Journal,* September–October 1986, pp. 409–421.

Abell, Derek. "Strategic Windows." *Journal of Marketing,* July 1978, pp. 21–26.

Abernathy, William J., and Kenneth Wayne. "Limits of the Learning Curve." *Harvard Business Review,* September–October 1974, pp. 109–119.

"AM International: When Technology Was Not Enough." *Business Week,* January 25, 1982, p. 62–68.

Buzzell, Robert D., and Frederick D. Wiersema. "Successful Share-Building Strategies." *Harvard Business Review,* January–February 1981, pp. 135–144.

Christensen, H. Kurt, Arnold C. Cooper, and Cornelis A. DeKluyver. "The Dog Business: A Re-examination." *Business Horizons,* October–December 1982, pp. 12–18.

Fierman, Jaclyn. "How to Make Money in Mature Markets." *Fortune,* November 25, 1985, pp. 47–53.

Fogg, C. Davis. "Planning Gains in Market Share." *Journal of Marketing,* July 1974, pp. 30–36.

Fruhan, William E. "Pyrrhic Victories in Fights for Market Share." *Harvard Business Review,* June 1972, pp. 100–107.

Hambrick, Donald C. and Ian C. MacMillan. "The Product Portfolio and Man's Best Friend." *California Management Review,* Fall 1982, pp. 84–95.

Hammermesh, R. G., M. J. Anderson Jr. and J. E. Harris. "Strategies for Low Market Share Businesses." *Harvard Business Review,* May–June 1978, pp. 95–102.

Kotler, Philip. "Harvesting for Weak Products." *Business Horizons,* July 1978, pp. 15–22.

Levine, Joshua. "Sorrell Ridge Makes Smucker's Pucker." *Forbes,* June 12, 1989, pp. 166–168.

Phillips, Lynn, Dae Chang, and Robert Buzzell. "Product Quality, Cost Position and Business Performance: A Test of Some Key Hypotheses." *Journal of Marketing,* Spring 1983, pp. 26–43.

Porter, Michael. *Competitive Advantage.* New York: Free Press, 1985.

Schnaars, Steven P. "When Entering Growth Markets, Are Pioneers Better Than Poachers?" *Business Horizons,* March–April 1986, pp. 27–36.

"What Is Dragging Anchor Down." *Business Week,* September 26, 1988, p. 54.

Woo, Carolyn Y., and Arnold C. Cooper. "The Surprising Case for Low Market Share." *Harvard Business Review,* November–December 1982, pp. 106–113.

Chapter 5

Assessing Competitive Intensity

An integral part of marketing strategy is coping with competition. Excessive competition drives down prices and hurts profits. A market where competition is less severe offers firms higher prices and more attractive profits.

Economists have long recognized that some markets are more fiercely competitive than others. The ferocity of that competition is rooted in the structure of the market (Porter 1980). The characteristics of some markets combine to either strengthen or weaken the level of competition. This chapter examines the mechanics of competition and shows how firms and events can conspire to change the intensity of competition.

Economic Models of Competition

The intensity of competition is rooted in the three basic types of competitive environments—perfect competition, pure monopoly, and imperfect competition. As Exhibit 5.1 illustrates, those forms of competition array themselves along a continuum ranging from no competitive pressures whatsoever to cutthroat price competition.

PERFECT COMPETITION

In the imaginary world of economic theory, some firms compete in markets characterized by perfect competition. Specifically, perfect competition describes markets where the following conditions are met.

Non-Differentiated Products

In a perfectly competitive market all products are identical or homogeneous. They are commodities, like wheat, eggs, and pork bellies. There

Exhibit 5.1   *Basic Forms of Competition*

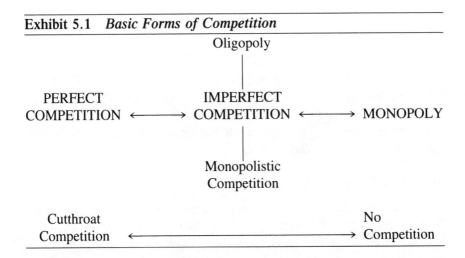

is no difference between them, except for price. Perfect competition is essentially pure price competition. Since there are no differences between homogeneous products—be they real or imagined—consumers choose the cheapest. Clearly, price competition in commodity markets is likely to be fierce.

Perfect Knowledge

All firms are created equal in a perfectly competitive market. All firms have equal access to the production technologies and techniques. There are no patents, proprietary designs, or special skills that allow an individual firm to do the job better than competitors. Firms also have equal access to the resources needed to make products. Raw materials are available to all and available on similar terms. There is no such thing as competitive advantage in a market characterized by perfect knowledge.

No Barriers to Entry

Firms can enter a perfectly competitive market at will. There are no barriers to entry. If a firm is making handsome profits in a particular market, no other firms can enter easily and share in the wealth. There are no brand names, expensive factories to be built, or limited distribution to keep competitors away.

The absence of entry barriers means that new entrants can build factories quickly, enter attractive markets, and expand capacity. As a result, supply quickly meets demand keeping strong downward pressure on prices. Profits decline to the point where firms no longer find the market attractive.

In the absence of entry barriers, no one firm makes extraordinary profits. Instead, many firms make a modest profit.

No Exit Barriers

If profits decline to the point where they are no longer attractive, firms can withdraw from the market at will. The fluidness of entry and exit means that profit margins will reach equilibrium at slightly above the rate earned on U.S. Treasury Bills.

Atomistic Competition

In a perfectly competitive market there are many buyers and many sellers. The market decides the price of products through the interplay of supply and demand. Neither buyers nor sellers have the power to influence prices.

In atomistic competition all firms are roughly the same size. There are no market leaders. High-share firms do not exist. Sellers are at the mercy of efficient market mechanisms. So are buyers. Since all buying firms are the same size, there is no such thing as a large important account demanding more favorable terms. Buyers and sellers compete on an equal footing. Firms are "price-takers." Like the farmer who sells his wheat at market, manufacturers receive only what the market will pay any one of many manufacturers. Finally, in atomistic competition all firms act independently. There is no collusion, industry coalitions, or other mechanisms to interfere with perfectly competitive markets.

Perfect competition makes for easy curve-fitting in elementary economics textbooks. Supply and demand curves can be neatly plotted. But it is an unrealistic view of markets. Few markets fit the model of perfect competition. Most markets are imperfect.

MONOPOLY

Monopoly lies at the opposite end of the continuum from perfect competition. In a monopoly there is no competition. There is only a single seller and that seller's product is unique. There are no substitutes for it. If a customer wants to buy that type of product he must buy it from that single seller.

With the exception of electric utilities, and a few other regulated industries, monopolies are as rare as perfect competition. Most markets have far greater freedoms than those presumed by the rigid control of monopolies. Most markets lie somewhere between perfect competition and monopoly.

IMPERFECT COMPETITION

Most competition is neither perfect nor monopolistic. Instead, it is imperfect—beset by a host of inequities that affect both the buyer and the seller. Those inequities lie at the heart of competitive marketing strategy. By understanding the factors affecting the level of competition in a market, a firm can assess the likelihood of earning higher-than-average profits. There are two distinct forms of imperfect competition, each of which gains competitive advantage in its own way:

Monopolistic Competition: Product Differentiation

Monopolistic competition holds that there are many sellers, but that each of them sells differentiated goods. Toothpastes, cosmetics, the retail trade, and most consumer product categories and services are characterized by real or imagined product differences. Those products do not compete on the basis of price alone. They compete, instead, on the basis of product differences.

The focus of monopolistic competition is on product differentiation. Firms minimize competition and earn higher profits by selling unique products, which are not direct substitutes for one another.

Oligopoly: Few Sellers

The term oligopoly means "few sellers." In this form of imperfect competition, a few large sellers dominate the market by selling homogeneous, or slightly differentiated, products. Steel, aluminum, and machinery products are largely oligopolistic. A few large sellers sell products that are largely the same.

An oligopoly lessens competition in a different way than monopolistic competition. The emphasis is on barriers to entry, market collusion, and other practices that ensure high profits for the few sellers that dominate the market. Competition is imperfect because of control of the market rather than the presence of unique products.

Marketing Strategy and Models of Competition

Over the years, marketing strategy formulations have embraced different components of imperfect competition in their search for extraordinary profits.

BCG AND COMPETITION

The BCG's growth-share matrix embraces many, but not all, of the central tenets of perfect competition. It relies heavily on pure price competition and the sale of homogeneous products. But it also embraces some key aspects of oligopolistic competition. Consider each of these characteristics in turn.

Pure Price Competition

The BCG approach to strategy assumes that all firms, regardless of their size, compete on the basis of lower prices derived from lower costs. Experience curves and the growth-rate share matrix are single-minded in their attention to declining costs and prices. A firm must keep its costs below the industry price or it will be shaken out of the market. In the BCG view, most competitors have no control over the prices that customers will pay for their products.

Homogeneous Products

The BCG approach views all products as commodities, another characteristic of perfect competition. There is no opportunity for product differentiation, nor is there the option of serving market segments with unique products. In the BCG view, products are essentially commodities.

Emphasis on Market Domination

The BCG approach does reject some of the components of perfect competition. It rejects the assumption of atomistic competition. Firms are advised to build dominant shares or withdraw from the market. The result is often a few large sellers, an oligopoly.

Experience Effects as Barriers to Entry

Experiences effects serve as barriers to entry. Firms that quickly build dominant shares of their market have greater efficiencies than those of lower-share firms. Those efficiencies keep other competitors out of the market. Again, the BCG approach embraces some aspects of oligopolistic competition.

Imperfect Knowledge

The BCG approach also rejects the assumption of perfect knowledge. It holds that experience effects are learned over time. Some firms attain them faster than others. Consequently, not all firms have perfect knowledge of the market, but some have a competitive advantage.

MARKETING AND MONOPOLISTIC COMPETITION

Monopolistic competition is the form of imperfect competition most akin to marketing. While the BCG approach seeks production efficiencies, marketers have long sought to minimize competition by creating unique products. Monopolistic competition can be found in most markets. Most sellers sell products that are differentiated on more than price alone. They compete on the basis of product features, branding, image, packaging, quality, design, and a host of other tangible and intangible factors that fall within the purview of marketing.

Product differentiation is not a new idea. It has its roots in the work of early economists such as Edward Hastings Chamberlin, a renowned Harvard University economist, whose 1933 book, *The Theory of Monopolistic Competition,* posted a definition of product differentiation that is almost identical to that used in marketing today. He argued that products can be differentiated on the basis of real or perceived dimensions as long as the point of differentiation is important to the consumer. In recognition of his contributions to marketing theory, Chamberlin was awarded the Paul D. Converse Award by the American Marketing Association in 1953.

The ramifications of product differentiation for business performance have also been known for decades. The English economist P. Sraffa presented a realistic representation of markets in the 1920s in a landmark article titled: "The Laws of Returns under Competitive Conditions." His work was extended by Joan Robinson in a 1933 book entitled *The Economics of Imperfect Competition.* Clearly, the use of product differentiation to gain competitive advantage is not a recent idea. It has a long history in early economics.

BROADENED VIEW OF IMPERFECT COMPETITION

In more recent years, Porter (1979, 1980) has broadened the view of competitive strategy to incorporate both forms of imperfect competition—monopolistic competition and oligopoly. Porter's primary contribution is the recognition that either form of imperfect competition leads to competitive advantage. The important point is that competition is less severe in markets that are less perfectly competitive. According to Porter, competition, and hence profitability, are rooted in the structure of an industry. Markets that approach perfect competition are less profitable than those that are imperfectly competitive. A firm gains competitive advantage by either selecting a market where imperfect competition already exists, or by changing that market to make competition imperfect.

Finding Imperfect Markets

Firms can use imperfect competition to their favor by searching for markets where the mechanisms of perfect competition are not working properly. They can decide to compete in markets where products are highly differentiated, or where production efficiencies are important.

Creating Imperfect Competition

An alternative strategy is for firms to influence market mechanisms to earn a higher profit. Marketers may be able to disrupt the mechanisms of perfect market competition. They might introduce greater differentiation into the market or strive to gain a large share of the market through lower prices. In either case, the firm intercedes and uses economic inequities to its own advantage. It is a view of economic phenomena that is strictly pro-business. The intention of business is to avoid competition. It is a view in tune with current pro-business times.

Five Factors Affecting Competitive Intensity

Five forces interact to influence the intensity of competition in an industry (Porter 1979, 1980), and together these factors determine market attractiveness. The five factors are (1) the threat of new entrants, (2) rivalry among existing firms, (3) the threat of substitutes, (4) the bargaining power of buyers, and (5) the bargaining power of suppliers. Exhibit 5.2 illustrates the relationship among them.

Some markets have particularly unfortunate combinations of these factors. As a result, competition is cutthroat and profits are poor. Other industries are more fortunate. The five factors combine in a manner that lessens the intensity of competition. Competition is less severe in those markets, and firms that compete in that market tend to earn a higher profit.

Firms should focus their attention on these five crucial factors, and by doing so, can identify attractive markets where competition is lessened.

Exhibit 5.2   Five Forces Affecting Competition

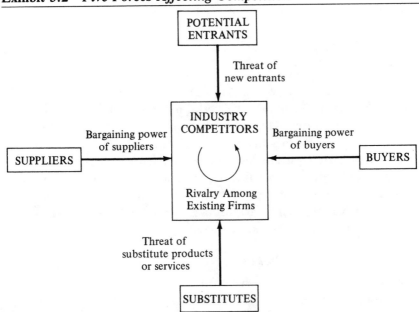

SOURCE: Reprinted with permission of The Free Press, a Division of Macmillan, Inc., from *Competitive Strategy: Techniques for Analyzing Industries and Competitors* by Michael Porter, p. 4. Copyright © 1980.

Or, they can change the combination of those five factors to their advantage.

The focus of these five factors is a more flexible view of strategy than that proposed by formula planning techniques such as the BCG growth-share matrix. It does not propose a single view of all industries, as does the BCG. Instead, it proposes that each industry is affected by the same set of factors, but that those factors combine in different ways. It focuses attention on the factors that affect competition rather than proposing a single model of competition that applies to all markets. The five factors affecting competitive intensity are described in the following sections of this chapter.

THREAT OF NEW ENTRANTS

The easy entry of new firms into an attractive market makes that market less attractive to incumbent firms. Incumbents want to keep others out. They can do so in two ways: (1) by erecting barriers to entry, so that others cannot enter the market, even if they want to, or (2) by threatening to fight vigorously against new entrants, persuading them to enter those markets instead.

Barriers to Entry

In a perfectly competitive market firms can enter and leave at will. There are no barriers. In the real world, however, markets usually have entry and exit barriers. Markets where firms cannot enter easily are more profitable for firms that are already in that industry. Firms that erect entry barriers ensure less competition and higher profits. Entry barriers are the modern business equivalent of moats around medieval forts. They protect incumbents from competition.

Eight key barriers to entry are discussed below. Four are drawn directly from marketing; the other four arise out of economics.

1. Product Differentiation

Marketers seek to destroy what economists propose as perfect competition. Product differentiation is a prime example. It lessens competition in a product category by offering products that consumers do not perceive as similar. As a result, product comparisons based solely on price are less meaningful.

Differentiation is widespread. Few products compete as commodities. Most products possess prominent brand names that are instantly recognized by millions of consumers. Campbell's soup, Quaker Oats, Coca-Cola, Heinz catsup, and myriad other popular products serve as effective barriers to entry for those wishing to enter those markets.

2. Access to Distribution

Distribution also serves as a potent barrier to entry. A firm that cannot find wholesalers or retailers to sell its products is at a severe disadvantage. Firms that can tie up distribution channels can preclude entry by others. Consider the strategic effect of distribution in the following examples:

The myriad brands of Coke and Pepsi, and the many offerings in laundry detergents (all owned by only a few firms), offer consumers a wide array of choices. But they also tie up limited shelf space from potential entrants. Many years ago, Timex could not find jewelers to carry its watches. It had to find a different channel of distribution. When Seven-Up introduced its ad campaign "no caffeine—never had it never will," Pepsi threatened to cut off distributors who went along with the campaign. It turned out to be a choice that never had to be made.

Pepsi introduced its own version of decaffeinated soda—Pepsi Free—shortly after.

In the early days of personal computers—the early 1980s—distribution proved to be a potent barrier to entry. Smaller firms could not find retailers who would stock their products. One of the earliest entrants, Columbia Data Systems, produced a fine product, but could not find dealers to sell the machines. Forced to rely heavily on mail order, Columbia went belly up in the mid-1980s.

3. Favorable Locations

Favorable locations also serve as a barrier to entry. K mart moved into mass-market discount retailing from its Kresge five-and-dime store operations shortly after World War II. Woolworth followed much later with Woolco, its entry, but had to settle for second-rate locations. Woolworth stores turned in a second-rate performance and were closed in the early 1980s.

4. Brand Switching Costs

Switching costs are sometimes engineered to thwart market entry. As designed, they tie buyers to a particular seller's product making it expensive or inconvenient for a customer to switch to another seller. Long-term contracts and product designs that are compatible only with a particular manufacturer's products are standard means of ensuring brand loyalty.

Consider the case of Baxter International Inc., a hospital supplier. Baxter offers large customers deep volume discounts, rebates, management consulting services, and free computer software if they agree to multiyear contracts. Forty percent of Baxter's sales come from such contracts. Hospitals, pressured to cut costs, trade the right to switch suppliers for lower prices.

Switching costs can sometimes backfire, however. Texet, a once-successful software supplier, has recently fallen on hard times (Jereski 1988). The electronic publishing software it sold was purposely designed to work only on the computers it also sold. Texet wanted both markets. Unfortunately for the firm, instead of erecting barriers to entry it erected a barrier to success. Consumers found the products too inflexible.

5. Patents

Patents can protect markets from competitors, but not as often as expected. Polaroid dominates the instant camera segment, after successfully suing Kodak when Kodak sold a similar product. Nutrasweet is also a protected product.

Patents are more pervasive in some industries than others. In the drug industry patents are common, and very enforceable. In many consumer product markets, and with services, patents are less potent, and thus copying is rampant.

6. Economies of Scale

Economies of scale preclude entry by smaller firms that do not have the starting volume of sales to achieve such effects. Scale effects can be found in production, marketing, and distribution. Production is most amenable to scale effects. It calls to mind the ubiquitous assembly line, where it costs less per unit to make many rather than a few. Oil refineries, auto production, and other large-scale industrial operations all benefit from economies of scale. A large producer has numerous production advantages over a smaller producer. Often, these advantages can be used to preclude entry.

Economies of scale can also occur in marketing. A beer company, for example, with a national brand can advertise more efficiently than a brewer with only regional appeal. It can take out ads on network TV without wasting dollars to reach consumers who cannot consume the product. And, its costs are spread over a larger volume of production.

Finally, there are economies of scale in distribution. It is less expensive (per unit) to distribute high-volume, widely distributed products than it is to distribute lower-volume products. Distributing Coca-Cola or Budweiser to retailers, for example, is far more efficient than distributing more obscure brands that are stocked only in scattered locations.

The major beer brewers possess tremendous economies of scale. It is difficult for a new entrant to match the benefits that arise from such effects. Smaller entrants have to find another way to enter.

7. Experience Effects

Experience effects can also serve as a barrier to entry, but only if they cannot be copied by later entrants. Experience effects were the key barrier to entry proposed by the BCG growth-share matrix, which was covered in the previous two chapters.

8. Capital Investment

Capital investment can scare off some entrants. Some industries require heavy investments to enter, which can serve as a barrier to market entry.

Expected Defense of Market Share

New firms are less likely to enter markets where incumbents will fight hard to defend their market share. They will be especially reluctant if the incumbent firm has the will and the resources to fight back.

Assessing the likelihood of a strong defense depends on the answers to the following questions:

Has the market leader defended share strongly in the past? Some firms have cultivated a well-deserved reputation for ruthless retaliation. To enter their markets is to invite disaster. At the very least, to enter is to raise th cost of entry and lower the likelihood of success. Coca-Cola, P&G, Hallmark, IBM, Anheuser-Busch, and a host of other savvy competitors are known to be strong competitors when it comes to defending their markets.

Often, strong competitors battle with one another. P&G, a superb marketer, entered the well-defended market for orange juice with its Citrus Hill brand with little success but tremendous costs. Tropicana, now owned by Seagram's, and Minute Maid, owned by Coca-Cola, have been unwilling to relinquish a piece of their markets. In the absence of any special product feature, P&G has failed to gain a profitable share of an attractive market for fruit juices. To date, retaliation by incumbents has been vigorous and effective at precluding P&G's Citrus Hill brand from gaining significant share of the market.

Does the market leader have the resources to defend share? Defending markets from attack is expensive. Large, well-financed firms seeking to enter new markets will often seek out opportunities where smaller competitors do not have the resources to retaliate.

Entry into home improvement centers by large firms, such as Supermarket General's Rickel's, and Home Depot steals share from mom-and-pop hardware stores, a group that is hard-pressed to respond. Similarly, moves into real estate by Sear's Caldwell Banker, and the entry of chain drug stores into the markets held by independent corner drug stores, pitted strength against weakness.

Is the market leader committed to defending share? Market leaders must also be committed to defending market share. Some firms do not have the desire to fight. Their attention may be focused on other markets; or, there may be some reason that the incumbent is not interested in defending his share of the market. Vigilant new entrants seek out undefended markets and hope to catch incumbents at their weakest moment.

Is the market leader "asleep at the wheel"? Some incumbents seemingly invite new entrants by appearing to be "asleep at the wheel." For a variety of reasons these firms either will not or cannot respond to attacks on their markets.

Will a sleeping giant be awakened? Sometimes, lackadaisical incumbents are awakened by the shock of a new entrant in their midst. In the early 1980s, for example, Coca-Cola entered the gentlemanly wine industry with the intention to gain share for its newly acquired Taylor brand. Coke conducted taste tests and other marketing practices unheard of in the refined business of selling wine. While industry incumbents were shocked, Taylor gained share. But, they also awakened a sleepy giant. Gallo, the industry leader, possessed overwhelming economies of scale. They even made their own wine bottles.

Gallo fought back vigorously. Coca-Cola divested Taylor a few years later. It was bought by Seagram's. Then, in the late 1980s, Seagram's too quit the business. The level of retaliation turned out to be more vigorous than either Coca-Cola or Seagram's had anticipated. Competition at the low end of the wine market turned out to be higher than expected.

RIVALRY AMONG EXISTING FIRMS

In some markets, firms fight hard with one another to gain market prominence. In other markets competitors coexist peacefully. Peaceful markets are more attractive than intensely competitive markets. Intense rivalry drives down prices, drives up promotional expenses, and otherwise negatively affects profits.

The following issues seem most important in assessing the intensity of rivalry:

Current Intensity of Rivalry

Sometimes, competition is so intense that competitors are driven to near suicidal strategies that hurt themselves as well as their opponents. Consider the rivalry that existed among airlines during much of the 1980s. After deregulation airlines were free to compete. Many airlines fought with lower prices. Consumers could fly across the country for less than $100. Often, kids flew free. Profits in the industry were low. Exacerbating the problem was the fact that the product they sold—a seat on an airline—was difficult to differentiate. All airlines sold essentially the same product. Price competition among near commodities is the most destructive type.

During the same period competition among cigarettes was mild by comparison. Although the market was shrinking slowly, manufacturers kept prices and profits high.

Outlook for Rivalry

Some markets go through short periods of intense rivalry and then settle down to a more stable pattern. It is important to ask whether the fighting is likely to be short-lived? Or whether intense competition is endemic to the market? The historical stability of market shares gives an indication of long-term rivalry. Stable market share is often the result of mild competition.

Presence of an Upstart

The presence of a firm that is determined to gain share increases rivalry. Both gaining share and defending share are expensive. In either case, credible attempts to change the make-up of market shares is likely to increase the intensity of competition and decrease profits.

Presence of a Benevolent Market Leader

Competition is reduced by the presence of a benevolent market leader, a high-share firm that sets a slow pace for the competition. In those markets smaller competitors follow the leader and strive to keep conditions stable.

Price Rivalry

Fighting with price is the most destructive type of competition as it instantly lowers profits for all competitors. Price cuts are easy to institute, and easy to match. Countering price cuts with increases in promotional expenditures is a more creative response to price cutting that can protect share and profits, and negate the efforts of the price cutter.

Excess Capacity

Rivalry tends to be higher when competitors have excess capacity. Often, firms are willing to cut prices to keep the factory running and pay fixed costs.

Markets That Offer Big Rewards

Rivalry can be especially high if the rewards for success are great and recognized by all competitors in the market. Consider the. fight for a leading national pasta brand. Currently, individual spaghetti brands serve only regional markets. There is no one dominant national brand. Firms have been fighting to build a national brand, and achieve economies of scale in production, advertising and distribution, but so far with only limited success. Acquisitions, regional roll-outs, and a host of other tactics have increased rivalry in pasta markets.

THREAT OF SUBSTITUTE PRODUCTS

Rarely do products sell in isolation. More often, they compete against substitutes. Sugar, for example, competes with artificial sweeteners in consumer markets. In commercial markets, it competes with corn syrups and other sweeteners derived from substances other than cane. Network television competes with cable TV—and both compete with video rentals. Soft drinks compete with fruit juices, fruit drinks, and bottled waters to quench consumers' thirsts.

In automobile production, plastics have substituted for steel in many applications. Steel has been hurt by substitutes as much as it has been hurt by low-cost foreign competition.

Broad Versus Narrow Definitions of Substitutes

Substitute products can be defined broadly or narrowly. Bayer aspirin, for example, competes with less expensive private aspirin brands. It also competes with aspirin substitutes such as acetaminophen and ibuprofen. Tropical islands compete with cruises, lush casinos, and ski resorts for the vacation dollars of some consumers. Consumers may even decide to spend their discretionary income on a personal computer rather than on a down payment for a car.

Clearly, defining substitutes can vary greatly. Substitutes are typically defined as "similar" products, but there is ample room for expansion and contraction in just what is covered. Substitutes greatly influence competition. Consumers can switch to close substitutes if prices are perceived as uncompetitive.

Technological Innovation

Technological innovations can drastically alter the competitive environment. The invention of the calculator, for example, made slide rules obsolete almost overnight. But predicting technological innovation is difficult, if not impossible. The process by which inventions are made and brought to market is not well known. The evolution of products is covered in a later chapter.

Price and Performance Comparisons

Predicting the likelihood of substitution is a more practical goal. Consumers switch products based on perceptions of price and performance. Substitutes that are declining in price vis-à-vis an existing product suggest the threat of substitution is imminent. Substitutes that offer performance advantages are also likely to gain customers. If the cost is less, they are especially threatening. But the balance between the two is most important.

Once again, consider the case of pain relievers. Tylenol (acetaminophen) costs more than aspirin. But Johnson and Johnson, the makers of Tylenol, have been able to convince consumers that the absence of stomach upset—improved performance—is worth the additional price. Tylenol has gained share in the pain reliever market—a broader definition. It has also maintained a monstrous share of the acetaminophen market—a more narrow definition. Clearly, Tylenol has made the pain reliever market less attractive to aspirin producers, such as Bayer.

Reduced Demand

A final variation of this pattern is a reduction in consumer consumption when prices are raised, even if there is no substitute. Consider what happened to coffee and sugar a decade ago. Consumers drastically cut back their consumption of those products in response to rapidly raised prices. Neither has regained its pre-price-rise position of dominance.

BARGAINING POWER OF BUYERS

A market characterized by powerful customers is less attractive than a market where customers have less power. The reason is simple: powerful customers can demand lower prices from a weaker seller. The seller has to acquiesce to the customers' demands or find another outlet for its goods. Powerful customers drive down the sellers' prices and profits.

Few Versus Many Customers

The presence of a few customers is less attractive to the seller than a large number of dispersed customers. Consider, for example, the power a strong retailer like Toys 'R' Us exerts over toy manufacturers. Nearly 25 percent of all toys sold today in the United States are sold by Toys 'R' Us. And the company's share is expected to double by the end of the 1990s. That large share of the market translates directly into immense power over toy manufacturers. If Toys 'R' Us dislikes a product, the product faces a bleak future and may be withdrawn. As *Business Week* noted in an article on the company: "Its decisions influence the whole industry" (Dunkin 1988, p. 58).

Imagine yourself as a salesperson negotiating a deal to sell a large lot of toys to Toys 'R' Us. When the discussion turned to terms of the contract, who do you imagine would hold the upper hand? In contrast, imagine the same set of negotiations with a small mom-and-pop, single-unit toy store. In the parlance of competitive strategy, Toys 'R' Us has strong bargaining power.

Consumer Versus Industrial Markets

Customers in consumer markets tend to have less power than industrial buyers. Individual consumers are dispersed and many. It is far more difficult for them to exert influence over manufacturers. There are fewer industrial buyers, but each places larger orders. Thus, they tend to be more important accounts.

Individual consumers also have less than perfect knowledge of the market. Myriad models of many types of products make it difficult to compare prices. Seiko, for example, sells 2,300 watch styles. It is difficult to bargain for better prices when product offerings cannot be compared easily.

Limits of Consumer Decision Making

Furthermore, a large body of research on consumer decision making suggests that individual consumers engage only in limited decision making when it comes to purchasing many categories of products. For many products consumers buy as much on habit as they do on price, and do not spend a great deal of time shopping for alternatives. Hence, they are less sensitive to higher prices. This is especially true in the absence of close substitutes. In the parlance of competitive strategy they are not powerful buyers.

BARGAINING POWER OF SUPPLIERS

The power of suppliers is the reverse side of the coin as the power of customers. Powerful sellers raise the price of raw materials, inventory, and supplies to the customers they serve. Powerful sellers can also dictate terms to the customer.

Consider the case of distributing paperback books to small retailers. Few sellers want to service those low-volume accounts, and those that do, offer terms that provide few services to the retailer and offer weak discounts. The small retailer has no alternative. He can either accept the meager service on the seller's terms or go without books. In such transactions the seller is powerful and the customer is weak. The seller protects his own profits at the expense of the customer's profits.

Paperback book publishers play a similar version of the same game with the distributors. In the mid-1970s discounting became a popular practice among large book retailers. Customers would get 20 percent off the cover price. Publishers encouraged the practice, but did not reduce their discounts to smaller wholesalers and retailers. To remain competitive with the larger chains (powerful customers), smaller firms were forced to discount their prices even though their costs remained the same.

Franchises: A Single Seller

The presence of a few sellers shifts power from the customer to the seller. The ultimate case of a powerful seller is a franchise, which is a single seller. Franchises are often required to buy only from that supplier. To do otherwise is to violate the terms of a contract.

An Important Seller

Finally, the seller of an important product—one that would be difficult for the buyer to do without—shifts power to the seller. The *New York Times,* for example, charges retailers a hefty deposit to carry the paper. Retailers either pay up or do without this popular paper, which brings in customers for other products sold in the store. Many of the brands carried by supermarkets possess similar clout with weaker buyers.

How Firms Use Competitive Analysis

According to Porter, firms can observe and manipulate the five forces affecting competitive intensity in the following five ways:

FITTING THE CURRENT ENVIRONMENT

A firm that understands its competitive environment can better position itself in the market to take advantage of the current configuration of the five factors affecting the level of competition as illustrated in Exhibit

5.2. A firm that has a small share of the market, for example, can avoid competition by focusing on a segment of the market rather than by trying to compete across a broad front. A low-share firm cannot hope to match market leaders in advertising, economies of scale, distribution, and a host of other areas. It can still find success, however, by competing in only part of the market.

ANTICIPATING CHANGES

Markets are perpetually changing. Innovations alter the competitive position of substitutes. Consumers demand different products. Competitors find new ways to serve those demands. A firm that knows how its market will change can better position itself to exploit those changes. Abell (1978) argues that market changes create opportunities for some firms and destroy opportunities for other firms. He draws an analogy with "strategic windows," which opens and closes with those opportunities.

PICKING AN INDUSTRY TO ENTER

The five forces affecting competition (Exhibit 5.2) can also be used to identify diversification opportunities. Firms, by looking for markets where the economic mechanisms are not working perfectly, might find a market where barriers to entry are low, but can be raised. Some product categories underspend on advertising, even though increased spending might promote much higher sales or serve to raise entry barriers. Existing competitors might be unable to respond.

CHANGING THE RULES OF COMPETITION

Firms can actively seek to change the markets in which they compete. They can raise entry barriers, decrease the level of rivalry, and otherwise change the rules of competition to favor their own firm's position. Actively interceding with the intent of changing the competitive structure of a market is a central component of marketing strategy.

PROTECTING THE STATUS QUO

Lastly, market leaders can protect a market from destructive changes that can lead to a destructive shakeup and diminish their position. While market challengers may wish to change the five factors discussed in the previous section to improve their own position, market leaders, with a favored position in a market, will resist such changes.

References

Abell, Derek F. "Strategic Windows." *Journal of Marketing,* July 1978, pp. 21–26.

Chamberlin, Edward Hastings. *The Theory of Monopolistic Competition.* Cambridge, Mass.: Harvard University Press, 1933.

Dunkin, Amy. "How Toys 'R' Us Controls the Game Board." *Business Week,* December 19, 1988, pp. 58–60.

Jereski, Laura. "The Texet Software Disaster." *Forbes,* October 31, 1988, p. 140.

Porter, Michael. *Competitive Strategy.* New York: Free Press, 1980.

Porter, Michael. "How Competitive Forces Shape Strategy." *Harvard Business Review,* March–April 1979, pp. 137–145.

Robinson, Joan. *The Economics of Imperfect Competition.* London: Macmillan, 1933.

Sraffa, P. "The Laws of Returns Under Competitive Conditions." *Economic Journal,* vol. 36 (December 1926), pp. 535–550.

Chapter **6**

Porter's Three Generic Strategies

An old adage states that the way to succeed in business is to "buy low *and* sell high." Porter (1979, 1980) disagrees. He argues that firms should *either* "buy low" *or* "sell high," but they *should not do both*. It is a current but controversial proposition. This chapter examines those two distinct marketing strategies, and assesses Porter's advice.

Exhibit 6.1 illustrates graphically the two strategic approaches that derive from that old adage. The first strategy earns profits by reducing costs. It is, in essence, the strategy employed by the BCG growth-share matrix. The emphasis is on "buying low" rather than "selling high." The second strategy focuses on raising prices rather than reducing costs. It is a strategy of product differentiation, by which a firm sells a unique product for which consumers are willing to pay a little more. It is a strategy based on "selling high."

Exhibit 6.2 illustrates Porter's generic strategies. Actually, there are three strategies, not just two; the third emphasizing market segmentation. But market segmentation focuses on reducing costs *or* raising prices. Firms target only part of the market with a product that is either priced lower than, or differentiated from, competitors' products.

A summary of each strategy is provided below. A detailed discussion of product differentiation, market segmentation, and the low-cost producer strategies are provided in other chapters.

Low-Cost/Low-Price Seller

Firms that follow a strategy of "overall cost leadership" focus on lowering prices to customers, which they are able to do by lowering their costs of production. The competitive advantage of low-cost, low-price sellers

Exhibit 6.1 *Prices, Costs, and Profit Margins*

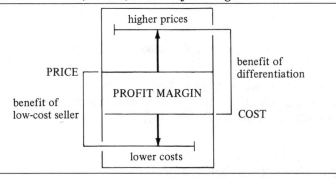

lies in their ability to produce goods cheaply and efficiently. They make standardized products, have more narrow product lines, and design products for efficient production. They avoid marginal accounts.

Low-cost, low-price sellers avoid heavy spending on R&D and advertising. In some cases, they may allow others to innovate and then imitate the designs of those higher-cost competitors. They then sell those designs at a more attractive price.

This strategy, a variation of the production concept presented in the first chapter, stresses costs rather than product differences. It is most akin to ideas espoused by the BCG's growth-share matrix, which was

Exhibit 6.2 *Porter's Three Generic Strategies*

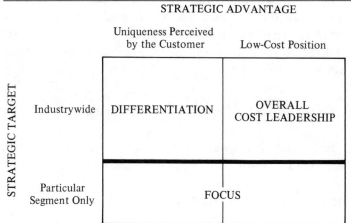

SOURCE: Reprinted with permission of The Free Press, a Division of Macmillan, Inc., from *Competitive Strategy: Techniques for Analyzing Industries and Competitors* by Michael Porter, p. 39. Copyright © 1980.

presented in a previous chapter. It competes on the basis of lower prices, which are gained through experience effects and higher share.

COSTS, PRICES, PROFIT MARGINS, AND MARKET SHARE

The low-cost, low-price strategy is based on the interplay of production costs, prices charged customers, profit margins, and market share. The strategy earns a profit by two distinct patterns based on lower-cost structures:

Lower Margins and Higher Share

Usually low-cost, low-price sellers earn lower profit margins than sellers of differentiated goods, but they gain a high share of the market. They have lower costs, but reduce prices to consumers, in turn. As a result their profits margins are small. But, what they lose on margin they make up for in volume. Many low-cost, low-price sellers are willing to trade high margins for high volume. Toys 'R' Us, for example, earns its money in this way, making very little on each sale but total sales volume is enormous.

Lower Costs and Higher Margins

Sometimes low-cost, low-price sellers lower costs faster than prices. The result is higher margins rather than high share of the market. In essence, they do the opposite of firms that differentiate. Private label supermarket items sell for less than national brands, but earn higher margins for retailers. They maintain a respectable share of the market but they do not dominate their product category. They earn higher margins by lowering costs.

HOW LOWER COSTS LEAD TO COMPETITIVE ADVANTAGE

A focus on lower costs and lower prices leads to many competitive advantages based on the structural analysis of industries.

Reduced Bargaining Power of Suppliers

High volume provides bargaining power against suppliers. Suppliers value large accounts and will be able to exert less pressure on them than they can against smaller volume accounts.

Reduced Bargaining Power of Customers

Lower prices reduces the bargaining power of customers. Customers have little room to bargain against the firm selling at the lowest prices.

Substitutes Are Less Attractive

Lower prices make substitutes less attractive. The low-price seller keeps the balance of price and performance tilted towards existing products.

Reduced Rivalry

Many firms retreat from competition with a low-cost producer with whom they cannot compete. Competitors are willing to relinquish the low end of the market to the low-cost, low-price seller.

PREVALENCE OF LOW-COST, LOW-PRICE SELLERS

Low-cost, low-price sellers exist in every corner of the economy. In retailing, discounters such as K mart, Filene's of Boston, Toys 'R' Us, and Syms have stolen customers from department stores en masse. Department stores cannot match the prices of these low-cost, low-price sellers, since their cost structures, and their prices, are much higher.

Low-cost, low-price sellers thrive in many consumer product categories. Suave, for example, sells shampoo on price while other manufacturers sell differentiated goods. Suave allows consumers to trade price for image. As in many markets, lower prices serve the needs of many shampoo consumers.

A dominant force in consumer electronics and low-cost, low-price sellers. Sharp and Sanyo, along with Matsushita, wait for Sony to pioneer markets then turn their manufacturing might towards large-scale efficient production. They sell large volumes on the basis of price.

Newer entrants from Korea have taken the low-cost, low-price strategy a step further. Lucky Goldstar, Samsung, and other producers sell products at even lower prices than Japanese competitors, threatening the historical advantage of the Japanese. To preempt their move, many Japanese producers have consumer electronics products now made in lower-wage rate countries in Asia.

In autos, Hyundai, a low-cost Korean producer, entered at the bottom of the market. The Excel, Hyundai's first and most popular entry, was first introduced in Canadian markets. It then moved into the larger American market after gaining experience in Canada. In its first year of business in the United States, Hyundai sold more cars than any other new entrant, ever. Hyundai successfully avoided real competition by focusing on the low end of the market where few competitors could match its lower costs and rock bottom prices. It avoided competition by matching its strengths with the needs of the markets.

PITFALLS OF A LOW-COST STRATEGY

A strategy based on lower costs and lower prices is not without risk. Two pitfalls are especially troublesome:

Entry of Lower-Cost Competitors

The competitive experience in consumer electronics and autos points up the potential problems with a low-cost, low-price strategy. Selling on the basis of price alone runs the risk that other manufacturers, with even lower cost structures will enter the market and gain position by offering even lower prices.

Reduced Flexibility

Another problem is this strategy's expense and inflexibility. Lower production costs usually require that firms invest heavily to gain production efficiencies. In the process, the firm ties itself to a single way of serving the market. Efficiencies are gained at the expense of flexibility to market changes. If consumer tastes shift suddenly, the low-cost, low-price seller may be stuck with an efficient means of producing obsolete products. Low-cost production is most advantageous in stable markets.

FINDING MARKETS WITH FEW LOW-COST SELLERS

Low-cost, low-price sellers perform best when other firms in the market are focusing on differentiation. The absence of a low-cost, low-price seller offers an opportunity to enter the market and serve an unmet need. Competition is increased if a market has many firms seeking to be low-price sellers. In such instances opportunity may lie in differentiation or segmentation. Coping with competition often means going where the crowd is not.

Korea's Jindo Corp., the world's largest fur coat manufacturer, is attempting just such a strategy. It is hoping to expand the consumer market for luxury mink coats into a mass market. Like Hyundai, it is aiming at the bottom of the market where it has inherent cost advantages. Jindo sells simply designed coats sown with low-wage Korean labor to first-time buyers, who do not notice the difference in quality and favor price over elegance. These consumers will buy a Jindo coat or they will buy nothing. Jindo is also the only vertically integrated fur coat manufacturer, which lowers costs further. Finally, market leaders, such as Chicago-based Evans, Inc., are reluctant to react. They fear compromising the upscale image that took years to cultivate. As the young owner of Jindo furs observes: "There's plenty of empty market, forty-six million cars are sold [worldwide] a year, but fewer than one million fur garments. Of ten women who purchase fur coats, one fur should be mine" (Trachtenberg 1988).

Product Differentiation

Many products sell on image as well as physical attribute. A strategy of differentiation, as the term implies, is concerned with making the tangible and intangible aspects of a product different from those offered by other sellers. Whereas the low-price strategy focuses on efficient production, differentiation focuses on creating a unique product offering.

Chapter 7 looks at product differentiation in detail. This section shows the elements of the strategy.

COSTS, PRICES, PROFIT MARGINS, AND MARKET SHARE

As Exhibit 6.1 illustrates, a strategy of product differentiation strives to earn higher profit margins by charging higher prices. It is often successful because consumers are willing to pay extra for special or superior products. As Hallmark Cards crows: "When it pays to send the very best."

Costs are not ignored by the seller or differentiated goods, they are simply not the central focus of attention. The idea is to set prices that are higher than the cost increases necessary to produce a superior product. Prices are pushed higher than the additional costs, if any, required to produce the better product.

Market share can vary greatly for the seller of differentiated goods, but two patterns are common.

High Margins and Low Share

Some firms earn huge margins on differentiated goods but possess only a small share of the market. Mercedes-Benz, for example, goes for the highest rung on the automotive ladder. High prices preclude purchase by more than a small share of the market. In fact, the exclusivity implied by that small share makes the differentiated product all the more appealing. The focus is on status. Production efficiencies come second.

Slightly Higher Margins and High Share

Some firms earn high margins, but also possess a huge share of the market. Coca-Cola, Campbell's soup, Quaker Oats oatmeal, Hellman's mayonnaise, Heinz catsup, and a host of other well-known branded products are in the fortunate position of doing both: earning higher margins and higher shares of the market. It is an enviable market position.

MARKETING AND DIFFERENTIATION

Differentiation is predicated on the following marketing precepts.

Brand Loyalty

Brand loyalty is a cornerstone of product differentiation. Firms sell unique products with the hopes of building loyal customers, who are less sensitive to price differences than consumers of commodities. That lack of sensitivity often translates directly into higher profits.

Product Quality

Product differentiation also relies heavily on product quality. Many firms earn higher margins by selling superior products, for which they charge more. Braun in coffeemakers, Sony in consumer electronics, and myriad other manufacturers command higher prices through higher quality. An image of status and style is usually grounded in product quality. It is not enough for marketers to merely focus on product intangibles. A quality strategy must offer truly better products.

Product Innovation

New and innovative products are often at the heart of a strategy of product differentiation. Spending on research and development is heavier for a seller or differentiated goods than for low-cost producers. New product development is often the path by which firms offer unique products.

Style and Image

Good style and image are coveted attributes. They are also cost effective. The price premium that can be charged for a nicely styled product usually far exceeds the additional costs incurred. Consequently, styling serves to boost profit margins.

HOW DIFFERENTIATION LEADS TO COMPETITIVE ADVANTAGE

Differentiation leads to competitive advantage by manipulating the five forces affecting the intensity of competition in a market.

Reduced Bargaining Power of Customers

The uniqueness of differentiated products lowers the bargaining power of buyers. Consumers either have to pay the price requested or settle for something else. Comparisons among products that are not direct substitutes lowers the bargaining power of customers.

Substitutes Are Less Attractive

Unique products are not direct substitutes. By design, differentiated products are different. The greater that difference, the less likely substitution will occur in response to price increases.

Reduced Rivalry

Differentiation is a variation of monopolistic competition, where competitors offer different products. Fierce competition, especially price competition, is reduced in a market where products are not directly comparable.

PREVALENCE OF PRODUCT DIFFERENTIATION

Most markets are heavily populated by differentiated products. McDonald's hamburgers, Hallmark cards, most cosmetics, Gray Poupon mustard, L'oréal hair color, Frusen Glädje ice cream, Merrill Lynch securities, Perdue chickens, Crest toothpaste, Ultrabright toothpaste, Nike running shoes, and L. L. Bean clothes are but a few of the items of firms that have successfully implemented product differentiation. Most markets can support many sellers of differentiated goods. The same is not true for low-cost producers. Markets populated by low-cost producers promote price wars, which are destructive to all players.

PITFALLS OF PRODUCT DIFFERENTIATION

A differentiation strategy is not without risk. Three pitfalls are especially troublesome:

Price Differentiations Is Too Wide

There is a limit to the price premium consumers will pay for unique products. If the price difference between the seller of differentiated goods and the low-cost producer is too great, then consumers will shift to the lower-priced goods. Coca-Cola at twice the price of C&C cola may be acceptable, but at $10 a six pack it is likely to lose many loyal customers. Sellers of differentiated goods learn the limits of price premiums quickly.

Shifts in the Point of Differentiation

Department stores used to offer consumers higher status, and a more pleasurable shopping experience but charged higher prices for the privilege. Years ago, only the well-to-do could afford to shop regularly in department stores. Slowly, but surely, times changed. By the 1980s, the idea of finding a bargain implied being a smart shopper, not being unable to purchase more costly goods. The point of differentiation changed over the decades. Department stores remained the same. As a result, many department stores lost sales to less-well-appointed stores that offer lower prices, but better bargains. Speciality shops stole upscale shoppers with special offerings. What was a strong point of differentiation in years past turned into a weakness. Constant change creates and destroys marketing opportunities.

Easy Imitation

Another risk is that competitors will copy the point of differentiation. A creative stroke of differentiation that proves successful with consumers will likely be quickly copied by less insightful but better financed competitors. Copying is rampant in most markets. Frusen Glädje followed Häagen-Dazs into the market premium ice cream. Coke and Pepsi followed

Royal Crown Cola into diet and caffeine-free sodas. Even Sharper Image, the upscale mail order catalog that carved a creative position in the market for itself, has been hurt by imitators.

Sharper Image found success by selling fancy gadgets to upscale consumers who were not price conscious. Its products were expensive toys for well-off adults. It was a strategy that allowed it to compete in a crowded market. But, in recent years, Sharper Image has been unable to sustain its competitive advantage. Other catalogs and retailers have stocked the same products. What was once a unique strategy of product differentiation is now commonplace. A competitor captures the quandary: "Sharper Image doesn't have the clear lead it used to" (Shao 1988). Such are the risks of differentiation.

Market Segmentation

It is well known that small firms are unlikely to win toe-to-toe battles with larger, more powerful competitors. But segmentation is a strategy that allows them to turn smallness into an advantage. Segmentation avoids competition by focusing attention on a portion of the market where the firm's strengths are highlighted and its weaknesses are minimized. Segmentation is covered in detail in Chapter 8. What follows is a summary of how segmentation can be used strategically to avoid competition.

Low Market Share

Segmentation relies on specialization. It does not seek to satisfy all consumers. Instead, it provides something special to a small, but defendable part of the market. According to Porter (1980), a firm can appeal to a segment through either product differentiation or by being a low-cost, low-price seller. What sets segmentation apart is its scope. Segmentation avoids competition across a broad market by focusing on part of the market. It appeals especially to consumers in that segment with either lower prices or unique products, which are designed specifically for them.

Differentiating to a Segment

Many firms succeed by offering specialized products to a unique group of customers. Oshkosh Truck, for example, specializes in the manufacture of emergency crash and rescue vehicles used at airports. The firm also makes specially designed cement mixers.

Segmentation through product differentiation has paid off for Oshkosh Truck by avoiding competition with the big three automakers. *Fortune* rated the firm one of the fastest growing companies on the fringe of the Fortune 500 (Gannes 1987). It made the list not by competing head-on with General Motors, but through a strategy of differentiating to serve a market segment.

Head and Shoulders shampoo also competes by differentiating to a segment. By focusing on consumers with dandruff, it avoids competition with shampoos that serve a larger market.

SELLING TO A SEGMENT AT LOWER PRICES

Some firms rely on manufacturing efficiencies to dominate a market segment. Their strategy is no different than that proposed by a low-cost, low-price seller, except that competition is constrained to a segment of the market.

AFG Industries, a speciality glass producer, makes most of the microwave oven doors sold in the United States. Its strategy avoids the pure price competition found in commodity glass markets aimed at a broader market. Similarly, Guilford Mills, a textile firm, controls more than half of the market for the material used to make lingerie. Competitors have shown little interest in the efficient knitting process used by Guilford, as it is considered an old-fashioned process. Guilford has even grown by finding new uses for its specialty products. It found new niche markets for its material as a liner for car roof interiors and mattress and box spring covers.

OVERLAP BETWEEN SEGMENTATION AND DIFFERENTIATION

There is considerable overlap between the concepts of market segmentation and product differentiation. They are different, but closely related terms. A detailed discussion of those differences is postponed until the next chapter. Suffice it to say that segmentation focuses on the market, while differentiation focuses on product differences.

The overlap occurs in those common situations where products are differentiated to appeal to segments of the market. Mercedes-Benz, for example, sells a differentiated product, but it sells that product to a small group of upscale consumers. Is it segmentation? Or, is it differentiation? It is differentiation. The focus of the Mercedes strategy is on producing a car that exudes engineering excellence. The attention is on the product. As a result of its differentiation, Mercedes appeals to a high-end segment. But the firm stresses product superiority rather than market segmentation.

In contrast, consider a firm that produces or sells maternity clothing to pregnant women. That firm is employing a segmentation strategy. The emphasis is on the market. The product is conceived and produced to serve that market segment.

In sum, differentiation stresses product differences while segmentation focuses on a defendable piece of the market. The terms themselves reveal their emphasis—it is *market* segmentation and *product* differentiation.

Marketers sometimes prefer the more precisely stated notion of "product-markets," which captures the relatedness of these two concepts. Product-markets focus on specific products sold into specific markets. It tries to capture both differentiation and market segmentation. It also illustrates the interrelatedness of the two concepts.

There is an inescapable definitional fuzziness to the terms differentiation and segmentation that arises out of their relatedness. They are slippery and elusive terms. Like many concepts in marketing, they are approximate notions rather than precise definitions. They also point up the artistic nature of marketing, and downplay the idea that marketing is a science.

How Segmentation Leads to Competitive Advantage

A segmentation strategy leads to competitive advantage in terms of the five forces affecting the intensity of competition.

Reduced Rivalry

A firm that successfully attends to the needs of a segment reduces rivalry in that segment by avoiding the larger competitors. The firm relinquishes the larger market for a more secure share in the smaller segment. At its essence, segmentation is a strategy based on avoiding competition.

Reduced Pressure from Substitutes

By focusing on the special needs of a segment a firm reduces the lure of substitutes. Substitutes appeal to either other segments or a broader market with a more diverse set of needs.

Pitfalls of Market Segmentation

A differentiation strategy is not without risks. Two pitfalls are especially troublesome:

Attracting Larger Competitors

The essence of a segmentation strategy is to avoid competition with larger firms. Often, however, as a segment grows, larger firms are attracted.

Blue Mountain Arts, a small Colorado firm, produces off-beat cards with expressive statements that are sent to friends and lovers even when no special occasion calls for a card. Over the past decade, the market for such cards has grown greatly. This growth attracted Hallmark Cards, the industry giant. Hallmark copied the cards closely and persuaded dealers to carry its cards and drop those made by Blue Mountain. Blue Mountain sued to save its segment—and won. Hallmark agreed to destroy its close copies and focus attention elsewhere.

Dependence on a Single Segment

The firm that pursues a segmentation strategy places its future on a single specialized market. Changes in the size and tastes of that segment can greatly affect their well being. A firm that appeals to a single segment is in a more tenuous position than a firm that serves a more diverse market. Specialty may raise the risks of market changes.

Prevalence of Market Segmentation

Myriad firms segment the markets they serve. It is often the only choice they have. While Coke and Pepsi rule the soft drink industry, "natural sodas," such as Snapple and Soho Soda, carved out niches for themselves among consumers who abhor artificial ingredients. In beer, Anheuser-Busch dominates. But myriad "micro breweries" successfully offer differentiated products to beer connoisseurs. Even in the steel industry, where economies of scale are crucial, specialty steel producers use lower-cost, nonunionized labor to make specialized products for special markets. In just about every other market, many sellers thrive by selling to segments.

Stuck in the Middle

Some firms have no strategy for combating competition. They seem to do nothing especially well. They are neither low-cost, low-price sellers, nor are they sellers of differentiated goods. Porter (1980) refers to such firms as "stuck in the middle." The results are devastating. He notes: "The firm stuck in the middle is almost guaranteed low profitability" (p. 41).

Exhibit 6.3 illustrates the concept of being stuck in the middle. It shows that profits are highest for firms that: (1) sell on the basis of price, and garner a large share of the market, or (2) sell differentiated goods—often higher-priced, premium quality, goods—that serve a smaller share of the market. The low-cost, low-price strategy earns a small margin of profit from a large share of the market. The differentiation strategy earns a higher profit margin from a smaller share of the market. The firm that is stuck in the middle is mediocre in terms of both profit margins and market share.

Exhibit 6.3   *Stuck in the Middle*

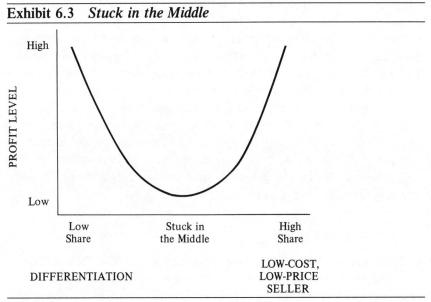

SOURCE: Adapted with permission of The Free Press, a Division of Macmillan, Inc., from *Competitive Strategy: Techniques for Analyzing Industries and Competitors* by Michael Porter, p. 43. Copyright © 1980.

WHY FIRMS GET STUCK

Unfortunately, many firms qualify as stuck in the middle, and end up in that position for a variety of reasons.

Inexorable Market Changes

Markets change perpetually. Those changes create opportunities for some firms but destroy the position of others. Consider the case of Woolworth—not the entire organization, which is quite successful—but the variety store from which the organization arose. Little has changed at Woolworth's variety stores over the decades. As a result, its competitive advantage has been severely eroded. Does Woolworth sell differentiated goods? Does the store sell something special? Are prices especially low? Are its costs exceptionally low? The answer to each question is no. Woolworth has its roots in the general store form of retailing that prevailed more than a century ago. In many respects, Woolworth's variety stores have evolved into the business equivalent of museum pieces. *Business Week* (1983) argued: "The stores are becoming an American Gothic" (p. 82). Woolworth shows how retailing once was, not how it is, and certainly not how it should be. Is there really a need for a five-and-dime as we approach the year 2000?

In steel, many large American producers were caught between low-cost, low-priced foreign steel and the small-scale speciality steel producers in the 1970s. They seemed to do nothing especially well. Their financial results mirrored those strategic shortcomings.

More recently, department stores have been stuck in the middle. Specialty retailers offer differentiated goods to upscale customers willing to pay higher prices for superior styling and service. At the same time, discounters offer bargain prices to the price-conscious consumer. The department stores lack either strategic focus as they struggle to find a way to deal with changes in the markets they serve.

Actions of Competitors

Competitors can force a firm to be stuck in the middle. Many popular, mass market brands have been pushed to the middle by rivals that strike from the top and the bottom of the market. Those brands, which once served a broad market, end up offering neither differentiated goods to consumers in search of prestige goods, or lower prices to consumers in search of bargains.

General Food's Sealtest ice cream, for example, has been hurt by the sellers of the superpremium brands, such as Ben and Jerry's and Häagen Dazs, and purveyors of high-price frozen yogurts. At the lower end of the market, the private label ice cream brands carried by most supermarkets offer a lower-priced alternative to the leader's products.

Similarly, Smirnoff vodka, still the number one brand in the U.S. market, has found its sales flat, while sales of premium brands, such as Absolut and Stolichnaya, have grown dramatically. It, too, has been pushed to the middle of the market by competitors' strategic actions.

Finally, competitors of Holiday and Ramada Inns have forced those firms to be stuck in the middle. Upscale, higher-service motels have pushed down from the top of the market, while bare-bones, no-frill motels sell clean but unadorned rooms to the price conscious traveler. Both firms have responded by introducing both higher-priced and lower-priced hotels/motels under different brand names.

In each instance, competitors forced market leaders to be stuck in the middle.

Poor Marketing

British Leyland, which made the MG and Triumph sports cars, was also stuck in the middle in the late 1970s. As a highly unionized manufacturer subsidized by the British taxpayer, the emphasis was not on market performance. Costs were high and reliability was low. During the energy crises of the 1970s, the company made small cars that got very poor gas mileage. As sales of small cars grew, British Leyland withdrew from the American market.

Fiat, the Italian auto producer, fell victim to a similar fate. It, too, was forced to withdraw from the American market due to severe competitive disadvantages. Fiat was also stuck in the middle.

Issues in Competitive Strategy

Three important issues have emerged in regard to Porter's three generic strategies. This section examines those issues.

Mixture of Strategies

The essence of marketing strategy is to avoid competition. Porter's three generic strategies imply that every market is best served when firms use a mix of strategies, rather than all competitors pursuing the same strategy. That is, competition is minimized when some firms serve as low-cost, low-price sellers, while other firms offer differentiated goods, or focus on market segments.

Problems arise when the mix of strategies becomes unbalanced. Competition is intensified, rather than reduced, if all firms follow a single strategy. That is especially true if many firms are attempting to compete as the lowest-cost producer. A strategy of low-cost production can exist, even prosper, in competition with differentiation and segmentation. In competition with other firms pursuing the same strategy, however, it looses appeal. It is the mix that is most important.

The mix of strategies also implies opportunity. If many firms are selling on the basis of price, an opportunity exists for differentiation. Conversely, if many firms are emphasizing highly differentiated, premium goods, an opportunity exists for a low-price seller.

PURSUING MORE THAN ONE GENERIC STRATEGY

The most controversial aspect of Porter's three generic strategies is the issue of whether a firm should pursue more than one of these strategies.

Following a Single Strategy

Porter is adamant on this point. He argues that success is ''rarely possible'' if a firm pursues more than one generic strategy. The reasons are simple and persuasive. Commitment and support ''are diluted if there is more than one primary target (Porter 1980, p. 35). The skills required by each strategy are so different that pursuing more than one strategy is likely to result in nothing being done well. Any firm so doing is likely to become stuck in the middle.

Following More Than One Strategy

The empirical evidence, however, contradicts those assertions. Most studies that have studied the issue have found that successful firms do both—they are low-cost producers *and* they sell differentiated goods. In a sense they ''buy low and sell high.''

Hall (1980) examined sixty-four firms in eight industries. Most of the firms he examined followed a single generic strategy. But the most successful firms in the sample seemed to follow *both* strategies simultaneously. A more recent study by White (1986) found similar results. Nineteen of the sixty-nine businesses he examined pursued *both* differentiation and low-cost production. Hill (1988) and Murray (1988) argue that Porter's two generic strategies are not mutually exclusive. In fact, a firm can use differentiation to achieve a low-cost position. The presence of both generic strategies leads to a sustainable competitive advantage.

A study by Phillips, Chang, and Buzzell (1983) examined 1,144 observations from 623 businesses contained in the PIMS database. They found no support for the hypothesis that differentiation is incompatible with a strategy of low-cost production.

Indirect evidence from the PIMS database also supports the contentions of those renegade researchers. Buzzell and Gale (1987) argue that high product quality is closely related to high market share. This suggests that differentiation, which relies heavily on the sale of higher quality products, *is related* to low-cost production, which relies heavily on high market share.

Reconciliation

Does the empirical evidence negate Porter's strategic advice? Not really. There is a difference between what very large successful firms *do* and what the majority of firms *should do*. One is a description of the current state of the premier firms in American business, the other is a prescription for strategic advice for a broad sample of firms.

Some firms that sit at the pinnacle of American business are fortunate enough to have achieved enviable cost positions and offer differentiated goods. IBM, for example, has among the lowest production costs in the computer business, extensive experience effects, a large share of the market, and goods that are surely differentiated in the minds of consumers.

Still, not all firms are IBM. Porter's advice holds true in most strategic applications. It is one thing to observe that some very successful firms pursue both strategies. It is another to advise that a broad cross-section of firms should pursue both strategies simultaneously. Most firms seeking to gain position are better advised to pursue a single strategy. A firm that tries to do everything, is likely to end up doing nothing well.

SUSTAINING COMPETITIVE ADVANTAGE

A competitive advantage is valuable only if it can be sustained over the long term. If competitors can imitate product innovations, learn quickly about special production techniques, and employ marketing tactics that counter a competitive advantage, then that advantage turns out to be short lived. It is contestable, not sustainable. An advantage that cannot be sustained is not an advantage.

Empirical studies have confirmed Porter's belief that competitive advantage rooted in the structure of an industry is sustainable. Ghemawat (1986) examined a sample of 100 firms that had outperformed others in their industry. Sustainable advantages fell into three categories, each of which is consistent with Porter's view. First, some firms excelled through the size of their operations. They earned economies of scale, experience effects, and the ability to share resources across a wide base of operations. They seemed to succeed as low-cost, low-price sellers. Other firms succeeded, however, by gaining special access to either raw materials or markets. Those firms competed in situations that were not easily copied.

Finally, the study found that some firms were protected because there was some impediment to competitor retaliation. In many cases competitors could not or would not respond. Coyne (1986) concurs. He contends that a competitive advantage is sustainable when there is some impediment to a competitor's retaliation.

In some industries, a sustainable advantage is easier to obtain than others. Fast-changing industries make it difficult to achieve sustainability. Changes destroy competitive advantage. Slower change promotes sustainable advantage.

The number of competitive advantages a firm has also affects sustainability. Some firms possess more than one advantage (Ghemawat 1986), enabling them to perform especially well. The more competitive advantages a firm has, the more sustainable its advantage over the long term.

In sum, Porter's advice has found widespread acceptance among both practitioners and academics. It has also found empirical support for many of the claims it makes. Porter's approach goes a long way towards understanding the competitive aspects of marketing strategy. Its contributions have been many and its roots in marketing run deep. The next two chapters expand on the strategies of differentiation and segmentation.

References

Buzzell, Robert D., and Bradley T. Gale. *The PIMS Principles*. New York: Free Press, 1987.

Coyne, Kevin. "Sustainable Competitive Advantage—What It Is, What It Isn't." *Business Horizons*, January–February 1986, pp. 54–61.

Gannes, Stuart. "The Riches in Market Niches." *Fortune,* April 27, 1987, pp. 227–228.

Ghemawat, Pankaj. "Sustainable Advantage." *Harvard Business Review,* September–October 1986, pp. 53–58.

Hall, William K. "Survival Strategies in a Hostile Environment." *Harvard Business Review,* September–October 1980, pp. 75–85.

Hill, Charles. "Differentiation Versus Low Cost or Differentiation and Low Cost: A Contingency Framework." *Academy of Management Review,* July 1988, pp. 401–412.

Murray, Alan. "A Contingency View of Porter's Generic Strategies." *Academy of Management Review,* July 1988, pp. 390–400.

Phillips, Lynn, Dae Chang, and Robert Buzzell. "Product Quality, Cost Position and Business Performance: A Test of Some Key Hypotheses." *Journal of Marketing,* Spring 1983, pp. 26–43.

Porter, Michael. *Competitive Strategy.* New York: Free Press, 1980.

Porter, Michael. "How Competitive Forces Shape Strategy." *Harvard Business Review,* March–April 1979, pp. 137–145.

Shao, Maria. "The Sharper Image May Need to Refocus." *Business Week,* November 21, 1988, p. 84.

Trachtenberg, Jeffrey A. "Moving the Mink." *Forbes,* April 18, 1988, pp. 86–88.

White, Roderick E. "Generic Business Strategies, Organizational Context and Performance: An Empirical Investigation." *Strategic Management Journal,* May–June 1986, pp. 217–231.

"Woolworth Is Still Rummaging for a Retail Strategy." *Business Week,* June 6, 1983, pp. 82–83.

Chapter 7

Product Differentiation

A. Schulman Inc. is a relatively small firm that sells plastics in an industry dominated by giants. It succeeds by avoiding competition with the likes of Dow Chemical and Monsanto. While industry giants concentrate on lowering the cost and price of commodity products, Schulman goes in the opposite direction. It avoids commodity products, works closely with customers to develop new specialty products, rushes orders to customers when they need them quickly, and builds long-term relationships with its customers. As the firm's president explains it: "We don't talk price, we talk quality" (Lappen 1990, p. 74).

A. Schulman's success is indicative of the value of differentiation in most markets. Its experience also reflects many of the most important aspects of differentiation. It can be based on tangible or intangible product attributes, involve different levels of product quality, and coexist with market segmentation. Most important, Schulman's success shows how firms can compete outside the arena of price competition.

Economic Basis

Product differentiation takes a competitor orientation, but it also provides consumer benefits. On the supply side, it allows firms to minimize competition and earn higher profits. On the demand side, it provides consumers with a greater variety of goods and services. This section examines the economic basis of differentiation.

MONOPOLISTIC COMPETITION

Product differentiation is rooted deeply in the economic concept of monopolistic competition. As was noted in a previous chapter, monopolistic competition is a form of imperfect competition that avoids price competition and increases profits by creating unique products that do not compete directly with one another.

Contrast the case of milk with that of coffee. At first glance, the two products seem to be pure commodities, which compete on the basis of price. But, a closer examination reveals a success and a failure at product differentiation.

Milk is a pure commodity. Few consumers shop for a specific brand. Since there are no perceived differences between brands, consumers buy the least expensive brand or the brand sold at the most convenient location. The industry relies on government regulation, price supports, and market protection schemes to avoid price competition.

Coffee, in contrast, is more highly differentiated. Brands like Sanka sell decaffeination. Other brands cultivate an image of exquisite taste. In fact, the high-price, high-margin, super-premium blends from exotic locales have grown fastest in recent years. Consumers, for example, will pay a premium for Hawaiian Kona, which is grown in volcanic lava. There is no equivalent in milk.

Beef versus chicken offers a similar difference in strategy. Beef is still an undifferentiated, largely unbranded, commodity product. Chicken, in contrast, has been successfully differentiation, thanks to the efforts to Frank Perdue.

Beers brewed with water from cold Canadian streams, mustard with wine added, and myriad other products with real or imagined differences have done likewise. All have successfully avoided price competition through differentiation, and the monopolistic competition that results.

Monopolistic competition increases profits by reducing the similarity of potential substitutes. It hints at the creation of monopolies, where each seller has some control over the prices they are able to charge. Whereas commodities compete vigorously with one another, differentiated products serve somewhat distinct markets. As a result, consumers are less likely to switch brands when prices are raised. Such is the basis of product differentiation.

CONSUMERS' PREFERENCE FOR VARIETY

Product differentiation is also rooted in the psychological observation that consumers prefer a greater variety of goods and services. That preference is partly driven by different tastes. The heterogeneity of demand ensures that a diversity of goods will be valued highly.

But, differentiation thrives even when consumer tastes are similar. Consumers often do not want products that are identical to those of their friends and neighbors, but want unique products and personalized service. Alfred P. Sloan, the former chairman of General Motors, made a similar observation. He recognized that consumers would pay extra for cars that were different than those of their neighbors. While Henry Ford offered consumers a single, low-cost, low-priced model in one color only, General Motors embraced product differentiation through greater product diversity.

Tangibles, Intangibles, and Differentiation

Products can be differentiated in many ways. The most common categorization is whether products are differentiated in terms of tangible or intangible attributes. Exhibit 7.1 illustrates the choices. There are two types of tangible product attributes that can be used to differentiate—fundamental product features and cosmetic, or incidental, product features.

FUNDAMENTAL PRODUCT FEATURES

The most obvious way to differentiate products is to change the fundamental properties of the product itself in order to stress a particular point

Exhibit 7.1 *Tangible and Intangible Differentiation*

	INTANGIBLE PRODUCT ATTRIBUTES	
	No Differentiation	Differentiation
TANGIBLE PRODUCT ATTRIBUTES — No Differentiation	perfect competition among pure commodities	same physical product differentiated on intangibles "pseudo-differentiation"
Differentiation	differentiation on tangible product attributes	complete differentiation on tangible and intangible attributes

of differentiation. Mercedes-Benz, for example, stresses engineering excellence, and strives to make the best engineered cars in the world. Sony does the same in consumer electronics by innovating new technological advances in order to justify the premium prices it charges.

Technological breakthroughs can create opportunities for differentiation. A firm that quickly and creatively adapts a new technology into its products gains competitive advantage. Backlit computer screens on laptop computers, for example, were used to differentiate early models. The extent to which technological advances can be kept from competitors determines the sustainability of that point of differentiation.

Technology can also limit opportunities for product differentiation. Producing a flat-screen, hang-on-the-wall television, for example, would be a potent point of differentiation. To date, however, it is not cost effective to do so.

COSMETIC PRODUCT FEATURES

Often, consumers are unable to evaluate fundamental product characteristics. The circuitry of a stereo system, for example, is meaningless to most consumers. Technical specifications are equally uninterpretable. Instead, consumers judge those products by relying on cosmetic product features. A stereo with many flashing lights, dials galore, and an attention to detail is judged superior to a stereo where less attention has been paid to incidental product features. In many instances, consumers buy stereo equipment not because they understand the distortion range of the speakers but because the incidental features signal product quality. Incidental features become surrogates for actual product performance. As a result, incidentals can often be used to differentiate.

Cars are often judged using similar criteria. To many consumers, the quality of the paint job, the styling, the sound of the radio, and the comfort of the seats are more important than engineering data. Few buyers buy a Mercedes because they understand the specifications on piston displacement. They buy a Mercedes because those specifications signal quality and high status.

Frank Perdue differentiates its supreme chickens using cosmetic product cues. Contract chicken farmers feed Perdue chickens marigold petals to make the meat yellow. Yellow chicken meat is not more nutritious or delicious but it is, however, visibly different.

Examples of differentiation on cosmetic product features can be found everywhere. Loud vacuums, lawnmowers, and leafblowers imply superior performance. Colored liquid window cleaners imply greater cleaning power than clear cleansers. Freeze-dried coffee was originally made with bigger flakes because consumer testing found that bigger flakes signaled superior product quality, even though the size of the flakes has no real effect on product quality. It is merely a physical cue.

Incidental product features can also serve as a negative point of differentiation. In the early 1980s, Tandy's Radio Shack personal computers had poor incidentals. Its TRS-80 was nicknamed the "Trash 80" because it was made of cheap gray plastic. Realistically, it was a fine machine in a poor package.

Packaging is a cosmetic product feature that can also serve as a potent source of differentiation. Perfume is more package than product, more sizzle than steak. Perfume bottles convey status and earn higher margins for the maker.

Brand names also serve as physical cues. Sunkist, for example, is a brand of orange soda pop that conveys a strong connection to orange juice even though the brand contains no juice.

Cosmetic cues are even more influential when there is no physical product. Services rely heavily on incidentals. The wood paneling in a law office connotes quality lawyers are at work at that firm.

Consider the way in which banks have used incidentals over the years to send different signals to customers. Earlier in this century, banks sought to convey an image of permanence. Older bank buildings still have the feeling of a fortress, meant to stand a thousand years, protecting depositor's savings. Modern banks seek to convey a different image— the personal touch and friendliness not normally found in the fortress of the past, and the impersonal electronic bank of today. Today's banks sell personal service.

PRODUCT INTANGIBLES

Differentiation does not have to rely on changes in the physical product itself. Often, as is the case with services, there is not even a physical product to change. Intangible product attributes are changed to signal that the goods are different.

Rarity of Commodities

Few products today qualify as pure commodities. Levitt (1980, 1981) contends that there is really no such thing as a commodity. Even products that are physically identical to one another are differentiated by intangible attributes. The physical products are mixed inexorably with the total product offering. Products are differentiated by company image and reputation, the salesperson with whom the customer interacts, and the services provided along with the physical product itself.

Intangibles and Salespersons

A product is often inseparable from its seller. Consider the purchase of 100 shares of stock in General Motors—a commodity that can be sought from many sellers. The product can be purchased from Merrill Lynch, a full-service broker, or Charles Schwab, a limited service, discount broker. One sells service, the other trades on price. They are clearly differentiated services, even though they sell identical products.

Often, salespersons serve as the primary point of differentiation. Tom Watson, the former head of IBM, recognized the importance of intangibles. IBM employees, including salespersons, wore white shirts to convey a professional image of the firm.

Sometimes salespersons convey the wrong image. A sportswear firm trying to convey an image of youthful activity that is represented by an elderly salesperson is likely to present a confusing image to the retailers that buy the clothing line. Fortunately for such salespersons, age discrimination laws protect against arbitrary forced retirements. Even in business, individual rights take precedence over strategic inconsistencies.

Intangibles and Image

By design or default intangibles create a product image that differentiates goods or services. Consider the case of American Express charge cards. Throughout the 1980s, both the number of cards outstanding and charge volume grew greatly. That growth came even though the firm charges both cardmembers and merchants more for the service. It happened because the firm sells prestige. Even though charge cards offer similar services, the American Express card offers superior intangibles. It even offers the extremely successful Gold Card, which implies even greater prestige. When asked to explain the difference between the green and gold cards, AMEX's chairman noted: "The difference is that the Green Card is green and the Gold Card is gold, and if you don't understand that then you don't understand this company" (Chakravarty 1989, p. 128).

Intangibles and Services

Services are tied most strongly to intangible cues of differentiation since there is no tangible product for the consumer to examine. What the customer sees is used to draw inferences about the service offered. A shabbily dressed accountant offers a different product to consumers than an accountant dressed in the required three-piece suit. An ineloquent financial planner conveys a different image than a planner that exudes wealth.

Accounting for Intangibles

Intangibles may be important but they wreck havoc with accounting methods. Accounting for intangibles is in its infancy. Consider the case of "Wheel of Fortune," one of the most successful programs in television history. The show successfully differentiated itself from game show competitors in the 1980s. What was its worth? Accountants valued it as the amortized cost of the rights to syndicate the program. By using that method the Wheel was worth nothing on paper, even though it has earned hundreds of millions. As Greene (1989) shows, "Traditional accounting methods, with their emphasis on bricks and mortar, no longer accurately reflect the importance of intangible assets to the service and idea industries of the 1980s" (p. 83).

Although intangibles contribute greatly to net worth, and add significantly to long-term profits, they are not considered assets on current balance sheets. Accounting rules do not permit it. Instead, intangibles are charged as expenses against current income.

Intangibles have long-term value. Advertising, contracts, patents, and R&D can all have long-term effects on shareholder equity. Coca-Cola, for example, possesses a world-class brand build mostly by advertising. Even King World, the syndicator of "Wheel of Fortune," "Jeopardy," and "Oprah Winfrey," had contracts that totaled $700 million in licensing fees. Yet, the company had a negative book value!

Clearly, intangibles are important. Just as clearly, intangibles lie in the realm of marketers, not in the realm of those who manage by the numbers. Marketing, more than most other disciplines, is more concerned with these less quantitative issues.

Fallacy of Pseudo-Differentiation

Some early economists held a view of intangibles similar to that of accountants. They considered differentiation based solely on intangible product attributes to be "pseudo-differentiation," a term meant to indicate that it was unreal and maybe less effective. Differentiation, they argued, cannot occur in the absence of real product differences. Image differences alone—created by brand names and skillful advertising—result only in pseudo-differentiation. It is a view that in more recent times counts few supporters among its ranks. Differentiation on intangible product attributes is a powerful and widely accepted strategic tool.

Quality, Price, and Differentiation

There is another way to categorize differentiation—depending on whether there are quality differences between the differentiated products. Economists refer to that type of differentiation as vertical and horizontal product differentiation (Lancaster 1979, pp. 27–29), which is illustrated graphically in Exhibit 7.2.

VERTICAL DIFFERENTIATION

When products differ in terms of quality they are considered to be vertically differentiated. Consider the case of automobiles presented in Exhibit 7.2. The Mercedes-Benz is surely differentiated from the Toyota Tercel. But it also differs greatly in terms of quality. That does not mean that

Exhibit 7.2   *Horizontal and Vertical Differentiation*

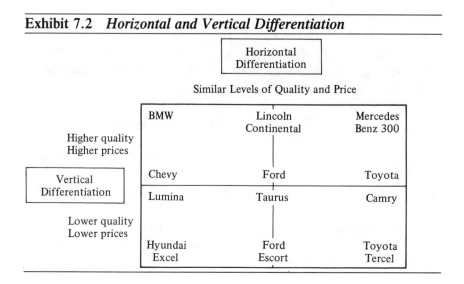

the Mercedes is more reliable than the Toyota; Toyota has an enviable record of reliability. The concept of vertical differentiation embraces a broader definition of quality. Quality means that there is agreement among consumers that Mercedes is "better" than Tercel in terms of most comparative measures—size, weight, leg and head room, status, luxury, appointments. Given the choice, the overwhelming majority of rational consumers would prefer the Mercedes over Toyota.

But, the Mercedes also costs more than the Toyota. In vertical differentiation, consumers must trade price for quality. They must decide whether to pay more for higher-quality products, or trade premium quality for a lower price.

Vertical differentiation captures the observation that sellers often differentiate their products by improving or degrading the quality of their products. In businesses as mundane as mustard, Gray Poupon increases quality (and price) as a way to differentiate its product from French's and Gulden's mustards. In autos, Hyundai's Excel differentiates its entry by degrading quality, and selling it at a lower price. In each instance, and myriad others, differentiation is vertical—quality (and price) are altered to reduce the similarity of substitutes and lessen competition.

A practical result of vertical product differentiation is that firms gain market position by selling either higher-quality, upscale products or services, or lower-priced downscale merchandise. In each case, the result is vertical product differentiation.

HORIZONTAL DIFFERENTIATION

Horizontal product differentiation keeps quality constant. Goods or services may be radically different, but they are similar in terms of price and quality. Consumers choose a horizontally differentiated product on the basis of other criteria.

As Exhibit 7.2 illustrates, the Chevy Lumina, Ford Taurus, and Toyota Camry are similar in terms of quality and price. Consumers make their choice based on other criteria.

Consider the many breakfast cereals on the market as another example of horizontal differentiation. There are cereals with oat bran, which appeal to consumers who value healthful morning eating; Count Chocula and Coco Puffs, aimed at children who prefer a sweeter taste; and Special K, for the calorie-counting, weight-conscious consumer. There is a cereal to satisfy seemingly every conceivable whim. Cereals may possess different features but they are of roughly equal levels of quality.

The fact that horizontally differentiated products or services are of equal quality and price means there is less agreement among consumers as to which cereal product is "better." Unlike the Mercedes/Toyota example, different cereals are favored by different consumer groups. A price cut on Count Chocula, for example, is unlikely to cause consumers of Special K to switch brands. As a result, horizontally differentiated goods and services do not compete on the basis of price.

Horizontal differentiation is closely associated with market segmentation. It implies heterogeneous demand patterns, where consumer preferences differ. Since consumers do not agree which products are "better," those products serve different segments of the market. Manufacturers differentiate their products to appeal to the needs of specific market segments.

Product Positioning Versus Differentiation

Product differentiation and product positioning are closely related terms. What economists refer to as differentiation, marketers often refer to as positioning. The two concepts differ mostly in where they place their emphasis.

DIRECTION VERSUS DIFFERENCE

Product positioning goes a step further than product differentiation. Whereas differentiation seeks merely to make products different in order to avoid competition, positioning steers product perceptions to a particular point in consumers' minds. Product positioning incorporates a sense of direction rather than simply a sense of difference. The difference is consistent with marketers' ability to intercede in the formation of markets.

A FOCUS ON INTANGIBLES

Positioning differs from differentiation in another way as well. Discussions of product positioning found in the marketing literature tend to rely more heavily on the intangible aspects of a product than do discussions of differentiation found in economics. The economic notion of differentiation focuses mostly on fundamental changes in the physical product.

Product positioning implies a greater concern with changes in product image as opposed to physical product changes.

The emphasis on intangibles is captured best by Ries and Trout (1981), who claim "it's incorrect to call the concept product positioning. As if you were doing something to the product. . . . [P]ositioning is not what you do to a product. Positioning is what you do to the mind of the prospect" (p. 3).

Differentiation Versus Segmentation

Product differentiation and market segmentation are widely used concepts in marketing. Remarkably, there is no generally accepted definition for either term. Dickson and Ginter (1987) reviewed the literature and concluded that different authors defined the concepts differently. Some authors even use the terms interchangeably.

There is general agreement that both concepts are consistent with the notion of imperfect competition. The ultimate strategic purpose of both differentiation and segmentation is to insulate a firm from price competition.

Most confusion exists over how the two strategies relate to one another. Do they mean the same thing? Must they be used together? Or, must a marketer choose one or the other? Consider the opposing arguments.

ARGUMENT FOR ALTERNATIVE STRATEGIES

Some marketers argue that product differentiation and market segmentation are alternative strategies. A firm picks one or the other but not both simultaneously. A landmark article by Wendell Smith (1956) epitomized that view. He made the following distinction: "Differentiation is concerned with the bending of demand to the will of supply" (p. 5). In other words, product differentiation focuses on the supply of goods. Demand is changed to fit supply.

According to that argument, differentiation is a "promotional strategy," which seeks to bring consumers to the product made by an individual firm. Segmentation, in contrast, focuses on the demand side of the equation. It is a "merchandising strategy," by which products are adjusted to serve a particular group of users. Supply is made to fit demand. Smith (1978) reiterated those ideas, more than twenty years after they were originally presented.

The difference between differentiation and segmentation is best drawn by an analogy with cutting a cake. Differentiation seeks a broad share of the total market, and seeks a horizontal layer of the cake. Segmentation seeks depth of market, and takes a deep slice of the cake.

CLAIMS FOR COMPLEMENTARY STRATEGIES

Many economists, especially those who studied differentiation in the 1930s, favor the argument that product differentiation and market segmentation can be used together. The two strategies are really two sides of the same coin. A firm, for example, might differentiate its product to appeal to a specific market segment. Selsun Blue, for example, sells a dandruff shampoo, which is clearly a differentiated product, to a segment of consumers who have that unfortunate malady. The product is differentiated. A segment is served.

The argument for complementary strategies is widely accepted by marketers today. Differentiation and market segmentation often work closely together in marketing strategies. Often they are used in tandem. Rarely are they viewed as alternatives, between which marketers must pick.

RELATIONSHIP BETWEEN DIFFERENTIATION AND SEGMENTATION

The relationship between product differentiation and market segmentation can be summarized as follows:

Segmentation Requires Differentiation

Segmentation requires differentiation. To appeal to a segment a firm must change something real or imagined about the product. It is impossible to appeal effectively to a segment of the market without goods that are different than those sold to the mass market. That difference can be real or imagined. It may even be based on offering lower prices, as was suggested by Porter.

Differentiation Does Not Require Segmentation

Differentiation does not require segmentation. Products can be made different without appealing to a segment of the market. Premium products are different from regular products but serve broad markets. Kellogg's corn flakes are different from a generic brand but do not target a segment.

Creating Differentiation, Discovering Segments

Another key difference between the two concepts is that differentiation is always created, it is man-made, whereas segmentation occurs naturally in markets. Firms differentiate their products on purpose, or force competitors' products to be differentiated. Differentiation does not exist on its own without the intervention of marketers. Segments are not always the result of marketers' creations. Markets segments exist naturally in the marketplace to be discovered by insightful marketers. Segments can also be created through marketing efforts, but they also exist on their own.

Competitor Versus Consumer Focus

Finally, there is a difference in the orientation between differentiation and segmentation. Differentiation focuses on competitors. It seeks to avoid competition by making products unique. Segmentation, in contrast, focuses on consumers. It aims to identify groups of customers that can be served in some special way. Those different orientations often lead to complementary strategies. They are also indicative of the different ways in which a firm can view the markets it serves. The difference is an example of the consumer versus competitor orientations discussed in Chapter 1.

Strategic Goals of Differentiation

Differentiation strategies may or may not rely on market segmentation. The following choices are available:

DIFFERENTIATION WITHOUT MARKET SEGMENTATION

The economic notion of differentiation does not employ the concept of market segmentation. Products are made different to avoid price competition, not to appeal to the particular needs of different groups of consumers. Differentiation without segmentation embraces the emphasis of monopolistic competition on simply making products different and has its roots in the work of early economists.

Exhibit 7.3 illustrates differentiation without segmentation. It shows three differentiated products serving a large, single group of customers. That single group of consumers may exist for a variety of reasons.

Exhibit 7.3 *Differentiation Without Market Segmentation*

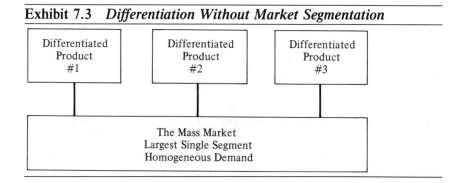

Homogeneous Demand

Often a market consists of consumers who have similar needs. The opportunity to benefit from segmentation in those instances may be limited or non-existent. In a sense, there is only a single segment to appeal to—what is commonly referred to as the mass market. In those instances, products are differentiated to appeal to that one large group. But, more important, products are differentiated so that they are unique, and different from competitive offerings.

Closer to the Ideal

Similar consumer needs imply that there is a single ideal product demanded by the market. In that instance, firms differentiate their offerings to appeal more closely to that ideal version of the product than the competitors'. Closing in on an ideal product is a common goal of product positioning.

Appeal to the Largest Segment

Some markets are dominated by a single segment. The practical result is that large firms pursue the bulk of the market, allowing smaller firms to serve the needs of smaller, specialized segments, which are less attractive.

When Segments Are Unreachable

In some instances, segments may exist in theory, but are unreachable in practice. The result is that firms must act as though there are no segments. Wind (1978), in a review of the segmentation literature, concludes: "It is not uncommon, however, to find markets in which no significant differences are found among various segments with respect to their demographic or other relevant consumer characteristics such as response elasticities to marketing variables" (p. 327). In such instances, differentiation without segmentation is the only choice.

DIFFERENTIATING TO REACH MARKET SEGMENTS

In many markets, there are clusters of consumers that have similar needs within each segment, but different needs between segments. In the parlance of marketing research, these segments are "homogeneous within" and "heterogeneous between." In such instances, differentiation and segmentation go together, and serve as complementary strategies.

Exhibit 7.4 illustrates differentiation to reach market segments. It shows three differentiated products, each aimed at serving a separate group of customers.

Matching Products with Segments

Differentiated products are often made different to match the needs of a market segment. Consumers in that segment will favor the product that best serves their particular configuration of needs. Sellers avoid competition by building dominant positions in separate segments.

Growing a Segment

When a firm establishes a dominant position in a segment it may try to attract more consumers to that segment. Volvo, for example, has long appealed to consumers who value safety in a car and are willing to pay extra for it. It has a strong hold on safety as a point of differentiation.

Exhibit 7.4   *Differentiation to Reach Market Segments*

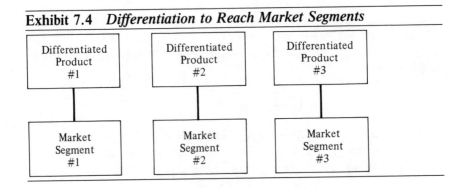

As consumers age and value safety for their families over sportiness and speed, Volvo hopes to attract more consumers to its segment.

Underalls, the underpants and stocking in one, followed a similar strategy. They offered convenience and the absence of panty lines to a progressively time-conscious and overweight populace. Underalls segment grew from a minor to a major part of the market.

Cascade, the dishwasher detergent, followed a similar strategy. It stresses no spots on dishes, a minor annoyance at best, But, with all products being physically similar, it proved to be a point of differentiation that was strong enough to shift consumer preference. All other things being equal, why not avoid soap spots on dishes?

SPECIFIC DIFFERENTIATION STRATEGIES

Product differentiation can be accomplished in many ways. The following patterns are typical.

HIGHER QUALITY

In recent years, many firms have decided to differentiate their products and services with higher quality. Quality is the topic of a later chapter, so an indepth discussion is postponed until then. For now, the discussion focuses on how quality affects differentiation. There are many facets of quality. Four types of quality are most important for differentiation.

The first way in which quality can be used to differentiate products is with a *performance enhancement*. Performance enhancement focuses on improving fundamental product features, which make a product superior to a competitor's offering. It is a strategy of engineering excellence. Mercedes, Sony, and Hewlett-Packard use performance enhancement as a point of differentiation. Each seller offers a technically superior product in their respective product categories.

Tropicana succeeds through superior performance in a completely different product category. It does not reconstitute its orange juice from concentrate. The juice is freshly squeezed. In each instance, a superior product commands higher prices and less competition.

Superior design and style is a point of differentiation that focuses on incidental product features. It is based on the commonsensical observation that consumers will pay extra for nicely styled products. In the 1980s Ford surpassed GM in products for the first time since the 1920s by offering more stylish cars, such as the Taurus. Ironically, it was with styling that GM passed Ford fifty years earlier.

Superior design and style also serve to differentiate products where styling has historically played a minor role. Style can be innovation. Drip coffee makers have similar performance standards. But, Braun, a European manufacturer, sells a well-designed product at a much higher price. It differentiates on style.

Better service can also be used to differentiate products. The high-service option is a strategy selected by Merrill Lynch and the other full-service brokers. Conversely, decreasing service and price—as is done by Toys 'R' Us in retailing and Charles Schwab in securities— and promoting self-service can differentiate a product in a market where most other competitors are peddling higher service. Hardware centers differentiated themselves from neighborhood hardware stores by lowering prices and service.

Greater reliability and durability can also be used to differentiate. Premium prices are often charged for products that do not break down. For years, Maytag has sold its large appliances on the basis of the lonely repairman. Its product costs more but is more reliable. Likewise, the Honda Accord, one of America's top selling cars, has an enviable reputation for both reliability and durability.

Higher Status and Image

Many products are differentiated on the basis of image. Rolex rarely sells watches because of their accuracy. They are bought because of the status they confer on the owner. Montblanc fountain pens, which cost well over $100, write only fractionally better than a Bic. But they come from West Germany, are nicely styled, and convey an image of success. Like many upscale European brands, Montblanc appeals to status and image.

Brand Names

Brand names serve as points of differentiation. IBM in computers, Campbells in tomato soup, Coca-Cola in soft drinks, and countless other well-known brand names are able to avoid price competition by offering consumers an easy way to assess product quality. Brand names signal consumers that quality goods are contained within. Performance enhancements, reliability, and other important aspects of product quality can all be conveyed via a brand name.

It is important to note, however, that differentiation is a broader concept than product branding. Branding can serve as an important way in which to differentiate products, but it is not the only way. Nor, is it the primary purpose of branding. Differentiation and branding often work together, but they are not synonymous terms.

CONVENIENCE

Time is especially valuable to today's consumers. Many products trade price for convenience. Gourmet frozen foods, such as Lean Cuisine, 7-Eleven convenience stores, McDonald's, and many services offer consumers the opportunity to make their lives easier and differentiate their goods in the process.

CHANGING DISTRIBUTION CHANNELS

Finally, many products differentiate themselves by selling through distinct channels of distribution. Timex in watches, Avon in cosmetics, and many other products offer consumers similar goods through different channels.

Issues in Differentiation

Some current issues concerning product differentiation are discussed below.

COMMUNALITIES IN DIFFERENTIATION STRATEGIES

Although differentiation is a broad marketing strategy with a long history in economics, it is often implemented by way of a single recurring pattern. In practice, differentiation often results in an appeal to upscale markets with higher status (and higher priced) goods. That is, differentiation usually entails a move to the high end of markets. Profit margins are increased by selling premium products to higher income consumers who are less price sensitive.

DIFFERENTIATION AND MASS MARKETS

Unlike segmentation, differentiation does not preclude serving a mass market. Differentiation, if coupled with segmentation, can result in a low market share. But, differentiation, by itself, does not necessarily portend low share. Differentiated goods often serve broad market demands. It is segmentation that restricts demand, not product differentiation.

PRICE AS A POINT OF DIFFERENTIATION

One argument holds that competing on the basis of price is not a distinct marketing strategy but merely a form of differentiation. According to that argument, lower prices serve as the point of differentiation. It is a persuasive argument. But price competition is so qualitatively different, and so directly and drastically affects margins that price is best treated as a distinct strategy. Furthermore, price cuts are easily matched and, hence, are not easily sustainable. Consequently, price competition is not a form of differentiation, but a distinct marketing strategy that requires special skills. Differentiation, by definition, dwells on non-price variables.

References

Chakravarty, Subrata. "A Credit Card Is not a Commodity. *Forbes,* October 16, 1989, pp. 128–130.

Dickson, Peter, and James Ginter. "Market Segmentation, Product Differentiation, and Marketing Strategy." *Journal of Marketing,* April 1987, pp. 1–10.

Greene, Richard. "Inequitable Equity," *Forbes,* July 11, 1989, p. 83.

Lancaster, Kelvin. *Variety, Equity and Efficiency.* New York: Columbia University Press, 1979.

Lappen, Alyssa. "You Just Work Your Heart Out." *Forbes,* March 5, 1990, p. 74–77.

Levitt, Theodore. "Marketing Intangible Products and Product Intangibles." *Harvard Business Review,* May–June 1981, pp. 94–102.

Levitt, Theodore. "Marketing Success Through Differentiation—of Anything." *Harvard Business Review,* January–February 1980, pp. 83–91.

Ries, Al, and Jack Trout. *Positioning: The Battle for Your Mind.* New York: McGraw-Hill, 1981.

Smith, Wendell. "Product Differentiation and Market Segmentation as Alternative Marketing Strategies." *Journal of Marketing*, July 1956, pp. 3–8.

Smith, Wendell. "A Retrospective Note on Market Segmentation." *Journal of Marketing Research*, August 1978, p. 316.

Wind, Yoram. "Issues and Advances in Segmentation Research." *Journal of Marketing Research*, August 1978, pp. 317–337.

Chapter 8

Strategic Market Segmentation

The basic premise of market segmentation is identical to that of military strategy. Segmentation strategy is rooted in the fundamental principle of military combat—the concentration of forces (Cohen 1986). In marketing, as in war, it is foolish for the smaller army to attack a larger, more powerful force across a broad front. Instead, the smaller firm (like the smaller army) should concentrate its forces at a point of attack where the opponent is weakest. Marketers and military commanders alike have won many battles in which they were outnumbered by concentrating their forces on that part of the battlefield where their own forces were strongest. As business strategists have long advised, they pitted strength against weakness.

Segmentation is not unique to military or business strategy. Early economists have long recognized that firms selling a homogeneous product in a market characterized by heterogeneous demand could earn higher-than-average profits by focusing on a distinct group of consumers. Those firms avoid competition focusing on a segment.

Clearly, market segmentation is not a new idea. It arises from at least three source: military strategy, business strategy, and early economics. All sources agree that segmentation is a powerful and effective strategy. This chapter examines market segmentation as it relates to marketing strategy.

Market Preference Patterns

Segmentation strategy is rooted in the observation that markets exhibit different preference patterns which typically lie between the extreme positions, as illustrated in Exhibit 8.1.

Exhibit 8.1 *Range of Consumer Preference Patterns*

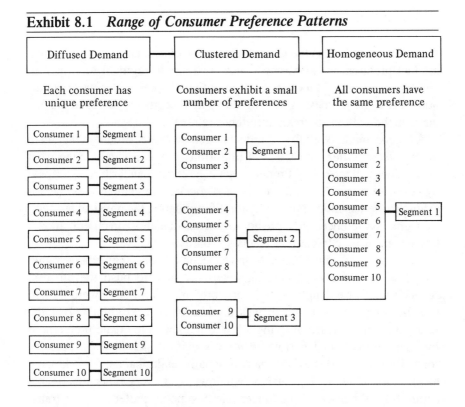

DIFFUSED DEMAND

At one extreme are markets where consumers exhibit widely dispersed, and possibly even unique, product preferences. In essence, each consumer serves as a single segment. The only way to fully satisfy each consumer is with custom-made products, an impractical idea in most markets.

In industrial markets, the demand for specialized machine tools represents diffused demand. Sellers are required to make one-of-a-kind machines in order to satisfy customers' needs.

In consumer markets, marketers may offer a wider variety of shapes and sizes. New Balance, for example, sells a nearly bewildering array of athletic footwear sized by widths, as well as by lengths. It differentiates its product by more closely fitting its customers feet.

Other clothing sellers follow a similar strategy. They offer a wider variety of sizes than competitors to appeal to many different figures.

HOMOGENEOUS PREFERENCES

At the other extreme is the market where consumers have nearly identical product preferences. In essence, there is a single segment to which all consumers belong. Marketers have only two choices under those conditions: (1) to be the best at serving that single segment, or (2) to change the demand pattern to create different preferences.

As some markets evolve, products become more similar rather than more diverse. Often, standards of uniformity are set, which define what the product will look like. Products that meet those standards are accepted by consumers, products that do not are rejected. In cement making, for example, there is little opportunity for differentiating the physical product. Consumer preferences are more homogeneous than those in other markets. Consumers want cement that meets standards.

Over the years most markets have become more segmented, rather than less. In some instances, marketers are able to push the process. At one time, for example, consumers' preferences for soap were limited to a bar of pure soap, which was used to clean everything. Over the years, a rising standard of living allowed marketers to create preferences for soap products that performed more specific tasks. Today, there are soaps for washing dishes, dry hair, oily hair, tender hands, a workman's hands, cars, clothes, dogs, faces, windows, and every other imaginable application. What was, is no longer. Homogeneous preference was transformed into market segmentation.

CLUSTERED DEMAND

Between the extremes lies clustered demand, which is most amenable to a segmentation strategy. It occurs when groups of consumers express a finite number of distinct product preferences. In breakfast cereals, for example, segments cluster on age and attitudes. Some consumers want a mix of healthful grains—the "twigs and sticks" segment. Younger consumers want extreme sweetness, and a prize in every box.

A similar pattern exists in autos. Some consumers want performance, others economy, or reliability. Suburbanites want stationwagons and Caravans. Men want pickups. Not all consumers have the same product preference. But they do not have unique preferences either. There is some commonality.

Clustered demand patterns are more common than the extreme positions represented by diffused and homogeneous demand. Most markets are segmented. They are characterized by clustered groups of preferences, which are served by different types of products.

Segmentation Strategies

It is one thing to discover segments. It is another to design strategies to serve them. Numerous strategies can be drawn from even the simplest market structures (Foote 1969). To illustrate those possibilities, consider the hypothetical market for breakfast cereals, and make three simplifying assumptions about that market.

First, assume the market for breakfast cereals consists of only *three segments* based on demographics:

1) children, under the age of 13, (the smallest segment)
2) the elderly, over 65, and
3) the rest of the market, all other ages (the largest segment).

Second, assume that market is served by only *three products:*

1) frosted flakes,
2) bran flakes, and
3) corn flakes.

Third, assume that market research has shown that *product preferences* are neatly distributed as follows:

1) children prefer frosted flakes,
2) elderly consumers prefer bran flakes, and
3) the rest of the market prefers corn flakes.

At least *eight basic strategies* are possible in a market described by those simplifying assumptions. Those strategies are representative of eight general types of segmentation strategies which are summarized in Exhibit 8.2.

BEST IN A SINGLE SEGMENT

The first five segmentation strategies target a single segment of the market.

Largest Segment

The *first* strategy a firm might pursue is to target the largest segment of the cereal market with the corn flakes product. It is an appealing strategy if the firm has the resources to be successful. Large segments are usually more attractive than small segments due to the higher volume

Exhibit 8.2   *Possible Segmentation Strategies*

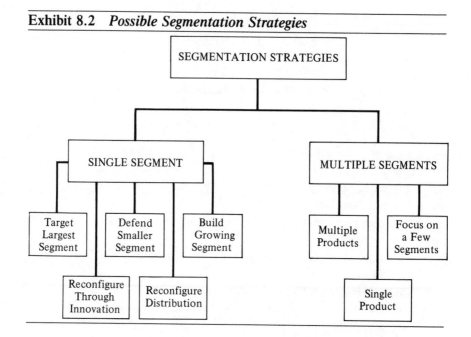

of sales they offer. Firms with the required capabilities often focus their attention on large segments, and willingly concede smaller segments to smaller firms. Their intention is to garner the lion's share of the largest segment.

In computers, for example, the "business" use of computers is more attractive than the "educational," "scientific," or "home" markets. IBM has focused its efforts on the business segment, where its strengths in brand and performance lie. Apple dominates the educational market. Smaller firms have focused on the smaller segments.

Emphasis on Avoiding Competition

The *second* strategy available to the firm competing in the cereal market is to build a solid reputation for selling the most favored brand of frosted flakes, serving only children. It is a strategy that trades large sales for a defendable market position.

The intent of emphasizing a smaller segment is to avoid competition rather than directly confront larger, more powerful competitors. The firm wishes to build a dominant position in a defendable niche of the market where its strengths are greatest.

Many smaller firms have succeeded by focusing on smaller segments of the market where they can exploit their competitive advantages. Consider the success of A&W root beer. From 1919 to 1971, A&W root beer was sold only at A&W root beer stands. In 1971, United Brands bought the rights to sell the brand, and operated it like a classic cash cow. It invested little, and withdrew much cash. United Brands sold out in 1983. In 1986, A&W management precipitated a leveraged buyout. It bought a low-share firm strapped with debt in a low-growth market dominated by giants. A&W recognized that it could not win a promotional war with market leaders. Competitors possessed all of the competitive advantages in that arena. A&W's only real resource was a trademark for a soft drink that held less than 2 percent of total soft drink sales.

Market conditions favor the giants. Sales and marketing expenses are immense. The large market shares of market leaders translate directly into more money for marketing.

A&W's strategy was based on three distinct actions. First, it convinced independent bottlers to add A&W root beer to their trucks, which were delivering Coke or Pepsi anyway. A&W root beer would supplement bottlers' product lines, not replace Coke and Pepsi. Second, A&W introduced a cream soda—a product where the A&W label could easily be transferred. At the time, there was no national cream soda. Hence, there was no direct competition. Third, A&W acquired two other niche players—Squirt, a grapefruit soda, and "The Original Vernors," a strange-tasting ginger drink with strong regional appeal. A&W also won the rights to distribute General Foods' Country-Time Lemonade. Competition was minimal in these markets.

The results of avoiding larger competitors have been impressive. While total soft drink sales rose only 4.5 percent in 1988, sales of A&W products rose a whopping 25 percent. Sales reached $100 million while profits soared to $7 million. As one industry analyst recognized: "The key to this business is knowing how to market, and these people are very good marketers" (Deutsch 1989, p. 10). A&W successfully served segmented markets by avoiding more powerful competitors.

Build Share in a Growing Segment

Recent years have seen a tremendous growth in sales of bran cereals. Much of that growth is due to favorable demographics. The *third* strategy available to the firm selling cereal is to build a defensible position among the growing number of elderly consumers with a superior bran cereal. That strategy would build a strong position in an increasingly attractive segment.

Building a dominant position in a growing segment is a cornerstone of many marketing strategies. In soft drinks, for example, Pepsi introduced Slice, a fruit-juice-based soft drink as the market grows older and larger. Pepsi is moving with natural changes in that market.

Reconfiguration

Firms can also influence market changes. The *fourth* strategy a firm could take in the cereal market is to introduce a new product that reconfigures the present cereal segments. The firm can pioneer another type of healthful cereal, which is preferred by consumers of all ages who are interested in healthful breakfast eating. The firm would redefine how sellers segment the market.

Miller Brewing's successful introduction of Miller Lite beer in the mid-1970s redefined how beer sellers segment their market. Lighter, lower-calorie beers moved from a small niche to a major part of the market.

The *fifth* strategy possible in the cereal market also relies on innovation, but it innovates in a different way. The firm might decide to pioneer a new channel of distribution, selling its cereals through health food stores located in malls, or by mail order. In many industries, firms have succeeded at segmentation by distributing products in new ways.

The videocassette business now has two distinct types of distribution. Most videocassette movies are sold to rental stores. The video rental stores purchase a few copies of many titles and rent them out to customers. Videocassette prices are high, as are profit margins for the studio. But volume is low. Few customers are willing to spend the $89.95 many tapes sell for, but prefer to rent them instead. In recent years, however, the studios have targeted hit movies, with the potential for huge sales, at consumers rather than rental shops. It is called the "sell-through." Studios have lowered the price, accepted lower margins, and sold tremendous volumes through mass market retailers. Many consumers are willing to purchase, rather than rent, a tape priced at $20. It is a move that has expanded the entire market. As one studio executive noted: "From our point of view, we regard the sell-through and rental businesses as two related but distinct businesses (Newcomb 1990, p. 41).

A POSITION IN MANY SEGMENTS

The final three segmentation strategies seek to build a position in more than one market segment.

Multiple Products to Multiple Segments

The *sixth* possible strategy for the firm selling in the cereal market is to produce all three cereals—corn, bran, and frosted flakes—to satisfy the demands of all three segments. It covers the entire market with all possible different products.

Many large firms follow a multiple-coverage segmentation strategy. For decades, Coca-Cola produced a single soda—sugared cola in a bottle. More recently, it began selling diet colas to the weight conscious, caffeine-free soda to the health conscious, "new" Coke to the young, Mountain Dew to rural teenagers, and Coke Classic to everyone else. Products are now packaged in twelve-ounce cans for individual servings and giant plastic bottles for families and "heavy-user" households. In addition, consumers are offered Minute Maid orange juice, orange-flavored soda, and many other thirst-quenching products. Coca-Cola covers every conceivable segment with a bevy of liquid refreshments.

Focus on a Few Segments

The *seventh* possible strategy is a variation of the sixth. The firm might sell only corn and bran flakes to the two largest segments, and ignore the small segment for frosted flakes. In that way it would focus on adults and avoid children. It is a strategy that targets a few, but not all, of the segments that make up the market. It is based on the belief that serving the smaller segment may not be worth the effort.

Single Product to Multiple Segments

The *eighth,* and final, strategy is to avoid segmentation entirely. The firm sells corn flakes to as many consumers who will buy them. Sales are often made on the basis of lower prices gained through the production efficiencies that arise from making only a single product.

Selling a single product is the least desirable approach for serving a segmented market. In effect, it ignores the presence of differing preferences. It hopes to partially satisfy the needs of all consumers without alienating the members of any segment. It is a strategy that appeases the internal pressures of the firm to increase efficiencies at the expense of consumer satisfaction.

The old-line sneaker manufacturers, such as Keds and P.F. Flyers, lost out to newcomers, such as Nike, with that approach. While they offered a single product, Nike offered dozens of different products targeted to different sports.

Basis of Segmentation

The number of possible segmentation strategies grows quickly as a market becomes more complicated. One way in which complications increase is with the number of ways in which to segment that market. The simple example of cereals presented above was segmented on the basis of age alone. It is but one of many other choices. Markets can be segmented in terms of the frequency and extent of product usage, price sensitivity, and innumerable demographic and regional characteristics. The alternatives are nearly endless. This section examines some of the ways in which a market can be segmented, and shows how they affect segmentation strategy.

REGIONAL SEGMENTS

Regional differences in demand and competitive advantage can have a profound effect on marketing strategy. Firms face many strategic choices. They can: (1) focus on a single geographic segment of the market, (2) exploit a national brand, (3) buy other regional brands, or (4) build a national brand.

Regional Focus

Many firms have succeeded against national competitors by focusing their efforts on a single geographic region. Hardee's, the fast-food chain, seeks market dominance in the Southeast and Middle West United States. It does not attempt to compete with McDonald's on a nationwide basis. To do so would be to spread itself too thin. It is a much smaller firm. As a result of its focus, Hardee's is the number two or three chain in 75 percent of the markets it serves. It competes on an equal footing with larger competitors, but only within its scope of operations. Hardee's tight focus allows it to move quickly against rivals in the markets it serves.

A more extreme example of regional focus is occurring in the brewing industry. National brands have grown at the expense of many large regional brewers. But, at the same time, very small "micro-breweries" have succeeded by serving small regional markets with a distinctive product. Those beers usually target an upscale market with a more expensive brew. Their volume is minuscule. They avoid competition with national brands by focusing on very small geographic segments.

Advantages of National Brands

Regional brands must compete against national brands, which possess many competitive advantages. National brands, such as Budweiser and Miller, for example, possess economies of scale in both production and advertising. They can wage a marketing war in one geographic segment with profits earned in other regions. A regional brand that serves a single segment is at a competitive disadvantage. It has no other source of funds upon which to draw except those generated in its home market. As a result, many national brands have grown at the expense of regional competitors that compete in a single geographic segment. Many regional brands are "stuck-in-the-middle."

Multiple Coverage with Regional Brands

Some regional brands have retaliated against national brands by buying other regional brands. Regional brewers, such as Heilman, have compiled a stable of strong regional brands that together cover a larger part of the national market. Heilman owns five popular regional brands: Old Style, Schmidt's, Ranier, Iron City, and Lone Star. Each brand serves a geographic segment. In addition, Heilman markets Colt 45, which serves not a distinct geographic segment, but a demographic segment consisting mostly of black consumers. Instead of one national brand sold to many segments, Heilman sells different brands to different segments.

Building a National Brand

The competitive advantages that arise from having a strong national brand has led some marketers to try and build a national brand in industries where no national brand currently exists. In spaghetti or pasta products, for example, firms have been fighting to build a single, dominant national brand. So far, no firm has been successful. Spaghetti still remains a market segmented by region. Prince dominates Boston. Philip Morris' Ronzoni brand is especially popular in New York, where, incidentally, consumption of pasta products is among the highest in the nation. American Beauty, which is owned by Hershey's, leads in California. Cremettes, Mueller's, and a bevy of other regional brands compete in local markets.

While no one has been able to build a single leading national brand of pasta, the industry has consolidated by buying successful regional brands. The power of regional brand names in pasta means that firms must sell different brands in different regions. They have succeeded with a multiple coverage segmentation strategy rather than a national brand.

Global Brands

The advantages of national brands over regional brands has recently moved to international markets. Firms in search of worldwide competitive advantages—economies of scale and advertising—have sought to sell a single standardized product throughout the world. Many firms have been successful in building global brands. The next chapter examines global brands in greater detail.

CONSUMER CHARACTERISTICS

Markets are often segmented on the basis of consumer characteristics. Segments can be characterized in terms of demographic, socioeconomic, and psychographic or lifestyle measures. Demographic and socioeconomic characteristics explain many differences in product preference. Age, gender, race, religion, income, and many other measurable characteristics greatly affect the types of products consumers desire. Younger consumers value soft drinks, personal computers, and stereo equipment, for example, while older consumers may pay more attention to investments and retirement options.

Many products are designed to appeal to distinct demographic segments. The Pontiac Sunbird, a GM C-type car, for example, is targeted primarily to lesser-educated young women who are purchasing their first car.

Firms that have a strong following among the members of one demographic segment may try to branch out and serve another segment. Cadillac, for example, sells mostly to older consumers. Younger consumers prefer sportier luxury cars such as BMW. Cadillac is trying to target younger, high-income consumers to expand its demographic base.

Sellers of cigarettes have had more success with expanding into other demographic segments. Cigarettes targeted towards women—such as Virginia Slims and Benson and Hedges—grew rapidly in the 1970s and into the 1980s as male smokers gave up the habit. Cigarettes successfully expanded into a demographic segment where they had previously been weak.

Psychographic segmentation—sometimes referred to as lifestyle or

AIO (activities, interests, and opinions)—compliments demographic segmentation. It is a recognition that consumers with similar demographic profiles often have very different lifestyles. Two twenty-year old, male college students with identical incomes, for example, may prefer very different types of products. One may whittle away the hours in the library pursuing scholarly activities, while the other may focus on dancing the night away at a local club.

PRODUCT USAGE

Product usage varies greatly among consumers. It is often possible to classify consumers into three groups: (1) heavy users, (2) light users, and (3) non-users. Marketers often segment on the basis of usage rate.

Heavy users consume most of the product. They are the embodiment of the age-old "80/20" principle, wherein 20 percent of the market routinely consumes 80 percent of a product's sales. In the beer industry, for example, Meisterbrau and Old Milwaukee, both owned by Miller Brewing, serve the heavy user segment with a low-end product. It is a strategy that seeks high volume with low prices.

Light users can also be an attractive market segment. Michelob by Anheuser-Busch, as well as Miller Brewing's Lowenbrau, both target the light user. It is a strategy that serves a lower-volume market of social beer drinkers with a higher-margin product. "Weekends were made for Michelob."

Non-users can also provide an opportunity for growth. Convincing those consumers to use the seller's product can create additional sales. The introduction of nonalcoholic beers, such as Miller's, Sharp's, and Anheuser-Busch's O'Doul's is an attempt to serve consumers a product more in tune with a society increasingly intolerant of drunk drivers, and clamoring for further restrictions on the consumption of alcoholic beverages.

BENEFITS SOUGHT

Many marketing experts believe that the best way to segment a market is with benefit segmentation, which allows a firm to target consumers who seek common benefits from a product. It is predicated on the belief that consumers purchase solutions to problems, or satisfactions of needs, rather than the mechanics of a physical product.

Benefit segmentation was popularized by Haley (1968), who, at the time, was a vice-president and research director for a major ad agency. First used in 1961 to segment the market for shampoo, its popularity has grown dramatically.

Haley argues that other bases of segmentation are descriptive not causal. They do not tell marketers why people buy products, they merely describe the people who buy them. In his own words: "The belief underlying this segmentation strategy is that the benefits which people are seeking in consuming a given product are the basic reasons for the existence of true market segments" (p. 31). It is a persuasive argument. Benefits are better predictors of purchase behavior than demographics, psychographics, and socioeconomic data.

Exhibit 8.3 illustrates a benefit segmentation of the market for toothpaste presented by Haley (1968). Four segments were discovered:

1. Children who like the taste of sweeter, more colorful toothpastes such as Colgate
2. Families and health-conscious consumers who favor decay-prevention dentifrices such as Crest, which carries the imprimatur of the American Dental Association
3. Teenage, single consumers who favor the appearance-enhancing benefits of whiter teeth and fresher breath from such toothpastes as Ultra Brite
4. Men who prefer whatever brand is on sale

Benefit segmentation is most useful when benefits can be linked to demographic, lifestyle, and product-usage characteristics. Linkages allow marketers to target specific consumer groups.

Configurations of Consumer Characteristics

Rarely do market segments differ by a single demographic, socioeconomic, or psychographic characteristic. Typically, clusters of consumers can be identified and described. Varying by more than a single measure, those clusters provide a vivid portrait of who buys particular products and what benefits they seek from them. It is those configurations of consumer characteristics that are most important in deriving market segments. As a market researcher might say: the real basis of segmentation should be multidimensional.

Exhibit 8.3 *Benefit Segmentation of the Toothpaste Market*

	SEGMENT NAME			
	Sensory Segment	*Sociables*	*Worriers*	*Independent Segment*
Principal benefit sought	Flavor, product appearance	Brightness of teeth	Decay prevention	Price
Demographic strengths	Children	Teens, young people	Large families	Men
Special behavioral characteristics	Users of spearmint-flavored toothpaste	Smokers	Heavy users	Heavy users
Brands disproportionately favored	Colgate, Stripe	Macleans, Plus White, Ultra Brite	Crest	Brands on sale
Personality characteristics	High self-involvement	High sociability	High hypochondriasis	High autonomy
Life-style characteristics	Hedonistic	Active	Conservative	Value-oriented

SOURCE: Reprinted with permission of the American Marketing "Benefit Segmentation: A Decision-Oriented Research Tool," by Russell I. Haley. *Journal of Marketing*, July 1968, p. 33.

[165]

Strategy Versus Market Research

Even a cursory review of segmentation research reveals a clear bias towards technique over substance. Myriad models have been proposed to identify market segments. Less effort has been expended on studying how segmentation can be used to gain competitive advantage. Most segmentation research favors the narrower perspective of market research rather than the broader perspective of marketing strategy.

A Priori Versus Clustering

Basically, there are two approaches to selecting market segments. One starts with management judgment, the other begins with mathematical techniques.

The first approach has management select the basis for segmentation beforehand, be it age, region of the country, or a configuration of characteristics and benefits. That selection sets the basis for subsequent analysis, which seeks to describe the segments. Selecting the basis of segmentation beforehand using management judgment is called the a priori approach.

An alternative approach is to allow a mathematical technique to decide the basis of segmentation. Generally, these techniques cluster consumers who have similar characteristics into the same segment. They "build" market segments from individual consumer profiles. The technique decides who falls into which segment. Judgment is still important. Someone must decides how many segments should be selected, and what their names should be. Often, segments with titles such as "upscale singles," "happy homemakers," and "young newlyweds" are the result of clustering consumers with mathematical techniques.

More recent advances in mathematical segmentation techniques have expanded on those two basic options. Some segmentation models match individual consumers with specific product features. Others allow managers to build segments based on responses to different product forms. Wind (1978) provides a review of that literature through the mid-1970s.

Aggregation Versus Disaggregation

In theory, segmentation lies between the two extreme positions illustrated in Exhibit 8.1. In practice, identifying segments starts at either end of the continuum and progresses through an aggregation or disaggregation process.

The aggregation approach moves from left to right in Exhibit 8.1. Individual consumers are matched with other consumers on the basis of profile similarities to build market segments. Many of the segmentation techniques found in marketing research build segments from the responses of individual consumers.

The disaggregation approach moves from right to left. It starts with the entire mass market and breaks down that market into distinct segments. Most discussions of market segmentation in strategy favor the disaggregation. The different perspectives reflect the macro-orientation of strategy in contrast to the micro-perspective of marketing research.

BEST WAY TO SEGMENT

The segmentation literature reveals one fact clearly—there is no one best way to segment a market. Instead, there are innumerable possibilities. Different approaches are often found within a single industry. One firm may target women, another may target the upscale market (both male and female), and still others may focus on the suburban consumer. The result is a market characterized by disjointed, overlapping, and often times inconsistently defined segments. Segmentation is not science at work. In one form or another, it is gradations of management judgment.

Picking market segments is guided not by a search for "what is best" but by what the firm is trying to accomplish. A firm trying to reduce switching behavior, for example, will segment the market differently than a firm seeking to reduce price sensitivity, or gain share against competitors. The goals of segmentation decide how segments should be selected: segments are not selected on the basis of some absolute truth.

How competitors view segments can also affect segment selection. Competitors can redefine a market and force a firm to attend to a previously unattended segment.

CRITICISMS OF SEGMENTATION

Two criticisms have been leveled against segmentation research. The first criticism is that segmentation focuses too intently on consumer characteristics and not enough on competitors. It is the same criticism that was leveled against marketing in Chapter 1. The result has been that some commercial users have become disenchanted with segmentation studies because they fail to consider the competitive environment in which segmentation must be implemented (Young, Ott, and Feigin 1978; Moran 1974). Many segmentation studies have been impractical and unrealistic, mistakenly assuming that segmentation strategy occurs in isolation.

The other criticism is that segmentation research has emphasized technique over strategy. The important question is not which mathematical technique is used to construct the segments, but of what strategic value those segments are once they have been formed. Moran (1974) claims the misplaced emphasis on complex mathematical techniques began in the 1960s with the advent of computers. He bemoans the shortcomings: "All this exotic segmentation research . . . [is] hooked up to inadequate marketing theory" (p. 15). His assessment is correct and remains undated after nearly twenty years.

Complaints about segmentation point up an important issue—segmentation is as much an art as it is a science. Technical advances in the methodology of segmentation have not reduced the importance of judgmental marketing decisions regarding how best to segment a market.

Issues in Segmentation

Numerous issues are salient to segmentation research. Five issues are examined below:

NATURAL VERSUS CREATED SEGMENTS

Segments are formed in one of two ways: (1) they either exist naturally in a market, to be discovered by astute marketers, or (2) they are created by marketers who see an opportunity. Unlike differentiation, segments are not solely the creation of marketers.

Many markets are characterized by naturally occurring clustered demand patterns, where different groups of consumers exhibit different product preferences. In such instances, the job of marketers is one of recognition. Marketers seek to discover segments and serve them with differentiated goods.

Segments can also be created. The need for underarm deodorants, which keep consumers "smelling fresh," versus anti-perspirants, which keep consumers "dry," have been created by marketers seeking to differentiate their products.

Which is more common in today's markets—created or naturally occurring segments? Moran (1974) argued: "More often then not, product market segments are made, not born" (p. 16). To support his claim, he cites the examples of Land's Polaroid camera, which created the segment for instant photoprocessing; and Clarence Birdseye's frozen foods, which created the segment for convenience foods.

Others disagree. They argue that those segments always existed; technological innovation merely made it possible to satisfy those segments better than had previously been possible.

Segments can be created, however, especially for line extensions and other variations on existing innovations. But discovery is more common. Usually, segments already exist, waiting to be discovered and exploited. Segmentation is more a process of discovery than it is a process of creation.

Overlapping Segments

Most segments are not mutually exclusive. Often the members of one segment can be classified in another segment as well. In the toothpaste example presented above, for example, families value decay prevention, while children favor flavorful toothpaste. But children, as part of families, fall into both segments. Families value decay prevention for their children. Similarly, targeting autos to women can overlap greatly with segments defined as "upscale" or "suburban." The boundaries of segments are roughly drawn, not ironclad.

Segment Stability

It is often said that change is the only certainty. That observation suggests that segments, once identified, will soon become obsolete. Segment solutions do not last for long. Benefits sought, segment size, and consumer profiles are in a state of perpetual flux. What is true today is not true tomorrow.

Few studies have examined the issue of segment stability. But the work that has been conducted suggests that market segments are stable. One study looked at how segments for retail banking services changed over a two-year period. It found three important results: (1) the benefits sought remained stable, (2) the size of the segments did not change much, *but* (3) the segments into which individual consumer households were placed did change (Calatone and Sawyer 1978).

As a rule of thumb, a more narrowly defined basis of segmentation is less stable than a segment defined in broader terms. Likewise, segment stability is related to market volatility. As common sense dictates, segments are less stable in markets where change is great.

COUNTER-SEGMENTATION

Segmentation is so pervasive that some markets may be over segmented. Some markets may be broken up into such small niches that opportunities exist for marketers to combine market segments and move back in the direction of mass marketing. That reverse process has been termed counter-segmentation (Resnick, Turney, and Mason 1979).

Consider the evolution of athletic footwear. In the 1950s and 1960s, sneakers served recreational athletes who engaged in many types of sporting activities. Keds and P.F. Flyers were popular brands. By the 1970s, coincident with the running boom, upstarts such as Nike began selling shoes designed specifically for the newly enlarged segment for joggers. By the 1980s the market was further segmented. There were aerobic shoes to serve aerobic enthusiasts, bicycling shoes for semiserious riders, and tennis shoes for the weekend athlete. Even obscure sports, such as wrestling, qualified for specialized shoes. Segmentation seemed to have reached its ultimate level of fragmentation. Then, there was a move towards counter-segmentation. Cross-training shoes gained popularity. These were sporting shoes that could be used for more than a single sport. What had once been sneakers were now cross trainers, which carried a price tag approaching $100.

FOR SMALL FIRMS ONLY?

Segmentation is often the only strategy available to smaller firms. But it is not limited to small firms. Large firms can also pursue a strategy of segmentation, particularly if they cover multiple segments with differentiated goods. Large firms have more options open to them than smaller firms.

Small firms are often limited to a segmentation strategy by the sheer fact that they must concentrate their scant resources on a part of the market that can be defended. It is not the strategy of segmentation that is limited, but the resources of the firm. Smaller firms simply have fewer options.

Consider the case of small software firms that have succeeded against larger competitors. Over the past decade, many small software firms tried to gain share on larger established software firms by making better spreadsheets, word processors, and databases. Most failed, even though they offered superior products. Small firms that sell specialized products to niche markets have had greater success. Programs that print output sideways, enlarge laptop cursors, and tell how much time is left in a laptop battery have succeeded by concentrating on niches and avoiding competition. As one niche marketer noted: "I'm like the barberfish that go into the jaws of big fish and clean their teeth. I get morsels that are too little for the big fish" (Ingrassia 1988, p. B1). Smaller firms often have no choice but to act like a small fish when it comes to marketing strategy. They must swim in smaller ponds if they are to survive and prosper.

References

Calatone, Roger, and Alan Sawyer. "The Stability of Benefit Segments." *Journal of Marketing Research,* August 1978, pp. 395–404.

Cohen, William A. "War in the Marketplace." *Business Horizons,* March–April 1986, pp. 10–20.

Deutsch, Claudia H. "A&W: Prospering by Avoiding the Big Boys." *New York Times,* January 15, 1989, sec. 3, p. 1.

Foote, Nelson N. Market Segmentation as a Competitive Strategy." In *Current Controversies in Marketing Research,* Leo Bogart (ed.). Chicago: Markham Publishing, 1969, pp. 129–139.

Haley, Russell I. "Benefit Segmentation: A Decision-Oriented Research Tool." *Journal of Marketing,* July 1968, pp. 30–35.

Ingrassia, Lawrence. "Small Software Companies Profit by Exploiting Niches," *Wall Street Journal,* October 11, 1988, pp. B1–B3.

Moran, William T. "Segments Are Made Not Born." In *Marketing Strategies: A Symposium* Earl L. Bailey (ed.), New York: The Conference Board, 1974, pp. 15–20.

Newcomb, Peter. "Can Video Stores Survive? *Forbes,* February 5, 1990, pp. 39–41.

Resnick, Alan J., Peter B.B. Turney, and J. Barry Mason. "Marketers Turn to Counter-Segmentation." *Harvard Business Review,* September–October 1979.

Young, Shirley, Leland Ott, and Barbara Feigin. "Some Practical Considerations in Market Segmentation." *Journal of Marketing Research,* August 1978, pp. 405–412.

Wind, Yoram. "Issues and Advances in Segmentation Research." *Journal of Marketing Research,* August 1978, pp. 317–337.

Chapter 9

The Standardization-Customization Debate in Global Marketing Strategy

An intense debate rages in global marketing strategy, centering on whether a firm should sell an identical product in all markets around the world or tailor its products to fit local tastes and desires. The argument contrasts standardized versus customized marketing strategies.

Standardization and customization parallel Porter's low-cost/low-price seller and differentiation strategies when applied to global marketing. The argument for standardization conjures up the global equivalent of a low-cost producer. It is a strategy that seeks to gain economies and efficiencies by selling the same product worldwide. Customization, in contrast, targets differentiated products to different countries (segments) in order to meet the unique needs of consumers in that country. Proponents of customization argue that products should be tailored to fit customers' needs. Proponents of standardization argue that customer tastes should be tailored to fit the firm's products. This chapter examines the standardization-customization debate.

The Argument for Standardization

Standardization is often referred to as "globalization" and "uniformity." It embraces a production orientation over the marketing concept. Standardization seeks competitive advantage through efficient production. It seeks to coalesce consumer needs around the firm's product.

Standardization assumes that successful products have, or can be made to have, worldwide appeal. It presupposes the existence, or the potential to create, fundamental worldwide consumer motives. It holds that a good product or product idea has universal appeal. It is an assumption that consumers are basically the same the world over. Standardization holds that similarities among consumers outnumber differences.

There are many examples of product standardization in world markets. Lego, the Danish seller of kids' building blocks, markets a nearly identical product worldwide. Children throughout the world enjoy the fundamental appeal of that basic product. Gillette sells the same razor worldwide, filling a fundamental need for shaving with as standardized product. American cigarettes have also been largely standardized. So have soft drinks. Pepsi and Coca-Cola sell their soft drinks throughout the world with few changes. These products, along with many others, are truly global brands.

HOMOGENEITY OF GLOBAL MARKETS

Proponents of standardization claim that the world is moving towards greater homogeneity. The growth of worldwide communications and media has exposed more and more of the world's consumers to the same ideas and products. Uniqueness among countries is being replaced by similarity. That trend bodes well for standardization. It means that products that are successful in one country can be successfully sold in world markets.

Levitt (1983) is one of the most strident proponents of standardization, and calls for the globalization of markets. His ideas have served as the sounding board for the entire standardization-customization debate. Levitt sees a clear trend towards greater homogenization of world markets. Consumers, he contends, are becoming more alike. As world markets become more similar, the opportunity for standardizing products becomes greater.

BENEFITS OF STANDARDIZATION

There are two primary benefits for standardization: (1) lower costs and (2) strategic consistency.

Lower Costs

The most widely mentioned benefit of standardization is the cost savings derived from economies of scale. Those savings arise from economies in production and advertising. A standardized product generates longer production runs, which leads to economies of scale in materials costs, machinery, and other aspects of manufacturing. A standardized product also spreads R&D expenditures over a larger volume of production, which lowers per-unit costs.

Economies can also derive from multinational advertising and promotional campaigns. The arguments for standardization made in the 1960s stressed the efficiencies that could be gained from the use of a single advertising campaign and a single advertising agency. Those efficiencies are real and commonplace. Quelch and Hoff (1986), for example, note that McCann-Erickson, the advertising agency, standardized Coca-Cola's commercials and saved $90 million over twenty years.

Still, standardizing a product leads to greater cost savings than standardizing an advertising campaign (Walters 1986).

Strategic Consistency

Standardization also leads to consistency in marketing strategy. The firm that sells standardized products worldwide is able to project a consistent image to all of its customers. That firm can also concentrate on its key competitive advantage. A firm that has built a reputation with one type of image, for example, can most easily maintain that image with a single product sold in all markets. The image can be carried over to global markets.

Consistency also aids in purchasing. In industrial markets a single product allows customers to purchase centrally. In fact, large customers may pressure the seller for product standardization so that they can gain that benefit.

Standardization and the Marketing Mix

Standardization can be found in each of the four P's of the marketing mix: promotion, product, place, and price.

Promotion

The earliest arguments for standardization came from advertising executives who called for universal advertising appeals. Even today, when many writers talk about standardization they are talking about the merits of creating a common promotional plan that can be used around the world. Hyatt Hotels, for example, uses the same image and the same advertising agency to sell its service throughout the world.

It is easier to standardize general advertising themes than specific advertisements. Specific ads and creative designs are more likely to be tailored to local markets. Most experts agree that the creative execution of ads in one country is more difficult to transfer to another country than the general appeal.

Product

Product standardization has been more widely standardized than promotion. Products sold in one country are often sold in another with only minor changes. Products that are not tied to a particular culture are particularly successful at standardization. Television sets, personal computers, and consumer electronics are sold worldwide with few modifications. They are sold on the basis of price and performance.

Household packaged goods and other products that have a stronger cultural component are less likely to be successfully standardized. Food products have an especially strong cultural appeal. Many food products appeal to specific consumer tastes. Consequently, many food products are tailored to the unique tastes of particular countries.

Brand names have generally achieved a higher degree of standardization. In many countries, brand names convey—or can be made to convey—a similar image. Wind (1986) argues that premium brands with a prestigious image have been especially successful at worldwide standardization.

Place

Distribution has also achieved a high degree of standardization. In many European countries, marketers use similar channels of distribution for their products. But, in less developed regions of the world, standardization is less likely.

Price

Standardizing price is more problematic than the other components of the marketing mix. Many countries have lower income levels than those found in the United States. Charging a uniform price for a global product can cut sales greatly. Consumers in international markets may simply be unable to afford the product. The problem is especially acute in less developed countries.

Customizing price, rather than keeping it the same in all markets, leads to other kinds of problems. Wide price differences create an opportunity for gray market transshipments. Gray marketers in one country where lower prices are being charged will transship the product to higher-priced markets for resale. A company that customizes prices may find itself competing with lower-priced versions of its own products. The practice is legal in the United States, and in some overseas markets. Firms cannot keep gray market goods out of the U.S. market.

Marketing Mix Strategies

The decision to standardize or customize can be combined with the elements of the marketing mix in many ways. More than twenty years ago Keegan (1969) proposed five strategic alternatives based on standardizing or customizing two elements of the marketing mix—product and promotion. Exhibit 9.1 summarizes those five strategies. In essence, he argued that a firm could adopt a strategy of:

1. pure standardization, where a *standardized product* is sold using a *standardized promotion* campaign,
2. a mix of standardization and customization, where a *standardized product* is sold, but a *customized promotion* campaign is developed for that particular foreign market,
3. a mix of standardization and customization, where a *customized product* is sold using a *standardized promotion,*
4. pure customization, where a *customized product* is sold using a *customized promotion,* and
5. a final form of pure customization, where an entirely new product invention is offered to the foreign market.

Exhibit 9.1   *Strategic Alternatives*

		PROMOTION	
		Standardization	Customization
PRODUCT	Standardization	Pure Standardization "one product, one message, worldwide"	same product with promotion tailored to specific countries
	Customization	same promotion with a product tailored to specific countries	Pure Customization New Product Invention

STRATEGIC IMPLICATIONS OF STANDARDIZATION

There are at least three important strategic implications of standardization.

Running with a Winner

Standardization is a strategy based on exploiting good ideas, and proceeds in the belief that a good product can be transferred to other cultures. If fundamental consumer needs are indeed universal, then a good idea will be widely accepted rather restricted to a single market.

Standardization is consistent with the success rate for new product introductions. Most new products fail. Standardization holds that transferring successful products to new markets is more likely to succeed than the process of inventing new products specifically for foreign markets.

Van Mesdag (1987) proposes a renegade approach to standardization called the "shot-in-the-dark method." He argues that many international products have succeeded by running with a winner. Those firms take a product that is successful in the home market and simply sell it overseas with few modifications. It is an approach to marketing that he calls "unmarketing," which is based on persistence rather than adaptation. Kellogg's, Coca-Cola, and McDonald's all took products that were successful at home and sold them overseas with few changes. Running with a winner is an approach predicated on the idea that a good product has fundamental and worldwide appeal.

Cross-Subsidization

Years ago, the beer industry in the United States was made up of many local brewers and a few, large national sellers. The national brewers possessed a potent competitive advantage—if a price war broke out (or was created) they could absorb losses locally with profits earned nationally. Local brewers had no such option. They were forced to compete on a much smaller scale. All of their profits were hurt badly if they lowered prices to match those of the national competitors. That is one of the reasons why there are so few regional brewers left today. Regional brewers competed locally while national brewers competed on a broader scale.

More recently, the same phenomenon has occurred in international markets. Global competitors have been able to absorb losses in one country with profits earned worldwide. In the sale of television sets, for example, large Japanese firms with brand names such as Panasonic,

Hitachi, Toshiba, and Sony have used their presence in global markets to dominate American markets. American firms such as RCA and Zenith retaliated by becoming low-cost/low-price sellers. Still, they lost share for the same reason as did the local beer brewers. While American firms sold only in domestic markets, Japanese sellers sold worldwide. A price war in the United States hurt the profits of the American firms more than it hurt the profits of the Japanese firms. All of the profits of the American firms were subject to the ravages of lower prices. The Japanese sellers had less exposure since they also sold their products in markets where the price war was not raging. The example illustrates the competitive advantage to be gained from cross-subsidization.

Hamel and Prahalad (1985) argue that lower costs alone will not lead to market success and competitive dominance. They believe that the discussion of standardization has focused too intently on lower costs. The goal, they believe, should be cross-subsidization, whereby a firm lessens vulnerability to competition in local markets by competing in global markets. In other words, firms should try to broader their scope of operations rather than simply lower costs.

Cross-subsidization occurs "when a global company uses financial resources accumulated in one part of the world to fight a competitive battle on another" (p. 144). It is a strategy that takes a long-term view of market dominance.

A variation of cross-subsidization is "thrust and parry" (Hamel and Prahalad 1985). Firms often expand by selling their products in foreign markets. Competing firms, whose home markets have been attacked, can successfully counterattack by concentrating their attack not on the market where the initial attack occurred, but in the attacker's home markets. It is a strategy based on sapping the financial strength of the attacking firm. The pattern of "thrust and parry" is common in global competition. It illustrates the real issue in standardization—to gain competitive advantage.

Product Value Versus Product Choice

In essence, standardization is a strategy that provides customers with product value over product choice. Levitt (1983) argues that consumers will usually choose lower prices and higher quality over customized products when given the choice. He contends that marketers should pursue a strategy of standardization. By doing so, they will really be better serving their customers. It is a persuasive, but controversial, argument.

Arguments in favor of standardization are similar to those made against the marketing concept in Chapter 1. Like Bennett and Cooper (see Chapter 1), Levitt bemoans the size and effectiveness of marketing operations in many modern American corporations. He, too, contends that marketing research cannot tell firms what consumers really want. It is limited by the experience of those consumers. He argues that "marketing means giving the customer what he says he wants rather than trying to understand what he'd like" (p. 97). Levitt argues for imagination, push and persistence, all bywords of modern marketing strategy.

The Case for Customization

Customization is often referred to as "adaptation" or "localized" marketing. Whatever its appellation, customization is more closely allied with the marketing concept than is standardization. It embraces the notion that products should be tailored to fit the individual needs of customers in different countries. Customization is more akin to differentiation and segmentation than it is to lowering costs. Consequently, many of the most ardent proponents of customization come from marketing.

CRITICISMS OF STANDARDIZATION

Proponents of customization find many criticisms in a standardization strategy. Some of those criticisms are presented below.

Ignoring the Customer

In essence, a strategy of standardization subordinates consumer needs to production efficiences. It gives consumers less than what they want in the hope that lower prices will be sufficient. Sheth (1986) argues that the trend towards global competition should not be confused with a trend towards global products. Global competition does not necessarily imply global products. Paying attention to consumer needs is still the preeminent goal of marketers.

Insensitivity to Local Markets

By ignoring consumers' needs standardization may be viewed as a strategy aimed at exploiting local markets from distant shores (Quelch and Hoff

1986). An unpleasant result of that unfortunate image may be regulations imposed in local markets to control that practice of perceived exploitation.

Anti-Segmentation

Similarly, standardization in global markets contradicts the trend towards segmentation in American markets. Most markets have been split into ever smaller segments. The central assumption of standardization is that many segments can be covered by a single product. It implies that global markets can be standardized, while American markets are best served with differentiated products aimed at increasingly smaller segments. It argues that global markets behave differently than American markets.

Eschews Decentralization

Wind (1986) criticizes standardization because it centralizes decision making at a time in history when decentralization of decision making is often advocated as the preferred approach for dealing with local tastes. Being close to markets, the flexibility and speed of entrepreneurial decision making, and the trend towards pushing decision making downward to lower levels in the organization are all favored approaches in the 1990s. Standardization goes in the opposite direction. It takes marketing decision making away from local marketers and moves it to headquarters. It is a strategy driven by production efficiencies rather than consumers' wants, needs, and desires.

Unrealized Cost Savings

Some critics even dispute the primary advantage of standardization—that standardization leads to lower costs through higher efficiencies. A study by Sorenson and Weichman (1975) examined twenty-seven multinational corporations selling products in European markets. It found that only one of those firms was able to confirm cost savings due to standardization. They contend that actual cost savings due to economies of scale may be less widespread than expected.

Wind (1986) takes particular issue with the purported cost advantages of standardization. Those advantages, he claims, can be overcome with flexible manufacturing. Small, efficient, flexible production runs, which provide consumers with a wide variety of products tailored to their specific needs, may be able to overcome the purported advantage of standardization.

MOTIVATION FOR CUSTOMIZATION

While standardization is a laudable goal, practical considerations often make customization a more likely alternative.

Voluntary Versus Mandatory Customization

Customization can be either voluntary or mandatory. That is, firms can actively decide to tailor products and marketing to fit individual markets, or the government of the host country can require them to do so. In the first case, the firm is motivated to customization by strategic concerns. In the second case, the firm is forced to do so.

Even if a firm wants to sell a standardized product in international markets it often cannot do so without making changes to that product required by local law. European car makers, for example, that wish to sell their cars in the United States must comply with local pollution laws and fit their cars with special equipment not required in European markets. Cars sold in California must meet even more strident requirements. The law requires that products be customized for those markets.

Voluntary customization, on the other hand, responds not to legal requirements but to consumer demands. Consumers in different geographic locales often desire different products. Most arguments for customization focus on voluntary actions where there is a choice to be made.

National Differences

Often, tradition overpowers efficiency. Although it has been thirty years since the first calls were made for standardization there are still major differences between international markets—even markets in Europe that are technologically advanced and in close geographic proximity. It might even be argued that those differences are becoming more, rather than less, pronounced. A growth in nationalism, a return to extreme religiosity, and a renewed pride in ethnic origins all suggest a trend towards heterogeneity rather than homogeneity of global demand.

Furthermore, many of the differences between countries are built into the physical structure of their economy. Europeans, for example, tend to live in smaller homes than Americans. Consequently, there is less kitchen space for the gadgets galore found in many American homes. Many other countries lack the plethora of retailers and the consumption orientation found in the United States. There may be fewer massive shopping centers or supermarkets. Those patterns are likely to change slowly, at best. They are likely to stymie the trend toward global products.

Competitive Advantage Through Customization

Businesses themselves may be promoting the trend towards customization. Boddewyn, Soehl, and Pichard (1986), for example, found that over the past two decades there has been a trend towards more customization and less standardization in international markets. That trend is motivated by firms with the desire to gain a competitive advantage by tailoring products more precisely to customers' needs. Similar to the trend toward greater segmentation found in U.S. markets, global markets are being targeted with goods designed specifically for those markets.

The Middle Ground

The standardization-customization debate is less divisive than it seems at first glance. The debate may be acrimonious but the two positions are really not that far apart. As proposed above, each approach is extreme and untenable. The criticisms of each approach tend to dwell on the extremes and spurn the middle ground. Conventional wisdom holds that it is not realistic for all elements of the marketing mix to be standardized. But, there are some advantages to standardization. As with other arguments in marketing strategy, the middle ground position seems the most reasonable.

Definitional problems explain part of the confusion. Standardization and customization mean different things to different people. Ironically, there is little standardization of the terms themselves. In absolutes they are easily defined. In practical terms there is considerable confusion.

Consider the case of a product that is sold throughout the world in essentially the same form, except for minor product differences—such as special colors or special sizes. Is that product standardized or customized? What about a product that is identical in every respect except it uses a different advertising claim in different countries? Is it standardized or customized?

Other confusions further compound the problem. A firm that sells the same product in ten different countries clearly sells a standardized product. But, what about a firm that sells five different products, each product sold exclusively in one of ten markets, for a total of fifty different markets? Is that firm also engaged in standardization, or is it customizing its products to meet special needs? (Rosen 1990). Often, standardization and customization are conceptually clear but practically muddled. Only the extremes are open for easy attack.

There is widespread agreement that total standardization is neither advisable, or even possible. After a thorough review of the literature up through the mid-1980s, Walters (1986) concludes: "From the available evidence it appears that policies of total uniformity . . . are relatively rare." He adds: "It would be naive to believe that unique recipes for success with universal validity have been, or are waiting to be, discovered" (p. 64).

More recently, John Quelch adds that standardization is "unattainable in its purest form for most companies and products" (Hammonds 1990, p. 84).

Quelch and Hoff (1986) also opt for the middle ground. They contend that both views are too extreme. Flexibility is the key. The marketing concept, consumer tastes, strategic considerations, and sheer practicality work against a strategy of complete standardization.

Even Levitt defines standardization in a way that does not preclude room for some degree of customization. He warns not to "mistake a difference for a distinction" (p. 94). His arguments seem to be more rhetorically strident than substantively extreme. His ideas have served mostly to attract attention to this important issue, and point up what he believes is the direction in which markets are moving. For that he is to be commended.

Levitt argues that people were taking him too literally (Hammonds 1990). He never meant to imply that all products should be completely standardized in all situations. He too has moved more towards the middle ground.

A recent examination of the success of Nestle, the world's largest food company, illustrates the merits of the middle-ground position. Nestle, a Swiss multinational, has owned Stouffer frozen foods for more than ten years. Stouffer's Lean Cuisine is a very successful product with diet-conscious Americans. In 1985, Stouffer introduced Lean Cuisine in England. The frozen entrees were customized for the English market—they came in curried chicken and cod in wine sauce. As Tully (1989) concludes: "While these products still have to be fine-tuned to local tastes, [Nestle succeeds] by selling similar products worldwide" (p. 74). Has it standardized or customized its frozen foods? Most likely, it has taken the middle ground.

Pluralization of Consumption

Levitt reconciles the standardization-customization debate with a concept called the pluralization of consumption. It is an intriguing idea. He remains committed to his original premise that the clear trend is towards the homogenization of global markets. Advances in communications and transportation are creating identical ideas, parallel preferences, and comparable consumption patterns. Global markets are converging.

But, at the same time, Levitt perceives a pluralization of preferences. Consumers the world over want an increasing variety of the same products.

Exhibit 9.2   *Standardization, Customization, and the Pluralization of Consumption*

STANDARDIZATION

Standardized Product

Country #1	Country #2	Country #3

CUSTOMIZATION

Customized Product #1	Customized Product #2	Customized Product #3

Country #1	Country #2	Country #3

PLURALIZATION OF CONSUMPTION

Standardized Product #1	Standardized Product #2	Standardized Product #3

Country #1	Country #2	Country #3

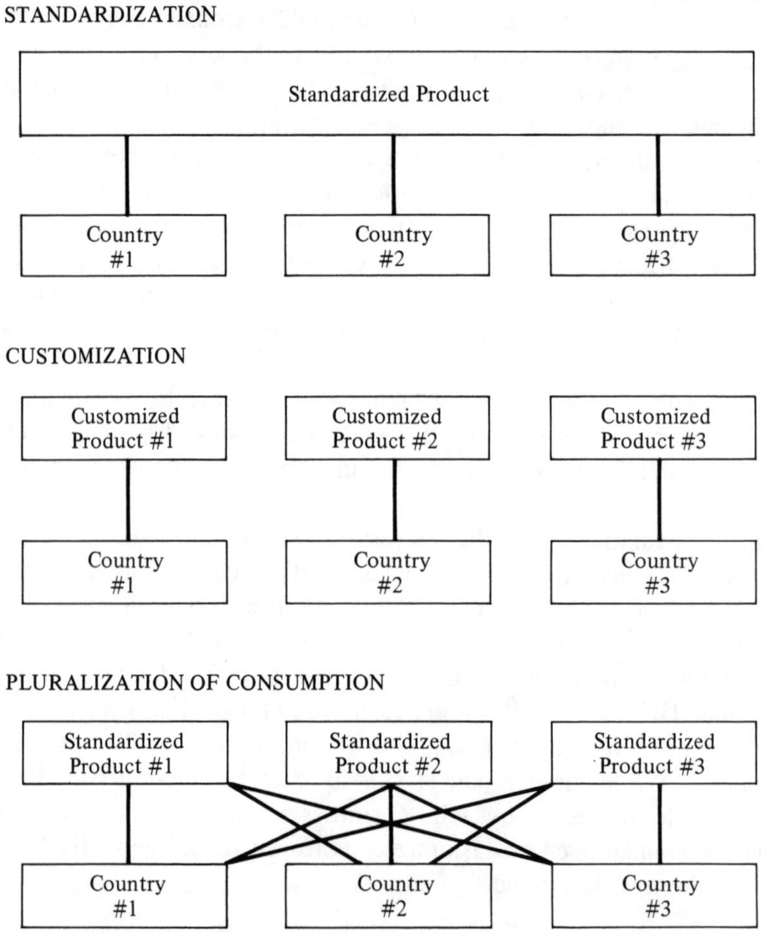

Consumers needs may be converging, but they are converging on a wide assortment of products that were once the purview of specialized markets.

Consider the case of ethnic foods. Standardization would advise that a single food product be sold the world over. American style hamburgers would be sold throughout the world. Customization would argue that a different food product would be required for sale in each country. Goya Spanish-style foods are for sale in Spanish-speaking markets. Pluralization argues that consumers the world over now prefer a variety of ethnic foods. Consumers in many markets want both hamburgers and Spanish foods, as well as Greek, Mexican, and many other ethnic foods. A firm can now sell Mexican food products, for example, throughout the world. Consumption, in short, is homogeneous throughout the world. But, the variety of products consumed in any one market is increasingly heterogeneous. As Exhibit 9.2 illustrates, Levitt contends that consumers now seem to be part of every conceivable preference segment.

Strategic Alternatives

Critics contend that a strategy of pure standardization or pure customization is not feasible. There are, however, opportunities to move towards standardization in those situations where it is most likely to succeed.

LOOKING FOR LIKENESS IN MARKETS

The benefits of standardization can be achieved by targeting standardized products to markets that exhibit similar characteristics. The important question is not if standardization should be used, but when should it be used, and how far it should be taken. It is not a new idea. Buzzell (1968) captured those constraints best when he asked: "Which elements of the marketing strategy can or should be standardized, and to what degree?" (p. 103).

Standardized products and promotions are most likely to be successful when targeted to markets that have similar profiles. Targeting standardization can offer the benefits without the problems encountered when applied in all markets.

Searching for similar markets in which to standardize product and promotion strategies is akin to combining segments in domestic markets. In global markets, as well as domestic markets, similar segments are more likely to respond favorably to a single product and/or promotion than markets that are different.

Targeting standardization is not a rare strategy. Sorenson and Weichman (1975) found that the degree of product and promotion standardization was highest among markets that were highly similar.

Looking for Likeness in Products

Standardization can also be targeted to similar products. Products like consumer electronics, calculators, hotel rooms, and gasoline are remarkably similar around the world. They serve fundamental consumer needs. Other product categories, in contrast, have distinctively national tastes. In those cases, customization is the only alternative. Just as firms can target standardization to markets that are similar, so too can they target standardization to products that in one form appeal to consumers worldwide.

Creating Similarity

Finally, marketers can promote standardization by attempting to coalesce demand around a single product. Levitt (1983) calls for "global convergence," whereby a firm creates worldwide demand for a standardized product. It is an achievable goal, he contends, given the worldwide pervasiveness of modern media and communications. Overcoming national fragmentation is a proactive strategy that corresponds to the observation that global products satisfy fundamental consumer wants, needs, and desires. The time may not yet be here when all products in all markets can be standardized, but through global convergence firms can push standardization to its natural limit, and reap the benefits it offers.

References

Boddewyn, J. J., R. Soehl and J. Pichard. "Standardization in International Marketing: Is Ted Levitt in Fact Right?" *Business Horizons,* November–December 1986, pp. 69–75.

Buzzell, Robert. "Can You Standardize Multinational Marketing?" *Harvard Business Review.* November–December 1968, pp. 102–113.

Hamel, Gary, and C. K. Prahalad. "Do You Really Have a Global Strategy?" *Harvard Business Reveiw,* July–August 1985, pp. 139–148.

Hammonds, Keith. "Ted Levitt Is Back in the Trenches." *Business Week,* April 9, 1990, pp. 82–84.

Keegan, Warren. "Multinational Product Planning: Strategic Alternatives." *Journal of Marketing,* January 1969, pp. 58–62.

Levitt, Theodore. "The Globalization of Markets." *Harvard Business Review,* May–June 1983, pp. 92–101.

Quelch, John, and Edward Hoff. "Customizing Global Marketing." *Harvard Business Review,* May–June 1986, pp. 59–68.

Rosen, Barry. "Global Products: When Do They Make Strategic Sense?" *Advances in International Marketing* (Greenwich, CT: Jal Press, forthcoming).

Sheth, Jagdish. "Global Markets or Global Competition." *Journal of Consumer Marketing,* Spring 1986, pp. 9–11.

Sorenson, R., and U. Weichman. "How Multinationals View Standardization." *Harvard Business Review,* May–June 1975, pp. 38–50.

Tully, Shawn. "Nestle Shows How to Gobble Markets." *Fortune,* January 16, 1989, pp. 74–78.

Van Mesdag, Martin. "Winning It in Foreign Markets." *Harvard Business Review,* January–February 1987, pp. 71–74.

Walters, Peter. "International Marketing Policy: A Discussion of the Standardization Construct and Its Relevance for Corporate Policy." *Journal of International Business Studies,* Summer 1986, pp. 55–69.

Wind, Yoram. "The Myth of Globalization." *Journal of Consumer Marketing,* Spring 1986, pp. 23–26.

Chapter 10

PIMS: The Search
for Strategic Principles

PIMS is an acronym for the Profit Impact of Market Strategy. The goal of PIMS is to discover how marketing strategy affects profits.

Just as the name Bruce Henderson is closely tied to experience effects and the Boston Consulting Group, so are the names Sidney Schoeffler and Robert Buzzell nearly synonymous with PIMS. PIMS emerged under the tutelage of Mr. Schoeffler at General Electric in the early 1960s. Since then it has grown greatly in both size and prestige. Equally important has been the contribution of Robert Buzzell, who has been one of the most prolific PIMS authors. It would be impossible to study PIMS without following the work of either author.

PIMS was first reported publicly by Sidney Schoeffler, Robert Buzzell, and Donald Heany in a 1974 *Harvard Business Review* article, which provided an overview of the project and presented its initial findings. A more detailed discussion, using more recent data, is provided by Robert Buzzell and Bradley Gale in a 1987 book entitled *The PIMS Principles: Linking Strategy to Performance*.

What Makes PIMS Different?

PIMS is unique among marketing strategy formulations for the following reasons:

EMPIRICAL DATABASE

Most strategic formulations are purely conceptual as they pose interesting hypotheses but lack empirical testing. PIMS is different. Its findings are based on real-world data rather than theoretical suppositions. PIMS collects and examines the experiences of 450 firms that compete in nearly

3,000 separate businesses. It is a large empirical database of actual business experience.

OBJECTIVE STATISTICAL ANALYSIS

PIMS is a statistical model. It applies multiple regression to analyze a large database of actual business experience to discover how strategic variables such as market share and product quality are related to profitability. As a result, PIMS implies greater objectivity than strategy formulations based on supposition. It is based on fact rather than opinion.

EXAMINATION OF MANY VARIABLES

PIMS looks at the effects of dozens of variables on profitability—thirty-seven in an early model, twenty-two in more recent discussions. In contrast, the BCG matrix relies on only two key variables—market share and market growth. Likewise, Porter focuses on the five forces that affect competition in an industry and the three generic strategies—differentiation, low-cost production, and segmentation. PIMS is more encompassing than most other marketing strategy formulations.

RANKING OF MOST IMPORTANT VARIABLES

As a statistical model PIMS is also able to assess which variables have the greatest impact on profits, and which have minor influences. Such rankings are possible because of the regression approach employed by PIMS researchers. Other marketing strategy formulations rely on opinions alone to assess which variables are most important.

SEARCH FOR GENERAL MARKETPLACE PRINCIPLES

Most important, PIMS has a bold and broad objective—the search for general strategic principles of the marketplace that affect most businesses, regardless of the industry or market in which firms compete. Those principles apply equally to businesses that make cosmetics, steel, or sell insurance. Strategic principles of the marketplace are derived using two controversial concepts—pooled business experience and the analysis of look-alikes.

Pooled Business Experience

PIMS relies on the use of "pooled business experience." Data is collected from many different types of businesses, entered into the computer, and analyzed as a single sample. Results such as "product quality is related to higher profits" emerge from the analysis. The approach assumes that the same factors affect different businesses in the same way.

Analysis of Look-Alikes

Equally important is the way in which PIMS defines "similar" businesses. Comparisons are not made within an industry. One auto company, for example, is not necessarily compared with another auto company. Instead, PIMS relies on the concept of "look-alikes." Companies that are similar in terms of market share, product quality, new product activity, investment intensity, and a host of other factors are compared. They "look alike" in terms of the PIMS database, even though they compete in different industries.

PIMS, for example, might compare the performance of firms that have a high share of the cosmetics industry with high-share firms in the housewares industry, if those firms have similar profiles in terms of PIMS descriptors.

Are the concepts of "pooled business experience" and "the analysis of look-alikes" reasonable? Or, is PIMS based on a flawed premise? Are there really "universal laws of the marketplace"? Before describing the model itself, consider the validity of that central PIMS assumption.

Generalizing Marketing Strategy

The most important and controversial issue about PIMS is whether there are in fact "universal laws of the marketplace." Not all researchers believe that there are. In fact, it is on this point that PIMS draws its most severe criticism. Some experts argue that businesses in different industries cannot be compared: the factors that affect them are unique to each industry and situation specific. To compare the steel business, for example, with the cosmetics business makes little sense. Each is affected by different factors—factors other than those measured by PIMS. At the very least, the same factors affect each industry in a different way.

The argument over universal laws of the marketplace is basic and fundamental to the PIMS approach. If you do not believe there are principles of strategy, you will not believe in PIMS.

There are two extreme positions that constitute the anchors of a continuum shown in Exhibit 10.1.

UNIVERSAL LAWS: ARE ALL BUSINESSES ALIKE?

The left end of the continuum in Exhibit 10.1 illustrates the position held by early PIMS researchers who once searched to "discover the general laws that determine what business strategy, in what kind of competitive environment, produces what profits" (*The Pims Program* 1980, p. 5). Initial findings created an enthusiastic response. PIMS researchers concluded: "All businesses are basically alike in obeying the same laws of the marketplace" (Shoeffler 1980, p. 2).

PIMS further stated:

> Businesses with similar such characteristics tend to have similar profitability, regardless of differences in the name of the industry. Businesses differing in these characteristics have different profitability, regardless of similarity on the name of the industry (*The Pims Program*, pp. 17–18).

PIMS clearly asserted that business laws were like the laws of physics. It was an argument that strategy is widely generalizable. In essence, it

Exhibit 10.1   *Perspectives of Marketing Strategy*

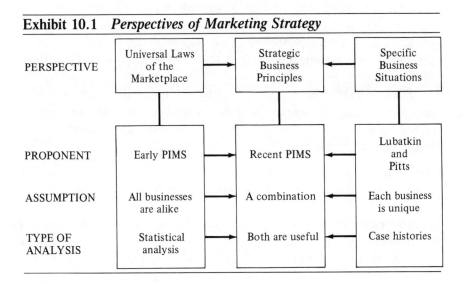

PERSPECTIVE	Universal Laws of the Marketplace	Strategic Business Principles	Specific Business Situations
PROPONENT	Early PIMS	Recent PIMS	Lubatkin and Pitts
ASSUMPTION	All businesses are alike	A combination	Each business is unique
TYPE OF ANALYSIS	Statistical analysis	Both are useful	Case histories

argued that all businesses are alike. It also implied that the statistical analysis of pooled experience is prefereable to the study of individual case histories. In support of that view, PIMS researchers offered the results of multiple regression. Proponents claimed that the model "explains" a substantial percentage of the variance in profitability among the businesses in the database. If businesses were affected in different ways, then the model would not perform as well as it does. The use of pooled business experience, they argue, is a defendable practice supported by the facts.

Specific Situations: Is Each Business Unique?

The right end of the continuum shown in Exhibit 10.1 is the argument "that no two businesses or industries are exactly alike: Each business represents a unique blend of internal competencies and market demands" (Lubatkin and Pitts 1985, p. 88). Consequently, the statisitcal analysis of pooled business experience is likely to be of limited value. It is specific situations that most affect profitability, not universal laws. The industry in which a business competes, and the way in which it creatively constructs a strategy, affects performance more than any set of immutable laws.

Critics of PIMS argue that the subjective and creative nature of strategy precludes the discovery of universal laws. Such laws might be useful in physics, where the phenomena under study behave in an orderly fashion throughout the universe, but in business, where irregularities occur regularly, laws are likely to be difficult to establish and surfeit with exceptions. PIMS critics contend that context is more important (Lubatkin and Pitts 1985). It is an argument for the case-study approach to the analysis of strategy over a statistical approach. Each business must be judged on its individual merits.

Critics of PIMS are also disturbed by the implication that universal laws of marketing strategy imply an easy way to win the game of business competition. They claim that in the past such simplifications have deceived more often than they helped.

Strategic Principles: A Realistic Compromise

More recently, PIMS has withdrawn from the extreme position that there are ironclad laws of the marketplace. Proponents now contend that there are "general strategic principles" but that those principles must be tailored to fit a particular business. It is not enough to merely know the principles; it is equally important to know the industry.

One empirical study found support for this more moderate position. Using data drawn from the brewing industry, it found that "Universal truths appear to be generalizable to specific industry sectors and over time" (Lubatkin and Pitts 1983, p. 42). It also found that an industry model performed about as well as the model using the entire PIMS database.

PIMS researchers do not admit to a change of position. They blame management consultants for overselling the universal laws proposed early on. Buzzell and Gale (1987) state: "We do not claim to have discovered universal or precise laws of strategy, like those of physics" (p. 6). Instead, they argue for general relationships and principles that guide management decisions. It is a fallback position to be sure, but it is a more accurate and defendable position given the empirical evidence.

The middle-ground position seems to be the most reasonable. Both extremes are too extreme. It is as ridiculous to claim that there are *no* principles of business strategy as it is to say that there are ironclad laws that hold in all cases. Clearly, some generalizations are possible. Market share, product quality, and investment intensity, to name but a few, affect all businesses. Today, PIMS reports on factors that affect *all* businesses and factors that are situation specific. It makes for a more complicated but accurate analysis. What follows is a discussion of the most important PIMS findings.

A Brief History of PIMS

PIMS began as the PROM program at the General Electric Corporation in 1960. GE competes in businesses ranging from nuclear power plant construction, gas turbines, consumer electronics, light bulbs, and refrigerators. Each business has different characteristics, different strategies, and different levels of profitability. GE sought to discover why some of its businesses were more profitable than others. For over ten years GE used the PROM project.

In 1972 PIMS was moved to the Marketing Science Institute, a powerhouse in the study of marketing, which is affiliated with the Harvard Business School. At this stage in its development, PIMS was expanded beyond GE to include many other businesses and grew rapidly during the 1970s. Most important, the strategic principles discovered at GE were supported using data from many companies. There was reason to believe that all businesses were affected by the same determinants of profitability.

In 1975 the Strategic Planning Institute (SPI) was formed to manage the PIMS project. SPI, located in Cambridge, Massachusetts, is a nonprofit organization made up of the very firms that provide data to the PIMS model. Firms were willing to contribute data to the project knowing that they would decide how that data would be used. PIMS has remained at SPI since 1975, and, over the past fifteen years, has grown and prospered.

Popular Uses of PIMS

PIMS is used to solve practical business problems and examine academic issues. Among the more popular uses are:

EVALUATING FINANCIAL PERFORMANCE

PIMS offers firms a point of comparison with other firms that face similar strategic situations. They can compare themselves with strategic "look-alikes."

ANALYZING STRATEGIC CHANGES' EFFECT ON PROFITS

PIMS allows firms to see how changes in marketing strategy will affect profitability before they actually make those changes. Using the PIMS model as a simulation, firms can observe how similar firms fared when they made those changes. They might, for example, see what will happen if they increase spending on new product development.

IDENTIFYING STRATEGIC OPPORTUNITIES

By observing the experience of other firms through the PIMS model it is possible to recognize opportunities to make strategic changes that will lead to higher profits. A firm, for example, might observe the results of firms that increased marketing and R&D expenditures.

EVALUATING DIVERSIFICATION OPPORTUNITIES

Firms can use the pooled experience of other firms to decide which new businesses to enter. They can evaluate the potential of other businesses before they actually diversify. Firms may discover opportunities to enter a business through acquisition and make strategic changes that may have led to higher profits in similar situations in other industries.

IDENTIFYING THE MOST IMPORTANT VARIABLES

Finally, and most important from an academic perspective, PIMS makes it possible to identify which strategy variables are most influential. To date, many studies have been published in academic journals and the business press using the PIMS database. Those studies have increased our understanding of marketing strategy.

The PIMS Methodology

PIMS is a statistical model. No discussion of PIMS would be complete without a discussion of the methodology upon which it is based. This section presents the sample, the key variables, and the method of analysis used in the PIMS model. It also shows the changes that have occurred in the model over the years since it was first reported to the public.

THE SAMPLE

The PIMS database has grown steadily over the years. Published reports of PIMS results show the following growth in the sample size:

Year	Companies	Businesses
1970	36	350
1972	57	620
1980	200	1,700
1984	450	3,000

Types of Businesses

The PIMS sample is skewed heavily in favor of large, mature American manufacturing businesses. Service businesses, Asian competitors, and small, high-technology start-ups make up only a small percentage of the sample. PIMS relies heavily on the bedrock of American manufacturing. Still, PIMS researchers' claim that strategic factors are more influential than the industry in which it competes implies that the focus on manufacturing does not overly restrict PIMS generalizations.

Definition of a PIMS Business

PIMS analyzes data at the business level, not company level. In other words, the sample consists of the nearly 3,000 businesses for which data are collected, a large sample by any standard.

PIMS defines a business in a manner similar to that of Strategic Business Units (SBU). A business must sell: (1) a distinct set of related products or services, (2) to an identifiable set of consumers, (3) in competition with an identifiable set of competitors, and (4) for which meaningful separation of strategic and accounting data can be made. To be included in the database, participating firms must meet those criteria.

Protecting Company Data

PIMS collects proprietary data that is not available to the general public. The way in which it ensures the confidentiality of that data is nothing short of ingenious. All dollar data are multiplied by a fraction that is known only to the firm providing the data. Even if competitors were able to obtain the original data, it would be of limited value.

Scaling the data does not affect the results. PIMS constructs financial ratios that are not affected by the multiplication. For example, a firm might earn $1,000 on sales of $10,000. Multiplied by 0.5, the firm might report earnings of $500 on sales of $5,000. In either case, the return would be 10 percent.

Furthermore, multiple regression, the statistical technique used by PIMS, examines relationships among variables, not the absolute value of the variables themselves. In this case also, the analysis is intransigent to multiplication by scalars. Finally, PIMS organizational structure— where member firms control the use of the data they submit—ensures that confidentiality is maintained.

Variables Examined

PIMS examines the effects of dozens of variables on profitability. In the mid-1970s the model examined thirty-seven variables that influenced profitability. In addition, combinations of those thirty-seven variables were constructed to measure "interactive effects," which resulted in a total of sixty individual measures. More recently, the model focuses on twenty-two variables.

PIMS variables fall into three categories:

1. *prevailing conditions in the market,* which includes variables such as the growth rate of the market, and the extent to which product differentiation is important
2. *the competitive position of the firm* providing the data, which includes variables such as the firm's market share, and the quality of the products it produces
3. *the strategy employed by the firm,* which includes variables such as pricing, R&D expenditures, and marketing expenditures

PIMS considers many variables which can also be classified according to whether they are of primary interest to marketing or not. Among the variables considered are:

Marketing-Related Variables	*Non-Marketing-Related Variables*
market growth rate	R&D expenditures
product differentiation	inventory expenditures
product quality	exports-imports
market share	fixed capital intensity
new product introductions	plant newness
marketing expenditures	capacity utilization
purchase concentration	vertical integration
pricing	employee productivity
rate of price inflation	unionization

PIMS also measures the financial performance of each firm providing data. The most important measure of financial performance is Return on Investment (ROI), the amount of resources expended by the firm to earn a return. ROI is calculated as:

$$ROI = \frac{Income - Expenses}{Investment}$$

where: Investment = Assets − Current Liabilities

PIMS employs two other measures of financial performance in addition to ROI—return on sales (ROS) and a more nebulous measure called "long-term value enhancement," which avoids the criticism that PIMS focuses on short-term preformance. For the most part, the findings are robust to the different performance measures. To simplify the discussion, the remainder of this chapter focuses on ROI.

DATA ANALYSIS

PIMS is constructed using a single equation, multiple linear regression analysis similar to that described in any basic statistics textbook. Multiple regression analysis designates one variable as the "dependent variable" (DV) and many variables as "independent variables" (IV). Using statistical correlations, regression analysis assesses which independent variables are most "related" to the dependent variable.

The dependent variable—ROI—is a function of twenty-two independent variables grouped into three categories—market conditions, the firm's competitive position, and its strategy. That is:

ROI = f(market conditions, competition position, strategy)

Changes in the market conditions, competitive position, and strategy of firms are hypothesized to affect profitability.

In the language of regression analysis, the IVs "explain" changes (variance) in the profitability from one firm to the next (the ROI of firms in the database ranges from -25 to 80 percent).

The measure used to assess the strength of those relationships is called "R-square," which ranges from 0 to 1. If R-square is close to zero, then the IVs are not correlated with the DV. If R-square is close to one, then changes in the IVs from one firm to the next closely mirror changes in the DV. Although statistics texts emphasize that correlations do not prove causality, the implication is that the IVs are influencing the DV.

How good is the PIMS model? In the mid-1970s, Schoeffler, Buzzell, and Heany (1974) reported an R-square of 0.8, an impressive result. Precisely stated, it meant that 80 percent of the variation in profits from one firm to the next could be accounted for by changes in market conditions, the firm's competitive position and strategy, which were measured by thirty-seven individual variables (and combinations of those terms to measure interactive effects). Only 20 percent of the variation in profits could not be accounted for by the model and, by inference, could be attributed to factors that were specific to individual firms or industries. There were, it seemed, universal laws of the marketplace. Strategy could be generalized broadly across many industries.

In more recent years PIMS reports less impressive statistical findings, but as a model, is more defendable in terms of "good" statistical design. Buzzell and Gale (1987) report on the results of a simple model that considers the direct effect of twenty-two IVs on ROI. An R-square of 0.4 was found—only 40 percent of the variation in profits from one firm to the next could be attributed to variation in the twenty-two IVs examined using this simple model. It is a less impressive result, but one that still has value.

Interactive Effects

A more complex version of the PIMS model includes additional IVs that account for statistical interactions. That model explains more variance, yielding an R-square of 0.7.

Direct effects, such as those measured in the simple model, are effects that hold for all businesses. As product quality increases, for example, profits tend to increase also.

Interactive effects are different. They allow PIMS researchers to account for effects that apply differently to different businesses. The inclusion of interactive effects is, in part, an attempt to overcome the criticism that there are no universal laws of the marketplace. Some industries are affected by the independent variables in different ways than others. It is also an attempt to capture the observation that the effects of the independent variables are not independent of one another. In many cases, they move together. There are three general types of interactive effects:

Offsetting effects occur when two independent variables affect profits in opposite ways. For example, heavy spending for investment leads to lower profits, but it also leads to higher productivity, which leads to higher profits. One variable pushes profits down, the other pushes profits up. In this case, the net effect is negative, investment intensity leads to lower profits.

Reinforcing effects occur when two independent variables combine to have a synergistic effect on profits. High market share, for example, leads to higher profits. Increasing product quality also leads to higher profits. But when both market share and product quality are high, ROI increases greatly. It is the strategic equivalent of the arithmetic impossibility $1 + 1 = 3$.

Reversing effects occur when individual firms are affected differently by IVs. PIMS has found, for example, that vertical integration—owning your buyers and suppliers—is best in low-growth markets, where change is slow. In such instances, owning the entire channel of distribution and production creates economies of scale. In high-growth markets, however, where change in rapid, vertical integration hurts profits. Vertical integration reduces the firm's flexibility to respond to market changes. They are tied into a single product and channel. Reversing effects capture the strategic moves may be good in some instances, but poor choices in others.

Interactive effects make theoretical sense but create methodological problems. They allow PIMS researchers to account for theoretical relationships. But they also provide fodder for those who claim that too many variables have been used in the equation, making the model unreliable and unbelievable. Armstrong (1970), for example, has shown that by using regression in a manner similar to that used by PIMS, it is possible to generate impressive R-square statistics using random numbers as the database. Large numbers of independent variables negate the very premise of the regression methodology. Armstrong argues persuasively for the greater use of a priori analysis, the use of fewer variables, and that more attention be paid to potentially useful theoretical relationships. By many accounts the PIMS model is flawed by the large number of IVs it incorporates. To some, it is indicative of bad statistical practice.

Cross-Sectional Analysis

Although PIMS has collected data for many years, the results are reported for cross-sectional data. That is, PIMS examines differences among firms at one point in time. PIMS does not, for example, trace changes in product quality over time for a single firm to see how it affects profitability. Instead, PIMS compares firms that currently have high product quality with firms that currently have low product quality. It is not a longitudinal analysis. On a positive note, cross-sectional analysis does allow PIMS researchers to use the most recent data to report results.

Selected PIMS Findings

PIMS findings have been remarkably consistent over the past twenty years. Since its early days at GE, the same independent variables have repeatedly shown up as the dominant determinants of business profitability. Such consistency supports the proposition that PIMS researchers have, in fact, discovered generalizable "strategic principles" of the marketplace. It lends credence to the advice they offer.

It is no accident that PIMS stands for the Profit Impact of Market Strategy. Marketing variables play an especially prominent role in explaining business profits. This chapter discusses three of the most important independent variables in the PIMS model: (1) market share, (2) product quality, and (3) investment intensity. Special attention is paid to the relationship between market share and product quality, a point where PIMS has made a particularly important contribution. The reader is referred to sources listed in the bibliography for a detailed discussion of variables that have a less important effect on profitability and lie mostly outside the domain of marketing.

MARKET SHARE

Consistent with the advice of the BCG, PIMS has found a strong correlation between market share and profitability. High-share firms in the PIMS database have consistently shown higher profits than low-share firms.

Measuring Market Share

PIMS measures market share in at least four different ways: (1) absolute share, the actual share of industry sales, (2) market share rank, (e.g., first, second, third), (3) market share "relative to largest" share firm, and (4) share "relative to three largest" firms in the market. Generally, the same results are found using any measure. Again, PIMS findings are robust to different measures of market share.

Five Times Share Equals Three Times Profits

The extent to which market share affects ROI has also remained constant over the years. Schoeffler, Buzzell, and Heany (1974) reported on the performance of the 620 businesses then in the PIMS sample: "Businesses with market shares above 36 percent earned more than three times as much, relative to investment, as businesses with less than 7 percent share of their respective markets" (p. 141). That is, profits went up by more than three times every time share went up by more than five times.

Five years later, Gale and Branch (1979) reported nearly identical results. Businesses with five times the share of smaller competitors had approximately three times the profits.

Schoeffler (1984) reported on the results of the expanded database of 1,700 businesses. A similar relationship was found between share and profits.

Finally, Buzzell and Gale (1987) describe the relationship between market share and ROI based on 2,611 sample businesses. They note:

Exhibit 10.2 *Market Share and Profitability*

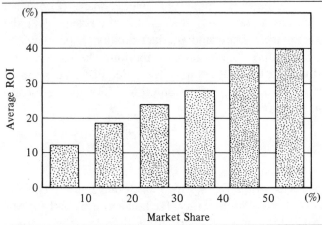

SOURCE: Reprinted with permission of The Free Press, a Division of Macmillan, Inc., from *The PIMS Principles: Linking Strategy to Performance* by Robert D. Buzzell and Bradley T. Gale, p. 9. Copyright © 1987 by The Free Press.

"Business units with very large market shares—over 50 percent of their served markets—enjoy rates of return more than three times greater than small-share SBUs (those that serve under 10 percent of their markets)" (p. 8). Their findings are presented graphically in Exhibit 10.2. Again, five times share leads to three times profits.

Reconciling PIMS' and BCG's View of Share

Although PIMS researchers agree that higher share leads to higher profits, they find a weaker effect than that proposed by BCG. BCG claims that market share has a profound effect on profits. PIMS argues that the effect is overstated. Buzzell and Gale claim: "The experience curve approach leads to exaggerated estimates of the effects of relative scale and experience" (p. 78). They note: "We agree with the assumptions of the Growth-Share portfolio system about the *direction* of impact of market share, but not about its *magnitude*" (p. 78). Market share leads to higher profits but it is not the only, or even the most important, influence on business profits.

In retrospect, BCG placed too much emphasis on market share. That approach to strategy proposed that gains in market share lead to tremendous gains in profits. PIMS, by studying the issue empirically, has established that market share is an important determinant of business profits but it is not the only factor to be considered.

Reconciling PIMS' and Porter's View of Share

Porter's view of market share and profitability is contradictory to both PIMS and the BCG. Recall from Chapter 6 that Porter postulates a "U-shaped" curve to explain the relationship between market share and profitability. High-share firms earn higher profits because of economies of scale, market power, and other competitive advantages. Small-share firms, however, also earn higher profits due to flexibility and ability to adapt to constantly changing trends. Medium-sized firms are "stuck in the middle." They possess neither advantage. It contradicts the view that profits do not increase with market share.

It is possible to reconcile that discrepancy by looking at the different ways in which PIMS and Porter define a market. PIMS looks at the served market, while Porter studies industries, a broader measure of markets. In the auto industry, for example, Mercedes, a very profitable maker of luxury automobiles, would have a low share of a broadly defined market under Porter's industry analysis. Mercedes would earn high profits even though it had only a small share of total automobile sales. Mercedes would be given a high share of the luxury auto market, its "served market," by PIMS researchers. It would have a high share and earn high profits.

Which definition is best? Buzzell and Gale argue persuasively for the served-market definition. They argue that Mercedes does not really compete with Volkswagen; Mercedes competes with other luxury car makers, such as BMW. It is a persuasive argument. The PIMS definition more closely mirrors the scope of competition. The most important observation, however, is that different views of how market share affects profitability are not as contradictory as they seem at first glance. Higher market share leads to higher profits.

PRODUCT QUALITY

Recently, business researchers have discovered the importance of product quality. It is not a discovery to PIMS. Product quality has always played a prominent role in the PIMS model. One of the major contributions of PIMS is its long-standing recognition that product quality has a strong effect on profits. While market share dominated the strategy literature for decades, to the near exclusion of other variables, PIMS consistently reported a central role for product quality. From the beginning PIMS has argued that higher quality leads to higher profits.

Exhibit 10.3 shows a typical relationship between product quality

Exhibit 10.3   *Product Quality and Profitability*

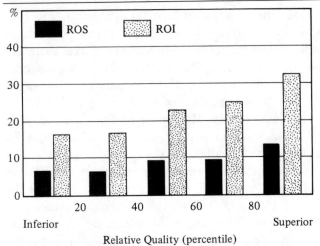

SOURCE: Reprinted with permission of The Free Press, a Division of Macmillan, Inc., from *The PIMS Principles: Linking Strategy to Performance* by Robert D. Buzzell and Bradley T. Gale, p. 107. Copyright © 1987 by The Free Press.

and profits. That relationship is not contingent on other factors. Higher product quality increases profits across the board, not just in selected situations. It is one of the most robust findings of the PIMS model.

Measuring Product Quality

Product quality is more ambiguous than most other PIMS concepts. It means different things to different people. Hence, it is more difficult to define and measure. That probably explains why it has been avoided by many researchers until recently. Most studies on product quality have focused on the more easily quantifiable concept of quality control. But, product quality is more encompassing than quality control. It includes the more marketing-oriented view of product quality as prestige goods— the finest product on the market.

The next chapter deals with the components of product quality in greater detail. This chapter focus only the PIMS view of quality.

PIMS employs a subjective measure of product quality. Since its early days at General Electric, PIMS has relied on ''the judgment of executives and staff specialists in the participating companies'' (Buzzell 1978, p. 2). The measure is admittedly imperfect, and an easy target for criticism, but it constitutes a valiant effort at measuring a slippery concept.

PIMS measured quality differently before 1980 than after 1980. In both cases, however, the PIMS view of quality has been more encompassing than the restrictive view of quality control. It is a concept of strategy more in tune with marketing's view of quality.

Before 1980, PIMS asked executives to estimate the percentage of the products produced by their business units that were: (1) superior, (2) inferior, and (3) equivalent to those sold by competitors. An "index of product quality" was then created by subtracting the inferior rating from the superior rating. Consider, for example, a business unit that makes and sells a complete line of baby carriages and strollers. Taking the consumers' perspective an executive might estimate: (1) 50 percent of the unit's carriages and strollers are superior to competitors' products, (2) 15 percent are inferior, and (3) the remaining 35 percent are equivalent in terms of quality. PIMS calculates 50 percent minus 15 percent for a product quality index of 35.

In 1980 PIMS switched to a standard multi-attribute model to measure product quality. The model consists of three parts:

First, executives list the attributes that consumers deem most important in evaluating the product. For baby carriages and strollers those attributes might be styling, availability of service, and reliability.

Second, executives give an "importance weight" to each attribute to denote how important each attribute is to consumers when they purchase the product. If styling is the most important attribute, it might be given 60 percent. Reliability might be weighted 30 percent and service, the least important attribute, only 10 percent.

Third, executives give a "rating" between 0 and 10 for their unit's products and those of leading competitors. The unit's strollers might be very reliable—score a 9—but offer less service than competitors do—score 3.

Importance weights are then multiplied by the ratings and summed to give a quality of profile for each competitor's products. A quality profile for the business unit that makes carriages and strollers might appear is presented in Exhibit 10.4.

RELATIONSHIP BETWEEN PRODUCT QUALITY AND MARKET SHARE

The greatest contribution of recent PIMS studies has been its empirical observations and theoretical suppositions about how market share and product quality are related to one another, as well as profits. PIMS is unique in its treatment of those two important marketing variables.

Exhibit 10.4   *Example of Quality Profiling for Carriages and Strollers*

Product Attribute	Importance Weight	Business "A" Rating	Rating × Weight	Business "B" Rating	Rating × Weight
Styling	.60	8	(× .6 = 4.8)	3	(× .6 = 1.8)
Service	.10	2	(× .1 = 0.2)	7	(× .1 = 0.7)
Reliability	.30	5	(× .3 = 1.5)	9	(× .3 = 2.7)
	1.00	Quality Score = 6.5		Quality Score = 5.2	

Conclusions:
1. Styling is more important to consumers than reliability.
2. Business "A" has better styling than Business "B."
3. Business "B" makes more reliable products than Business "A."
4. Business "A" has higher quality products.

High Share and High Quality Go Together

Since its initial disclosure to the public in 1974, PIMS has reported that market share and product quality are related. High-share firms tend to have higher quality products.

The relationship is by no means rare. Over the years, up to 50 percent of the firms in the PIMS database have reported both a high share of their served markets and a high-quality profile! In the PIMS sample there is a large, but elite, corps of firms that seem to do everything well.

High Share and High Quality Offset Each Other

Exhibit 10.5 summarizes the relationship between product quality, market share, and profitability that have been reported by PIMS since the mid-1970s. It shows the consistency of those relationships, even though PIMS switched measures of quality in mid-stream.

The table also shows that share and quality exhibit offsetting effects. High-share firms with low-quality products have earned, on average, an ROI of 23 percent since 1974. In contrast, low-share firms with high-quality products have earned 18 percent, a similar rate of return. It seems that either share or quality can increase profits. Consistent with Porter's notion of pursuing a strategy of either differentiation (low-share/high-quality) or low-cost producer (high-share/lower-quality) can lead to business success.

Exhibit 10.5 *ROI by Product Quality and Market Share*

MARKET SHARE

PRODUCT QUALITY		Low	High
	Low	1974 4% 1978 11 1987 10 Average 8	1974 20% 1978 23 1987 26 Average 23
	High	1974 17% 1978 20 1987 18 Average 18	1974 28% 1978 35 1987 37 Average 31

High Share and High Quality Reinforce Each Other

But, unlike Porter's view, and consistent with criticisms of Porter, the most important observation to be gleaned from Exhibit 10.5 is the reinforcing effect between share and quality. PIMS has repeatedly shown that having a high share of a served market *and* high-quality products leads to the highest level of profits, an average of 31 percent over the years since the study was first reported. Apparently, as critics argue, there is an elite group of very successful firms that are able to compete as sellers of high-quality goods and low-cost producers.

Theoretical Connections

Based on results using PIMS data, Phillips, Chang, and Buzzell (1983) propose a theoretical framework for explaining the relationship between quality, share, and profitability. Exhibit 10.6 illustrates the proposed theoretical connections, and shows the following patterns of causality.

Market Share Leads to Lower Costs

PIMS and BCG both agree that higher market share leads to lower costs. But the BCGs heavy reliance on the experience curve overstates the effect of lower costs on profits. PIMS agrees that higher market share leads to lower costs, which, in turn, leads to higher profits. But, as Exhibit 10.6 illustrates, PIMS views higher share and lower costs as only part of the explanation. In fact, PIMS views both as a byproduct of achieving higher quality.

Exhibit 10.6 *Theoretical Framework for PIMS Variables*

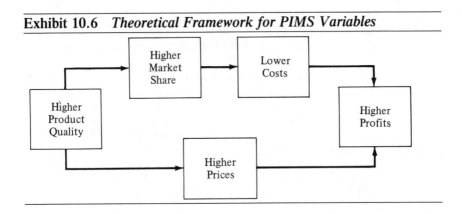

Higher Product Quality Leads to Higher Prices

PIMS contends that higher quality leads to higher prices, which, in turn, leads to higher profit margins. It is higher prices, in addition to lower costs, that causes higher margins.

Higher Quality Leads to Higher Share

The most controversial proposition offered by PIMS is the causal ordering of market share and product quality. PIMS goes farther than to observe that the two go together, arguing that higher product quality *leads to* higher share. Making and selling superior products offers a competitive advantage that draws consumers to the firm's products, thereby increasing the firm's share of the market. That is, quality leads to share. Higher share is not a goal to be pursued, as was argued by the BCG, but a result of pursuing a strategy aimed at producing higher-quality products. That is the essence of PIMS strategic advice: aim for higher-quality products and share gains will follow.

PIMS does not dispute the fact that higher market share has an important impact on profits. PIMS continues to believe that scale effects, reducing risk for consumers, market power, and good management accrue to high-share firms and increase profits. Researchers simply believe that another relationship is more important. Quality supercedes share as the goal of good marketing strategy.

In recent years, PIMS argument for focusing on product quality over market share has become more forceful. Those arguments have increasingly found a more receptive audience. Today, as never before, product quality has moved to the forefront of modern marketing thought. Whether PIMS is the cause of that new-found interest, or merely a reflection of it, is difficult to assess. PIMS is, however, discussing current issues indeed.

Finally, it is important to note that PIMS theoretical assertions explain empirical observations better than other marketing strategy formulations. Specifically, it is better able to account for the observation that high share and high quality go together, a key criticism of Porter's three generic strategies, which argue that a firm should pursue either differentiation (a rough surrogate for product quality) or go for high market share through lower costs.

Product "Value"

PIMS researchers have also been interested in a variant of the product quality issue—the topic of product value. Product value is concerned with the price that is charged for high-quality products. Exhibit 10.7 illustrates four possible pricing strategies and their effect on market share and profit margins.

High-quality products can command premium prices, which increase profit margins. It is an acceptable strategy, but it is not the best. Chussil and Schoeffler (1983) contend that moderately higher prices combined with higher-quality products lead to the highest profits. Firms that charge a moderate price premium for high-quality products gain two distinct benefits: (1) they earn slightly higher profit margins, and (2) much higher market share. They provide consumers with better product value.

A recent study by Anterasian and Phillips (1988) for the Marketing Science Institute argues even more forcefully for the product value. Those researchers found that delivering "value" to consumers leads to

Exhibit 10.7 *Pricing Product Quality*

		RELATIVE PRICE	
		Low	High
PRODUCT QUALITY	Low	Low-Price Seller low margins high share	Poor Value high margins low share
	High	Product "Value" somewhat higher margins high share	Premium Pricing high margins low share

higher market share. In contrast, they found no support for the proposition that higher market share leads directly to higher profits. They claim that market share does not now, and never did, increase profitability. Similar to PIMS, but even more extreme, they contend that product value rather than market share is the key determinant to profits.

Advertising and Pricing

Marketing expenditures play an important role in explaining profitability. A study by Farris and Reibstein (1979) examined the question: How much should be spent on advertising? Their results show that advertising expenditures should be *consistent* with pricing. Higher-priced, higher-quality products that are supported by higher levels of advertising are most profitable. So are lower-priced, lower-quality products that receive lower levels of advertising. Both strategies are consistent. Heavy advertising for low-quality products or little advertising for high-quality products are inconsistent strategies that lead to lower profits. Consistency is the strategic principle to follow when it comes to advertising.

INVESTMENT INTENSITY

Not all factors considered in the PIMS model increase profitability. Investment intensity negatively affects profits. Businesses that require large amounts of fixed investment (plant and equipment) and/or working capital relative to the sales they generate usually earn a lower rate of return on that investment than businesses that require more modest investments. Chemical and mining companies, for example, require large investments. As a result, they earn, on average, only one-third to one-half of what supermarkets earn, which are much less investment intensive. Exhibit 10.8 shows the typical relationship between investment intensity and profits.

   Since its inception, PIMS has found investment intensity to be one of the three major determinants of business profits. It is especially important to marketers, because it leads to a destructive form of price competition.

Why Investment Intensity Hurts Profits

The problem with investment intensity can be illustrated with a simple example. Assume for a moment your firm competes in two distinct businesses: business "A" and business "B." Business "A" is investment

Exhibit 10.8 *Investment Intensity and Profitability*

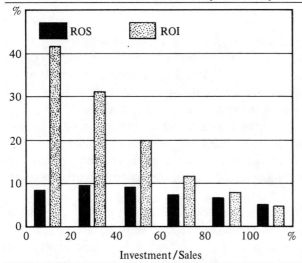

SOURCE: Reprinted with permission of The Free Press, a Division of Macmillan, Inc., from *The PIMS Principles: Linking Strategy to Performance* by Robert D. Buzzell and Bradley T. Gale, p. 139. Copyright © 1987 by The Free Press.

intensive, requiring a $1 million piece of machinery to make the necessary products. Business "B" is not investment intensive, requiring a machine that costs only $100,000. After a year, business "A" earns $80,000, while business "B" earns $10,000. Business "A" has earned more in absolute terms but it has earned a lower return on investment. One million dollars employed to earn $80,000 is an 8 percent return. One hundred thousand dollars employed to earn $10,000 is a 10 percent return. Therein lies the quandary for business investments. If business success is measured in terms of ROI, then large sales volume is required simply to cover the huge investment. It is not that investment-intensive businesses are unprofitable. It is that they cannot earn back the return to justify the large investment that must be put up front.

Changing Face of Competition

Investment intensity hurts profits for another reason as well. For more than a decade PIMS has observed that the nature of competition in investment-intensive businesses is different. That difference is most apparent in the case of an industry that is in the process of becoming more investment intensive—through increased expenditures for automation, for example, or other forms of expensive equipment.

Schoeffler (1983) presents a controversial interpretation of the data. He notes that conventional wisdom holds that large expenditures on advanced technology result in cost savings for the firm through improved productivity and economies of scale. Such expenditures are deemed to be good business practice grounded in firm economics. He argues otherwise. Such expenditures increase the level of investment intensity in an industry. The firm now has higher fixed costs to pay for that machinery, and the industry has a greater capacity to produce goods.

In times of economic expansion competitors perform well. In times of recession, however, when demand falls, severe problems arise. It is then that the nature of competition begins to change. Firms, which now have high fixed costs, must keep volume up to pay for the capacity they have added. To do so, they are forced to compete on the basis of price. Prices fall to fill capacity. Competition shifts from a focus on earning higher profits to a focus on keeping sales high. The industry degenerates into "volume grubbing." As a result, expected gains in productivity and economies of scale are passed on to the consumer in the form of lower prices. Lower costs were expected, but lower prices were the result.

Implications of Investment Intensity

The implications of PIMS findings in regard to investment intensity are profound and disturbing, as well as controversial. They imply that American business should pursue low-investment opportunities, such as services, and avoid large segments of basic manufacturing, such as steel and chemical processing. Public policy experts question whether that is a wise decision. Should American business desert heavy-investment businesses? Proponents point to two counter arguments: (1) the U.S. economy is already predominantly service oriented, and (2) a free-enterprise system encourages investments where the potential for returns are greatest. It is a difficult issue to resolve.

Improving Productivity with People

Many firms invest in expensive machinery to achieve gains in productivity. PIMS contends that those gains are usually not realized. Schoeffler (1980) refers to such investments as "bad productivity." Instead, more money should be spent improving worker productivity. "Good productivity" consists of inexpensive expenditures on: (1) worker training programs, (2) increasing worker morale, and (3) reducing restrictive union work rules. Productivity based on people is superior to productivity based on machines. It is advice that is in sync with modern times.

Criticisms of PIMS

PIMS has many critics. Most criticisms focus on the methodological shortcomings of the model itself. Some of the more common criticisms of PIMS are detailed below.

MULTICOLLINEARITY

A central assumption of multiple regression analysis is that the independent variables—market share, product quality, investment intensity—are independent of one another: they are uncorrelated. When that assumption is violated a condition known as multicollinearity is present. Statisticians contend that multicollinearity can cause peculiar results to occur that cast doubt on the findings.

Critics contend that multicollinearity is a perennial problem in the PIMS model (Naylor 1978; Anderson and Paine 1978). Lubatkin and Pitts (1983) in an empirical test "found that out of a possible sixty-six relationships, 38 percent of the relationships in the industry group suffered from high multicollinearity (p. 42).

Buzzell and Gale (1987) present contrary statistics. A correlation matrix of PIMS variables shows no strong correlations between any of the variables (p. 276). No correlation is over 0.30.

The figures are puzzling. Arguments made by Buzzell and Gale imply that there is strong multicollinearity in the PIMS database, even though the correlations show otherwise. They state: "Relative perceived quality and market share are correlated" (p. 108). An earlier study reported that 50 percent of sample firms had both a high share and high quality, an indication that at least some PIMS variables are correlated (Schoeffler, Buzzell and Heany 1974). Likewise, Phillips, Chang, and Buzzell (1983) propose the model shown in Exhibit 10.6 that holds that higher product quality *causes* higher market share, a clear implication that the two constructs are not statistically independent.

Are PIMS findings severely tainted by multicollinearity? Not really. The multicollinearity issue is of minor importance; it moves the argument from substantive to methodological issues. Furthermore, multiple regression is a robust statistical technique that performs well in the presence of all but the most severe cases of multicollinearity. PIMS variables may be correlated, but that does not discredit the findings. Multicollinearity is a nettlesome but relatively unimportant criticism.

RELATIONSHIPS DUE TO METHODOLOGICAL ARTIFACTS

The most surprising and controversial finding of the PIMS model is the negative effect of investment intensity on profitability. Critics offer an alternative explanation based, again, on methodological shortcomings of the PIMS model. Critics contend that the negative relationship between ROI and investment intensity is due to similarities in the measures, not a correlation based on substantive issues. For example, ROI is measured as follows:

$$ROI = Income/Investment$$

The large denominator in investment-intensive firms serves to lower ROI. A firm with a $10 million investment will tend to have a lower ROI than a firm with a $1 million investment.

In contrast investment intensity is measured as follows:

$$Investment\ Intensity = Investment/Sales$$

In this instance, a large numerator is present in investment-intensive firms. The firm with a $10 million investment will tend to have a higher investment intensity than a firm with a $1 million investment.

Anderson and Paine (1978) argue that the large numerator in one equation contrasts with the large denominator of the other equation to create a negative correlation due solely to similarities in the two measures. There is some support for that alternative explanation. A much weaker relationship is usually found when investment intensity is correlated with return on sales (Buzzell and Gale 1987). Similar methodological criticisms of PIMS ratios have been offered for other variables considered in the model.

LACKS PREDICTIVE VALIDITY CHECKS

A more serious criticism is that PIMS lacks meaningful tests of predictive validity. Naylor (1978) suggests that PIMS should be used to predict the ROI for sample firms one year into the future based on specific strategic advice. Then, when that year has ended, it would be possible to see how well the model and the firms did. Such a test would constitute a stronger test of "predictive" validity than the "face" validity the model now has. Face validity merely tests whether the relationships uncovered are reasonable. The more stringent test of predictive validity has not yet been performed to the satisfaction of critics.

RETROSPECTIVE RATHER THAN FORWARD LOOKING

Critics contend that PIMS strategic advice is based on what has happened in the past, not what will happen in the future. It is an argument that PIMS is retrospective—it shows what worked in the past—rather than what will work in the future.

At the heart of this issue is whether strategic advice is enduring or whether strategies that are successful in one time period are useless in another. Is past experience valuable? Or, do things change negating the paths to success that were once successful?

The consistency of PIMS findings over nearly two decades suggests that the generalizations offered by the model are enduring rather than transient. The fact that the same key variables have consistently proven to be the best predictors of ROI, even though separated by decades, lends support for PIMS findings. Even though PIMS is retrospective, its advice has value for future competition.

FOCUS ON WHAT IS MEASURABLE

Although PIMS has made great strides in trying to quantify and consider ill-defined variables such as product quality, critics contend that there are many other intangibles that are not considered by PIMS. The model does not consider differences in corporate culture, the presence of a charismatic executive, like Lee Iaccoca, or a host of other important, but qualitative, items.

ACCOUNTING DIFFERENCES AMONG FIRMS

Critics contend that accounting differences among PIMS firms make comparisons meaningless. Firms, for example, use different means of allocating expenses to SBUs. A vertically integrated firm may force one unit to buy from another of the firm's units. At what price should it buy? And, how should those prices be tabulated? PIMS researchers reply that accounting differences are minor and not systematic, and hence they have little effect.

DOES DATA FOLLOW POPULAR OPINION?

PIMS has been accused of confirming commonsense (Naylor 1978). More precisely, PIMS findings seem to mirror the popular issues of the day. Market share, a point of focus in the 1970s, was preeminent in the PIMS model of the 1970s. Schoeffler, Buzzell, and Heany (1974) note: "We shall limit our discussion to just three major determinants of return on investment" (p. 141). Market share was listed first. Quality was not even one of the top three. Instead, quality was considered a reinforcing variable for market share. PIMS considered product quality, but considered it subservient to market share.

By the 1980s the order of precedence had reversed. Product quality had moved to the forefront. Market share was deemed of secondary importance. Quality leads to higher share, not the other way around. PIMS proponents would argue that PIMS is leading popular opinion. But often, PIMS seems to be reacting to the major issues of the day as much as shaping them.

Whatever the order of precedence, PIMS still serves an important function in marketing strategy. Be it the discoverer or the popularizer of relationships, PIMS offers valuable insights into the current state of business strategy.

References

Anderson, Carl R., and Frank T. Paine. "PIMS: A Reexamintion." *Academy of Management Review,* July 1978, pp. 602–612.

Anterasian, Cathy, and Lynn Phillips. *Discontinuities, Value Delivery, and the Share-Returns Association: A Re-examination of the "Share-Causes-Profits" Controversy,* report no. 88–109, Cambridge, MA: Marketing Science Institute, 1988.

Armstrong, Scott. "How to Avoid Exploratory Research." *Journal of Advertising,* August 1970, pp. 27–30.

Buzzell, Robert. "Product Quality." *The Pimsletter,* no. 4. Cambridge, MA: Strategic Planning Institute, 1978.

Buzzell, Robert, and Bradley Gale. *The PIMS Principles: Linking Strategy to Performance.* New York: Free Press, 1987.

Chussil, Mark, and Sidney Schoeffler. *Pimsletter,* no. 5. Cambridge, MA: Strategic Planning Institute, 1983.

Farris, Paul, and David Reibstein. "How Prices, Ad Expenditures, and Profits Are Linked." *Harvard Business Review,* November-December 1979, pp. 173–184.

Gale, Bradley, and Ben Branch. "The Dispute About High-Share Businesses." *The Pimsletter,* no. 19. Cambridge, MA: Strategic Planning Institute, 1979.

Lubatkin, Michael, and Michael Pitts. "The PIMS and Policy Perspective: A Rebuttal." *Journal of Business Strategy,* Summer 1985, pp. 88–97.

Lubatkin, Michael, and Michael Pitts. "PIMS: Fact or Folklore?" *Journal of Business Strategy,* Winter 1983, pp. 38–43.

Naylor, Thomas. "PIMS: Through a Different Looking Glass." *Planning Review,* March 1978, pp. 15–32.

Phillips, Lynn, Dae Chang, and Robert Buzzell. "Product Quality, Cost Position and Business Performance: A Test of Some Key Hypotheses." *Journal of Marketing,* Spring 1983, pp. 26–43.

The Pims Program. Cambridge, MA: Strategic Planning Institute, 1980.

Schoeffler, Sidney. "Good Productivity Vs. Bad Productivity." *The Pimsletter,* no. 11. Cambridge, MA: Strategic Planning Institute, 1980.

Schoeffler, Sidney. "Market Position: Build, Hold or Harvest?" *The Pimsletter,* no. 3. Cambridge, MA: Strategic Planning Institute, 1984.

Schoeffler, Sidney. "Nine Basic Findings on Business Strategy." *The Pimsletter,* no. 1. Cambridge, MA: Strategic Planning Institute, 1980.

Schoeffler, Sidney. "The Unprofitability of Modern Technology and What to Do About It." *The Pimsletter,* no. 2. Cambridge, MA: Strategic Planning Institute, 1983.

Schoeffler, Sidney, Robert Buzzell, and Donald Heany. "Impact of Strategic Planning on Profit Performance." *Harvard Busines Review,* March–April 1974, pp. 137–145.

Chapter 11

Product Quality

Product quality has emerged as one of the most important concepts in marketing strategy. It is based on the belief that improving product quality leads to competitive advantage. The connection between product quality and other strategic concepts is clear. Differentiation, product positioning, and segmentation often take the form of providing consumers with higher-quality products than competitors. Building long-term customer satisfaction also relies heavily on improving product quality.

Most research on product quality does not take a marketing perspective. More often, it focuses on a particular type of product quality, such as statistical quality control or quality assurance. This chapter reviews and interprets the literature on product quality from a marketing perspective. It places less emphasis on statistical quality control and quality assurance. Instead, the focus is on the broad-based strategic implications of total product quality.

Why Product Quality Is More Important

Before defining product quality, consider why it has become more important.

COMPETITIVE PRESSURES TO INCREASE QUALITY

In recent years, manufacturers the world over have been forced to focus more intently on product quality. It is especially true in the United States where the sheer choice of products available means that consumers can bypass products they perceive to be of low quality. Providers of goods and services alike are being forced to increase product quality in order to survive. It is no longer feasible, if it ever was, to simply place products on the market.

QUALITY ADVANTAGE OF IMPORTS

After World War II the American auto industry held a virtual monopoly over the world's largest market for automobiles. German and Japanese factories had been reduced to rubble. There was no competitive pressure for American firms to compete on the basis of quality. Consumers bought an American car or they bought nothing. There were far fewer options. Competition was less severe.

Compounding the problem was the fact, as well as the perception, that the quality of imports was generally lower than that of American goods. Toyota's first entry into the American market was the Toyopet, a less than memorable product. In fact, "made in Japan" was synonymous with shoddy goods in the 1950s. But, the quality of imports increased faster than the quality of most American products. By the 1970s, Japanese products were no longer perceived as shoddy. Instead, they provided "Oh, what a feeling," as Toyota's ads once crowed. Foreign producers garnered a growing share of American markets by providing American consumers with better built products.

THE MOVE TOWARDS GLOBAL MARKETS

The trend towards global markets and global competition means that American markets are no longer captive to domestic manufacturers. Furthermore, American consumers are not especially loyal to domestic products just because they are produced domestically. Campaigns like "Crafted in Pride in the USA," which attempt to persuade American consumers to buy American-made goods, have been only marginally successful. American consumers are more persuaded by product quality than country of origin. An American firm that cannot compete on the basis of quality cannot expect to be favored by American consumers.

QUALITY IS MORE IMPORTANT TO CONSUMERS

Much of the emphasis on product quality has been brought about by consumers themselves, who today are willing to pay more for products that are better made. L. L. Bean, for example, charges more for its products, but finds consumers are willing to pay for the higher quality provided. The firm has been immensely successful.

The demand for higher quality has accelerated in recent years. Consider, again, the auto industry. In the 1950s and 1960s consumers valued superficial styling over reliability. Attractive "fins" were more important to consumers than the frequency of repairs. Consumers were so enamored of styling and so undemanding of quality that American manufacturers were routinely accused of "planned obsolescence." Automakers would make autos that fell apart, or fell out of fashion, after a few years. Consumers would then be forced to return to the showroom to buy another model, keeping sales high and the useful life of the product low. The arrogance of such a plan, whether real or imagined, illustrates the minor role product quality played in earlier decades. It also indicates how consumer demands for quality can change markets.

QUALITY IS SUSTAINABLE

Competitive advantage is easy to propose but difficult to sustain. Most competitive advantages can be easily copied by competitors. Innovations can be reverse engineered, price cuts can be easily matched, and unique selling propositions can be quickly rendered commonplace.

Quality advantages, however, are more difficult to copy over the short term. Perceptions of product quality take longer to form and carry a heavier psychological component. Competitors who have historically offered consumers lower-end, lower-quality products, which have produced dissatisfied customers, have an especially difficult time wooing back customers lost because of a bad experience. Even when quality is raised (as measured by objective standards), consumers' negative perceptions will linger. There is often a long lag in consumers' perceptions of quality. Just ask the American auto industry.

Flint (1989) observes that owners of Japanese imports are often reluctant to switch back to American brands. As satisfied customers of Japanese products, they will even pay a premium for what they perceive to be higher-quality products. Those consumers are especially reluctant to switch back to brands with which they had a bad experience in the past. As one Cadillac-Oldsmobile dealer noted: "It's easy to lose a customer; it will take time to bring him back to us" (p. 266).

Buick has faced an equally nettlesome problem with perception. In 1989, Buick captured two out of the top ten positions in the prestigious J. D. Power survey for the fewest breakdowns in the first ninety days of ownership (Levin 1989). American automakers are now producing cars of near-equal quality to imports. Still, many consumers base their opinions on perceptions drawn from past experiences with American cars. They continue to judge Japanese cars as being better. That inertia can be used to gain a sustainable competitive advantage.

LEGAL LIABILITY

A final reason why product quality has become more important is the dramatic rise in the amount of money paid out by firms held liable for making shoddy, defective, or dangerous products. Firms are now forced to pay dearly afterwards for products that they do not make well beforehand. Product safety and design has improved greatly.

What Is Product Quality?

Product quality is a slippery term that when examined closely means different things to different people. Everyone recognizes a quality product when he or she sees one, everyone wants such a product, and consumers agree it is a good thing. But what is product quality, really? Is it a product that breaks down less frequently? That makes Casio a high-quality watch. Or, is it a premium good? That makes Alpha Romeo a quality car, even though its reliability has been less than that of Japanese imports. Is it providing consumers with products they want? That makes Chrysler's Caravan a high-quality car. Or is it a combination of all those qualities?

There are four broad views of product quality, each of which is closely related to one of the "orientations towards markets" presented in Chapter 1. Each view focuses on either consumers, producers, or engineers. In addition, there are eight elements of product quality that characterize each of these viewpoints (Garvin 1987, 1988). Exhibit 11.1 summarizes the four viewpoints and eight elements of product quality.

PRODUCTS THAT WORK: A PRODUCTION ORIENTATION

The first view of quality focuses on the reliability and durability of products. It is a manufacturing-based view of product quality that embraces the production concept. Quality products are those that need fewer

Exhibit 11.1   *Viewpoints and Elements of Product Quality*

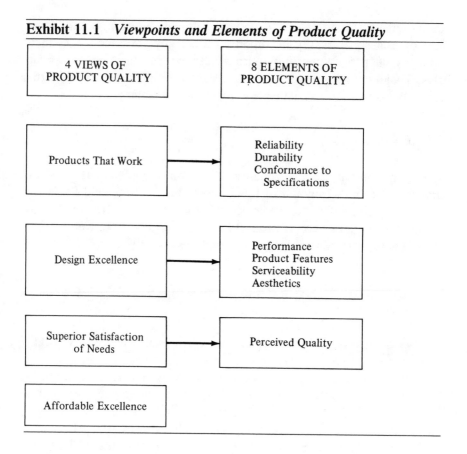

repairs and last longer than competitors' products. Improving product quality is accomplished by implementing procedures that make products work better for a longer period of time.

1. Reliability

Reliability is concerned with the number of breakdowns a customer experiences after purchasing a product. It is an objective measure of quality that can be tracked with greater precision than the more subjective measures of product quality.

Reliability tracks rework—the extent to which products are rejected and then fixed; and scrappage rates—the waste generated by defective products. Port (1987) estimates: "The typical factory invests a staggering 20 to 25 percent of its operating budget in finding and fixing mistakes" (p. 132). More ominous, he notes: "As many as one-quarter of all factory hands don't produce anything—they just rework things that were not done right the first time'' (p. 132).

Measures of reliability rely heavily on statistical quality control and assurance procedures, and include mean time until first failure (MTFF) and mean time between failures (MTBF).

Consumers assess reliability not only in absolute terms—the sheer number of breakdowns; but in relative terms—in comparison with competitors' products. In the 1920s, for example, all autos were unreliable and broke down frequently. Today, standards of reliability are higher, and still rising. Products are held to prevailing standards of the day. Firms compete against prevailing, not historical, standards of product quality.

2. Durability

Durability is a different concept than reliability. It is a measure of a product's lifespan. It measures how long a product lasts, and what its useful life will be. This is more difficult to measure than reliability. Products that are unreliable can be scrapped early to avoid additional repair costs. Conversely, lifespan can be extended with frequent repairs, preventive maintenance, and complete overhauls. Durability and reliability are distinct but interrelated terms.

Durability is dependent on product category. Consumers always want more reliable products. But, in our throwaway society, they may not value products that last forever. Robert Hall, for example, the discount seller of durable men's suits that went out of business in the early 1970s, failed, in part, because the firm's marketing strategy was to sell suits that lasted a long time. In earlier decades, when styles changed more slowly, and a suit was a luxury item, it was a successful strategy. By the 1970s, however, consumers were more concerned with fashion than durability. Few consumers wanted a suit that lasted for decades (Hartley 1981).

3. Conformance to Specifications

Reliability and durability are often judged against specifications set by the firm. One firm, for example, might be willing to accept a 10 percent rework rate. Another may set higher specifications. Lower standards are easily met but lead to lower levels of quality. Higher standards are more difficult to meet but lead to higher levels of quality.

Standards are often set to achieve a point of differentiation for marketing strategy. Maytag, for example, stresses the highest standards of reliability and durability. But, meeting standards for quality is a different concept than producing uniformly high-quality products.

Prevalence of Reliability and Durability

Consumers often define product quality in terms of reliability and dependability. Before purchasing an automobile, for example, consumers will consult *Consumer Reports* and J. D. Power and engage in word-of-mouth discussions with friends, relatives, and neighbors in order to assess the reliability and durability of available autos. No one wants a car that breaks down frequently or falls apart after a few years of ownership.

Incomplete View

Even though reliability and durability are prevalent consumer measures of product quality, they are incomplete. In autos, for example, a Chevette was clearly a low-quality car. Consequently, it is no longer made. A Toyota, in contrast, is much more reliable, and breaks down less often and requires less maintenance. Saab and Volvo, in contrast, require extensive and expensive servicing. Does that mean they too are low-quality products? Unlikely. The Toyota is simply more reliable. It scores higher on a single dimension of product quality.

DESIGN EXCELLENCE: THE PRODUCT CONCEPT

The second view of product quality is based on the product concept, which seeks to provide consumers with the "best" product on the market. A product can be made "best" in at least three ways: (1) it can perform its designed function better than competitors' products, (2) it can have better styling, or (3) it can offer customers higher levels of service. In each instance, it is a strategy predicated on uncompromising standards. Consumers are offered state-of-the-art products.

Premium Goods Strategy

Design excellence is often implemented as a premium goods strategy. It offers premium-priced, higher-quality goods or services positioned at the high end of the market. In autos, Mercedes employs performance enhancement. In ice cream, Haagen-Dazs does the same.

Price is an important component of a premium goods strategy. It is a view of quality that charges a premium price for premium products. Amoco, for example, advertises Amoco Ultimate as the highest-quality gasoline on the market. It is a premium product with a premium price.

A premium goods strategy combines premium products, higher quality, and premium pricing. Quelch (1987) holds similar sentiments. He contends that a premium product is "of excellent quality, high priced, selectively distributed through the highest quality channels, and advertised parsimoniously" (p. 39).

Four of the eight elements of product quality correspond to this second view of quality. Each element can be used to differentiate a product from competitors' offerings.

4. Performance

Design excellence stresses superior performance. Goods and services are differentiated in terms of how well they perform the task they were designed to perform. European autos, for example, offer superior acceleration and handling. Japanese imports stress greater reliability. In television sets, Sony stresses picture quality.

Superior performance can take many forms. It can be comfort in furniture, sound quality in audio components, or air-midsoles in athletic shoes. In each instance, product quality is improved by enhancing product performance. Like reliability and durability, performance can be measured objectively. Acceleration, picture quality, and most other dimensions of performance can be easily measured. The importance of performance to consumers, however, requires a more subjective assessment.

5. Product Features

Products judged by consumers to be of higher quality usually perform more tasks than lower-quality products. Higher-end telephone answering machines, for example, allow for a wider range of operations. Top-of-the-line VCRs have in-screen viewing, picture-in-picture, and a host of other features not contained in bare-bones models. Consumers tend to impute quality from the presence of additional features.

6. Superior Service

Better service is an integral part of better product quality. Higher-quality products tend to have higher levels of service. Consumers often impute product quality with the service attached to the product.

7. Aesthetics

Styling also affects judgments of quality. Gucci watches, designer fashions, and even the Ford Taurus and Mercury Sable are examples of products that imply quality through better styling. When competitors have let designs become stale, styling can be especially important. The Ford Taurus and Mercury Sable are less innovative in performance characteristics than they are on unique styling.

Styling can serve other aspects of product quality as well Nussbaum (1988). First, styling can differentiate on the basis of "ease of product use." Hamilton (1988) shows how products have been designed specifically for elderly consumers. Products from door knobs to detergent boxes are being redesigned to accommodate the physical problems of the elderly.

Second, styling can be used to impute safety. Shorter cords on small appliances, redesigned baby products, and many other design features ensure greater product safety and seek to minimize legal liability.

Third, styling can be used for ease of assembly. Many sellers have redesigned products so that they can be manufactured with greater reliability (they usually have fewer parts) and less expensively. We return to this issue in a later chapter.

SUPERIOR SATISFACTION OF NEEDS: THE MARKETING CONCEPT

The third view of product quality is a consumer-based perspective that arises from the marketing concept. According to this view, consumers decide which products are of the highest quality. In keeping with the basic philosophy of the marketing concept, it defines high-quality products as those that best meet consumers' needs.

Most authors agree that it is essential to take the consumers' perspective of product quality. Garvin (1987) contends that "managers need a new way of thinking, a conceptual bridge to the consumer's vantage point" (p. 104). Takeuchi and Quelch (1983) voice a similar refrain, stating that many managers are not in sync with consumer perceptions. Finally, Hauser and Clausing (1988) contend that product quality may be motivated by competitive pressures, but "quality begins with the customer, whose requirements are called customer attributes" (p. 65).

This view of product quality is more ambiguous and subjective than the other views. It is difficult to measure, impressionistic, and subject to individual differences. Furthermore, consumers change their preferences regularly. As a result, this view of product quality is more difficult to implement than the ones previously discussed because it is based on perception rather than fact.

8. Perceived Quality

Of the eight elements of quality listed in Exhibit 11.1, perceived quality is the most akin to the consumer-based view. Perceived quality arises from consumers' experiences before, during, and after the sale.

Consumers often have well-formed opinions about product quality before purchase. Their opinions are based on brand names and company image, previous experience with similar products, word-of-mouth communications with friends and neighbors, and evaluative information gleaned from *Consumer Reports* and the general media.

Opinions are also influenced during the sale. Auto manufacturers, for example, have courted women customers with vigor in recent years, only to earn low marks when women visit the showroom, and are poorly treated by salesmen who remark: "Come back with your husband or boyfriend when you want to talk about the serious matters."

Similarly, after-sale experiences can also influence perceptions of quality. Objective criteria such as reliability, speed of service, and the absence of unpleasant "surprises," can all influence opinions. So can more subjective criteria, such as the reaction of friends and neighbors and post-purchase dissonance.

Long-Term Customer Satisfaction

Product quality, when viewed from the perspective of superior satisfaction of needs, is tied closely to the notion of long-term consumer satisfaction. It is a broader view of quality that includes more than merely providing more reliable products. It is a view that mirrors the rising standard of quality incorporated in today's products. Competition is moving to the broader concept of "satisfying the customer in every way before, during and after a sale" (Finkelman 1989, p. F3). A narrower view of quality as simply reducing defects is no longer enough.

The primary difference between the marketing and production views of quality is one of scope. Conformance to specifications focuses on a narrow view of quality as that which reducing defects. Superior satisfaction of needs looks at the broader issue of long-term customer satisfaction through higher product quality.

AFFORDABLE EXCELLENCE: THE CONCEPT OF PRODUCT VALUE

A final definition of product quality is a variation of design excellence. It combines price with performance in recognition that consumers will buy excellence only if they deem it to be of good value. The concept of product value was introduced in the PIMS chapter. It recognizes that premium quality products command higher prices in the marketplace. But, it holds that raising the price of those products too high destroys product value. A moderate increase in price, along with an increase in product quality, leads to the greatest profits. Consumers are satisfied because they obtain product value, while the seller earns a higher profit due to increased market share.

The notion of affordable excellence is attracting increasing attention for at least two reasons: First, value is the best defense against foreign competitors, most of whom have gained entry into American markets by selling superior quality products at affordable prices. Second, product value promotes long-term customer satisfaction, a goal clearly related to product quality. The relationship is so strong that almost by definition the firm that offers high-quality products at affordable prices is likely to keep those customers.

Quality Mix: The Need for Multiple Perspectives

Total product quality consists of more than one element of quality. It consists of a combination of the four views and eight elements of quality listed in Exhibit 11.1. Garvin (1983) refers to that combination as the quality mix—the blend of elements of product quality contained in a particular product offering.

The multidimensional nature of product quality is illustrated in a recent *Fortune* cover story that identified the 100 products that American firms make best (Knowlton 1988). To be included on that list a product "had to be state of the art—that is, at the height of innovation and technological advancement. It also had to be the most durable of its kind and provide good to great value for the price" (p. 40). That definition captures three views of product quality: (1) design excellence (performance), (2) reliability and durability, and (3) product value. America, incidentally, is the world's highest quality producer of aerospace products, agricultural equipment, computers, pharmaceuticals, and medical technology.

REINFORCING EFFECTS

The elements of quality do not exist in isolation. Higher quality on one element often implies higher levels on other elements as well. Greater reliability and durability, for example, are often associated with perceptions of higher quality among consumers. Similarly, superior service and styling often affect ratings of perceived quality. Many of the elements of quality also exert a reinforcing effect on long-term satisfaction.

Product design can reinforce reliability. Simplicity in product design, where fewer parts are used in the manufacture of goods, usually means fewer breakdowns. General Electric, for example, improved reliability and lowered costs by reducing the number of parts in its refrigerators from fifty-one to twenty-nine (Nussbaum 1988). Port (1987) estimates that fully 80 percent of quality errors are due to product design, while only 20 percent are due to poor workmanship.

OFFSETTING EFFECTS

Not all effects are reinforcing. Some marketing actions can serve to lower elements of the quality mix. Increasing the variety of products offered for sale, for example, is often the enemy of reliability. (Garvin (1983) notes: "Product proliferation and constant design changes may keep the marketing department happy, but failure rates tend to rise as well" (p. 71). It is a controversial issue to which we return in Chapter 13. Adding product features can have the same effect. More complicated products may work to lower reliability.

QUALITY MIX ISSUES

The quality mix is affected by five important issues.

Relative Versus Absolute Quality

Quality can be measured in both absolute and relative terms. Absolute quality is measured against an established benchmark. Conformance to standards, and other precisely stated, quantitative measures, are calculated within the firm, in isolation of competitors' products (although standards themselves can be set in accordance with prevailing expectations of quality in the market).

Relative measures consider the quality of competitors' products. PIMS, for example, measures "relative" perceived product quality, which is a measure of how one firm's products compare to competitors' products. Relative quality measures the rising level of quality in the marketplace. To fall behind in relative quality is to gain a competitive *dis*advantage.

Objective Versus Subjective Measures

Some elements of the quality mix can be measured more objectively than others. Objective measures focus on the more quantitative elements, such as reliability, durability, and conformance to standards. Quality is assessed by tabulating the number of defects, measuring the percent of output that is rejected for sale and must be reworked, and the number of service calls required during the warranty period. Objective measures also focus on performance characteristics of product, such as the horse-power of a car, or the processing speed of a computer.

The more ambiguous elements of quality require more subjective measures. Consumers' perceptions of product quality and measures of style are less amenable to precise quantitative measures than reliability. PIMS, for example, uses expert opinion to assess product quality.

Combinations of elements into the quality mix also lean more towards subjective measures. The quality mix—like the marketing mix—is a qualitative phenomenon.

Differences Among Product Categories

The quality mix can vary greatly from one product category to the next. Reliability and durability are important elements of the quality mix for some products, such as large appliances, where styling is of lesser importance. In clothing, by contrast, styling is weighted more heavily, and durability plays a more minor role.

Changes in Valued Elements

In some instances, the important elements of the quality mix are timeless. In other instances, they change over time in response to shifting consumer demands. Takeuchi and Quelch (1983) document the well-known changes that have occurred in the auto industry. In the 1960s consumers valued styling most highly. And, that is exactly what domestic producers provided them with. In the 1970s, consumers changed their minds. In response to the oil crisis, consumers wanted cars that got good mileage. American firms hurried to catch up with Japanese manufacturers, who already produced fuel-efficient cars. By the 1980s, when American manufacturers had succeeded in greatly lowering the overall fuel consumption of their fleets, consumer preference switched to reliability. The case of the auto industry is extreme but not unusual, and illustrates how the quality mix can change over time.

Consensus Versus Idiosyncratic Views of Quality

In some cases, consumers agree as to which products are of the highest quality—those products that have a high degree of innate excellence. It is a view of quality that is similar to the concept of vertical differentiation presented in a previous chapter. In other cases, consumers may have more idiosyncratic views of quality. That is especially true when quality is defined as being in the "eye of the beholder." That view of quality is more akin to horizontal differentiation. Two distinct quality mix strategies emerge from those two views.

Quality Mix Strategies

Quality mix strategies focus on two separate issues. Like vertical differentiation, the first strategy trades price and quality. Sellers increase the overall level of product quality in return for higher prices. The second strategy, like horizontal differentiation, emphasizes different elements of the quality mix. Creating a quality mix that is tailored to idiosyncratic tastes, it is the quality-based counterpart of segmentation.

INCREASING OVERALL LEVEL OF QUALITY

The most obvious quality mix strategy follows the pattern illustrated in Exhibit 11.2. It increases the overall level of product quality by raising every one of the eight elements of quality. Superior quality is defined broadly, meaning better on all elements of quality. Consumers agree that a product higher on all elements of quality is superior to a product lower on all elements. There is a consensus of opinion among consumers on what constitutes a quality product.

Price plays an important role in the quality mix. Higher quality comes at a higher price. Consumers expect to pay a premium price for higher-quality products. Alternatively, they can purchase a product of acceptable quality at a lower price. Consumers must trade quality for price.

Exhibit 11.2   *Increasing Overall Level of Quality*

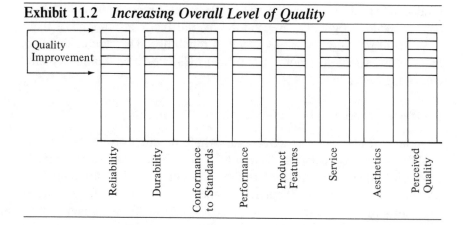

Competitors define quality similarly, and must decide which level of quality to provide—the highest quality at highest prices versus acceptable quality at lower-prices.

Trading Quality and Price

Exhibit 11.3 illustrates the tradeoff between price and quality for different levels of the same quality mix. Assume a starting point at point "X." Firm "A" moves upscale, offering premium goods, which carry a higher price tag. Firm "B" moves towards lower prices, offering less-expensive, less-premium goods. Each firm offers consumers the same "value." Consumers simply trade price for quality. Price is an important attribute of this form of the quality mix.

Cutting Price and Holding Quality Constant

Firms can break the price-quality tradeoff. Improving product quality is not the only strategy available to a firm. Clark (1961) found that some firms excelled by following the low-cost producer route while maintaining an equal level of quality. Firm "C" in Exhibit 11.3 offers equal quality at a lower price using a strategy that embraces affordable excellence.

Cutting price and holding quality constant does not embrace differentiation. To the contrary, firm "C" wants to make its products seem the same as competitors' offerings, merely less expensive. It is a strategy that relies heavily on process innovations, a type of innovation that strives to gain efficiencies and advances in the process of production, rather than the product itself.

Exhibit 11.3 *Trading Price and Quality*

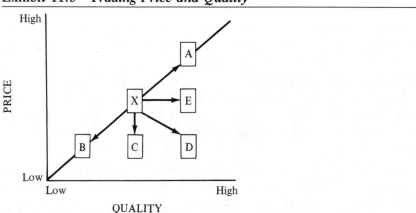

Increasing Product Value

Product value is another form of affordable excellence. It too breaks the bond between price and quality. Gale and Klavans (1984) offer two additional strategies for increasing product value.

As Exhibit 11.3 illustrates, firm "E" has increased quality while holding prices constant, and is able to offer consumers higher quality at the same price. How feasible is that strategy? Before considering that question, consider firm "D" which has managed to increase quality slightly and lower costs and prices. It has pushed the prevailing tide of product quality to a higher level, and, in so doing, has gained a competitive advantage.

Does Quality Lead to Higher Costs?

It is widely believed that higher quality is more expensive. Higher-quality products require a firm to purchase better materials at higher prices. It also adds the expense of quality control and assurance procedures, and the increased costs of better design. The tools of superior customer satisfaction, such as the "800" numbers, liberal return and refund practices, and prompt service surely add to the expense of producing and selling a product. In fact, the added expense of selling higher-quality, differentiated products is so inconsistent with the emphasis required of a lower-cost producer that some strategists, most notably Porter, argue for two distinct marketing strategies.

Proponents of product quality disagree. They claim that the additional money spent on quality is more than offset by a number of equally obvious positive influences. There are three reasons why higher quality may not lead to higher costs.

First, higher product quality leads to savings in error rates. Products made right the first time do not have to be reworked. Consequently, there is less waste. That helps to lower costs, in some cases enough to negate the added costs of checking for and assuring higher quality.

Some authors contend that quality itself is not that expensive to begin with. Reddy (1980), for example, argues that firms should focus on low-cost quality not technological wonder. Quality can often be produced inexpensively. Garvin (1983) makes the same claim. He argues that firms should not rely on capital-intensive investment to improve quality. Simple, basic training, based on people rather than machines, is usually the best and least expensive place to start.

Second, higher quality leads to a number of distinct marketing benefits that, as a group, make up for the high costs required by quality.

Third, quality leads to higher prices. Superior satisfaction of consumer needs, design excellence, greater reliability, and improvements in any of the other faces of quality is welcomed by consumers, who will pay extra for such products.

So, yes, quality does lead to higher costs, but it also leads to many sources of savings which offset those increased costs. Consequently, it is a mistake to equate product quality with higher costs on all but the most superficial levels. The benefits of quality to the firm are far greater than the costs that must be incurred to achieve it. If there is any strategic advice that is widely accepted today, it is this—improve product quality.

QUALITY SEGMENTS

Exhibit 11.4 illustrates a quality improvement strategy focused on only two elements of the quality mix. Idiosyncratic views of product quality offer opportunities for market segmentation. A quality mix can be tailored to appeal to the needs of a particular segment. One group of consumers may favor a quality mix strong on reliability and durability; another segment might favor a mix high on style.

Garvin (1988) argues for a strategy based on quality niches, which implies the option of different firms offering different quality mixes. He contends that firms should "single out a few dimensions of quality as their focus instead of striving to be number one on all categories (p. 62). Japanese cars, for example, have a strong record on reliability, but have a poor record on safety. Volvo, in contrast, has a good safety

Exhibit 11.4 *Focusing on a Quality Segment*

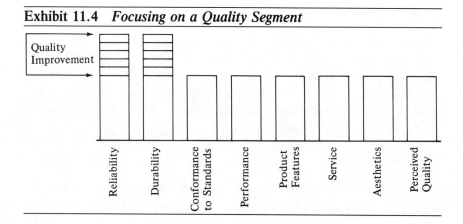

record but only an average record on frequency and cost of maintenance. Each has its own defendable position in a particular quality segment.

Quality segmentation offers most of the benefits of traditional segmentation strategy. It is a focused strategy that avoids head-on competition.

Requirements for Quality Improvements

The business press has focused mostly on the issue of how to improve product quality. Most discussions incorporate the following seven issues.

1. Long-Term Commitment

A product quality strategy is not a quick fix, but a long-term strategy with long-term payoffs. Dreyfuss (1988) notes that quality requires patience. It is difficult and time-consuming to implement a quality improvement strategy. It is often too easy to fall back on platitudes rather than a true commitment.

2. Employee Involvement

A quality strategy must have the active support of lower-level employees. Quality is embodied not by top executives but by those who actually make the product. Employees must be involved in quality improvement. In fact, the best ideas for improving quality often come from lower-level employees who have direct contact with the manufacture and sale of the product.

3. Worker Training

Quality improvements should rely on people, not machines. Some firms attempt to solve quality problems through automation, and are usually less successful than firms that invest in worker training. Investing in workers is better than investing in robots. It is also less expensive. Spending on employees has a rare dual benefit: lower costs and superior outcome.

4. Product Design

Product design plays an integral part of a quality improvement strategy. Superior design can improve reliability and enhance product styling.

5. Product Value

Improving quality requires more than cutting costs or enhancing performance. It requires product value. The ultimate success of a quality improvement strategy rests on whether the firm provides the consumer with product "value."

6. Marketing–R&D Interface

A quality improvement strategy requires extensive communications within the firm. Most important is the interface between the marketing function and research and development, connections that are especially crucial for product quality. The importance of product design and long-term customer satisfaction necessitates such action.

7. Long-Term Consumer Satisfaction

Product quality requires a customer focus. In fact, it is part of the larger issue of long-term customer satisfaction. Finkelman (1989) contends that improving long-term consumer satisfaction is the most important task in improving quality. To do so, three elements are necessary:

1. To really understand the importance of satisfying the customer
2. To treat customer problems as a serious signal for action not an annoyance
3. To give employees greater responsibility to solve customer problems

CONCLUSIONS ABOUT PRODUCT QUALITY

The following conclusions can be drawn about a strategy predicated on product quality.

Quality as a Long-Term Strategy

Product quality is a long-term strategy, not a quick fix. It takes much longer to change the quality component of a product than it does to lower prices. As Jack Reddy notes in his 1980 article, it takes years to implement a quality improvement strategy into production. Much planning is required. Furthermore, it takes years for consumers to recognize, no less accept, that quality has been improved.

Quality as a Unique Strategy

Not every seller can sell the highest-quality goods. As with most strategic positions there is room for one, or at most a few, highest-quality sellers. Not everyone can be the best. Not all sales can climb above the industry average. If many firms attempt to increase quality at once, as has happened in recent years, the average not the relative position moves up. In many markets, it is necessary to run faster just to stay in place. It is possible, however, for firms to offer different quality mixes.

Quality Does Not Restrict Market Share

There is a debate over whether higher product quality—and the exclusivity that it implies—precludes higher market share. Not everyone can drive a Mercedes, own a Philip Patek watch, or possess hand-crafted furniture. Likewise, premium ice creams, gourmet coffees, and Gucci loafers will never possess the largest shares of the markets they serve (defined broadly). Their exclusivity forces them to the top of each market. But, exclusivity, top-of-the-line, premium-product marketing strategies encompass only one view of product quality. Given that narrow definition of product quality, market share may well be restricted.

The other definitions of quality, however, do not imply lower market share. Greater reliability, durability, performance, service and others, strongly imply a greater consumer demand for high-quality products. In those instances, as observed by PIMS researchers, quality leads to greater market share.

Marketing Benefits of Product Quality

Many benefits accrue to the seller of higher-quality products. Consumers tend to be more brand loyalty, they make more repeat purchases, and they are less likely to switch brands if prices are raised. For the firm, consumer loyalty means higher profit margins, market-share gains, and partial immunity to price wars. Together those benefits lead to higher profits.

Consequences of Cutting Product Quality

If improving product quality leads to wondrous results, then cutting quality leads to disaster. The business press is littered with the wreckage of firms that cut quality to save money. Consider what happened to Maxwell House coffee and Schlitz beer when each cut quality.

As of 1989, Maxwell House coffee had been losing market share for five full years. Sales and profits were dropping steadily. To make matters worse, fewer Americans were drinking coffee, and those that still did were drinking less of it. One reason for the decline of Maxwell House was that they cut its advertising budget drastically in the face of increased competition. More important, in 1985 it cut the quality of the beans used to make the coffee, using fewer of the more expensive, but more flavorful, Central American beans and substituting cheaper, more bitter African beans. Maxwell House switched back shortly after it realized the gravity of its mistake, but consumers did not switch back from other brands. What had taken decades to build into the number one brand was lost seemingly overnight (Levine 1989).

A similar fate felled Schlitz beer. In the 1970s Schlitz was the number two brand in the U.S. market. Then, managers decided to substitute cheaper ingredients. It was well known that consumers could not tell the difference anyway. It was all perception. It proved to be a disastrous decision. Schlitz moved rapidly from second to seventh place in the industry. It too switched back to a strategy of the highest-quality ingredients, which its ads featured prominently. It even hired the head brewmaster of a large competitor to reinforce the quality image. But it was too late. Schlitz never regained its lost market share.

Those examples point up the importance of product quality in today's markets. Gale and Klavans (1984) sum it up best. They note: "It is time to swing the pendulum away from the experience-curve drive for market share and towards effective quality control and customer-perceived quality" (p. 9). In that endeavor, marketing has an important and a growing role to play.

References

Clark, John Maurice. *Competition as a Dynamic Process*. Washington, D.C., Brookings Institute, 1961.

Dreyfuss, Joel. "Victories in the Quality Crusade." *Fortune*, October 10, 1988, pp. 80–88.

Finkelman, Daniel. "Quality Is Not Enough: If the Customer Has an Itch Scratch It." *New York Times,* May 14, 1989, p. F3.

Flint, Jerry. "Habit Dies Hard." *Forbes,* May 29, 1989, pp. 246–266.

Gale, Bradley, and Richard Klavans, "Formulating a Quality Improvement Strategy," *Pimsletter,* No. 31. Cambridge, MA: Strategic Planning Institute, 1984.

Garvin, David A. "Competing on the Eight Dimensions of Quality." *Harvard Business Review,* November–December 1987, pp. 101–109.

Garvin, David A. *Managing Quality.* New York: Free Press, 1988.

Garvin, David A. "Quality on the Line." *Harvard Business Review,* September–October 1983, pp. 65–75.

Hamilton, Joan. "Gray Expectations." *Business Week,* April 11, 1988, p. 108.

Hartley, Robert. *Marketing Mistakes.* Englewood Cliffs, NJ: Prentice-Hall, 1981.

Hauser, John, and Don Clausing. "The House of Quality." *Harvard Business Review,* May–June 1988, pp. 63–73.

Knowlton, Christopher. "What America Makes Best." *Fortune,* March 28, 1988, pp. 40–53.

Levin, Doron. "Quality Survey Has Buick Smiling." *New York Times,* June 6, 1989, p. D5.

Levine, Joshua. "Drip, Drip, Drip . . . Drip." *Forbes,* April 17, 1989, pp. 196–198.

Nussbaum, Bruce. "Smart Design: Quality Is the New Style." *Business Week,* April 11, 1988, pp. 102–117.

Port, Otis. "The Push for Quality." *Business Week,* June 8, 1987, pp. 130–135.

Quelch, John A. "Marketing the Premium Product." *Business Horizons,* vol. 30, no. 3, May–June 1987, pp. 38–45.

Reddy, Jack. "Incorporating Quality in Competitive Strategies." *Sloan Management Review,* Spring 1980, pp. 53–60.

Takeuchi, Hirotaka, and John Quelch. "Quality Is More Than Making a Good Product." *Harvard Business Review,* July–August 1983, pp. 139–145.

Chapter *12*

Theories of Product and Market Evolution

O ver the years theories of how products and markets evolve from birth to decline have themselves evolved. This chapter is about those changes. It begins with the product life cycle, which early in its own life cycle proposed that products followed similar patterns. The discussion then moves to the current emphasis on the "drivers," or causes of changes in patterns in product sales histories.

Product Life Cycle

One of the most durable, yet controversial, concepts in marketing has been the Product Life Cycle (subsequently referred to as the PLC). Since its inception in the 1950s, the PLC has dominated how marketers view product evolution.

In essence, the PLC is a pattern-based approach which tracks trends in product sales histories from their inception to their demise. It assumes that products follow a common sales pattern. According to advocates, knowing the common pattern can help marketers understand how a particular product will evolve.

SINGLE PATTERN

Originally, hopes were high for the life-cycle approach. It was proposed that a single pattern served as an adequate model for explaining the evolution of many products. That basic pattern is well known and exhibited in Exhibit 12.1. It holds that new products are introduced into the marketplace, enter a period of rapid growth, stabilize at "maturity," then decline when replaced by superior innovations. Textbooks still chronicle

Exhibit 12.1   *Idealized Product Life-Cycle Pattern*

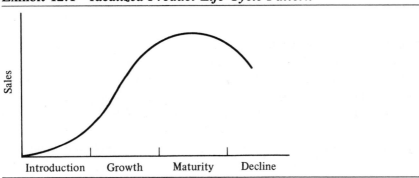

the pattern as though it were widespread and generalizable to many different kinds of products.

FAMILY OF PATTERNS

It quickly became apparent to early marketing theorists that not all products followed the idealized lifecycle. In the 1960s this led to a search for additional patterns. Maybe, it was reasoned, instead of a single dominant pattern, there was a family of patterns. Many aberrant patterns were observed, and, today, those patterns are part of the life-cycle concept.

There is "scalloped demand," wherein new uses are found for a product entering maturity, "cycle-recycle," wherein decline is transformed into renewed growth by the actions of creative marketers, and "extended maturity," where a product remains stuck in maturity for decades.

In the 1960s numerous empirical studies searched for life-cycle patterns. Cox (1967) fit six life-cycle patterns to sales of 258 prescription drugs. Nearly half of the series (48.2 percent) exhibited a cycle-recycle pattern, or an earlier stage in the pattern. Cox contends that the cycle-recycle pattern is common in the drug industry. Increased promotion is used to stave off decline. In the process, a recycle is created.

At about the same time, Polli and Cook (1969) tested two assumptions of the PLC: (1) whether the sequence of stages was as expected (i.e., maturity follows growth), and (2) whether the timing of stages was equal. They were looking for inconsistencies in the theory based on a study of 140 nondurable goods. Their results were inconclusive. The PLC did significantly better than chance in only 34 percent of the cases tested, but fully 92 percent of the sales series showed greater consistency than a matched, simulated series of random numbers. They conclude: "While the overall performance of the model leaves some question as to its general applicability, it is clearly a good model of sales behavior in certain market situations" (p. 400).

Rink and Swan (1979) reviewed the literature and found some twelve different life cycle patterns that had been identified over the years since the concept was first proposed. Many of those patterns were variations of one another. Most of the studies examined found support for the idealized version of the cycle. The second most common pattern was cycle-recycle. A few studies found a rising trend, declining trend, extended maturity, growth maturity, innovative maturity, high and low plateau, growth-decline plateau, and rapid penetration. Rink and Swan conclude that there is strong support for the basic, bell-shaped, product life-cycle pattern. Others disagree vehemently.

CRITICISMS

Severe criticisms of the PLC began to appear in the 1970s. Today those criticisms are still voiced. Consider six commonly stated criticisms of the PLC concept.

Pattern Variability

"Curve-fitting" as an approach to verify the PLC was abandoned by the early 1970s. It seemed to prove little. Researchers would fit many curves to many sales series and report which curves fit what percentages of those series. The more curves that were applied to actual data series, the more patterns that fit at least some of those series.

The curve-fitting approach violated many rules of good research design. But more important, it seemed to obscure, rather than highlight, the most important observation—that there is great variability in how products evolve. Anyone who has examined simple plots of yearly sales series quickly becomes appreciative of the wide variability in the evolutionary process. The differences among series seem to overpower the similarities.

No Predictive Validity

Equally important, and a criticism of the curve-fitting approach, is that it is not possible to know *beforehand* which pattern a particular product will follow. Curves are fit only to events that have already occurred. The theory of the PLC offers little indication as to what the future holds. Consequently, the PLC is limited to "post-hoc" explanations of evolutionary behavior. It tells what has happened; it offers no power to predict.

Difficulty in Estimating Current Status

It is often not even possible to identify which stage of the PLC a particular product is currently in. Which stage of the PLC is the microwave oven, facsimile machines, or personal computers currently in? How did you make that assessment?

Exacerbating the problem is the considerable variation around that trend line shown in Exhibit 12.1. Neat and orderly patterns that give clear signals are rare outside textbooks. Does a sales downturn, for example, signal the onset of maturity? Or, does it signal a temporary slowdown due to an impending recession? The choice is often difficult to make.

Skipped Stages

At its heart, the PLC is rooted in the aging process of individual organisms. It holds that products, like people, are born and grow old. But, unlike biological aging, which is immutable and irreversible, the evolution of products is replete with rejuvenations, reversals, and skipped stages. Some products—like CB radios—to straight from rapid growth to rapid decline. Other products spend decades in maturity, and never decline.

Erratic Timing

The amount of time a product spends in each stage also varies. Some products grow for short periods, while others grow for years at a time. There seems to be no rhyme or reason to the timing of life-cycle stages. Again, variability seems to be the rule rather than the exception.

Theory Versus Tautology

One of the most damning criticisms is that the PLC is a tautology, that is, it proves itself. Consider first the case of deciding which stage of the cycle a particular product is in. How can you tell a product is in the growth stage of the cycle?—because it is growing. In the decline stage?—because it is declining. Such explanations are not explanatory. They are tautological. The stage of the life cycle is identified by the trend in sales, which, in turn, is identified by the stage of the life cycle.

The concept proves itself and nothing else. Shelby Hunt (1976), the noted marketing theorist, puts it best: "If the level of sales determines the stage of the life cycle, then the stage in the life cycle cannot be used to explain the level of sales" (p. 55).

Critics contend that the PLC is tautological when it comes to patterns as well. Consider the idealized PLC broken into two parts: (1) introduction to maturity and (2) maturity to decline.

Introduction to Maturity

The first half of the PLC postulates that sales will follow an S-shaped curve. That is, after experiencing a slow start, sales grow rapidly as the product gains widespread consumer acceptance. Then, growth slows as the market saturates. Two problems arise.

First, many S-shaped patterns have been observed. Low-tar cigarettes, for example, were on the market for many years before sales soared. Other products, such as 100mm cigarettes, grew immediately upon introduction. Like children learning to print the alphabet, the shape of "S's" varies greatly from child to child and from product to product. Products also mature at different levels. Telephones and refrigerators reach well over 90 percent of households. Cornpoppers, in contrast, have penetrated less than 10 percent. Finally, the length of time required for products to reach their ultimate penetration level varies greatly.

Support for the proposition that products follow an S-shaped curve is insured by the sample used to test it. The PLC is applied only to products that have exhibited growth for an extended time period. It is never applied to product failures, such as the picture phone, CB radios, or artificial leathers. Consequently, by definition, sample products exhibit an upward trend in sales. The growth stage is insured by the nature of the sample selected, and the fact that all observations are made post-hoc. As a result, the PLC offers little explanatory or predictive power of product evolution during the growth stage. It simply says that there is growth in sales because the concept has been applied to successful product innovations.

Maturity to Decline

The second half of the PLC has attracted even more criticism than the first. Myriad patterns are possible once growth seemingly abates. Sales might: (1) remain in maturity for decades (extended maturity), (2) resume growth (cycle-recycle), or (3) decline slowly or precipitously (the basic pattern). Numerous examples of each pattern have been observed. Exhibit 12.2 illustrates those possible patterns.

Exhibit 12.2   *Outcomes After the Growth Stage*

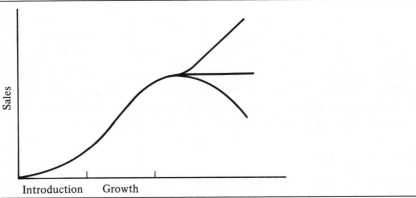

Critics claim that such observations offer little in the way of explanatory power. Instead, it reinforces the claim that the PLC is a tautology. It simply states: (1) sales may go up, (2) sales may go down, or (3) sales may remain the same. With a theory like that you cannot go wrong. In violation of the basic principles of scientific theory-building, that version of the PLC concept cannot be refuted. No matter what the outcome, the theory holds. But, in the absence of any mechanism to select which pattern a product will follow beforehand, the concept offers little in the way of worthwhile explanations. It is indeed a tautology.

CRITICAL EVALUATION

It is often said that if cigarettes, or even aspirin, were introduced as new products today they would be declared dangerous, and be controlled or made illegal. They are with us today only because of their long presence on the market. The PLC has followed a similar pattern. Its dominance today owes more to its historical presence than its theoretical or practical value. Its benefits and drawbacks must be couched in those constraints. Still, the life cycle does offer some benefits.

General Guide

To many marketers, the PLC is an intuitively appealing notion that has merit only in the most general of terms. It serves almost as a language by which marketers communicate fundamental ideas such as growth, maturity, and decline. As such, the PLC serves a useful, if limited, purpose. In addition, the PLC also communicates some basic generalizations that apply to most products.

First, the PLC holds that most products have limited life spans. This is especially true for product forms—versions of a product category that are most vulnerable to technological innovation. VHS VCRs (a product form) replaced Betamax (also a product form) in the VCR product category. Second, the PLC relates the idea that most products progress through stages, which characterize different marketing environments that require different marketing efforts. That benefit is examined next.

Stage Strategies

Probably the most useful contribution of the PLC is its recognition that different life-cycle stages require different marketing strategies. A growth market, for example, requires a different set of strategies than a mature, or a declining, market. As such, the life cycle fits nicely with the larger literature on competition in growth, mature, and declining markets.

No Pattern

As a reaction to criticisms of life-cycle patterns, some researchers argue that there are no generalizable patterns of product evolution. Instead, they argue, each product is unique, affected by events and decisions that unfold with the product. Sales histories are not predetermined. Unlike the life cycle of individual organisms, from which the concept arises, products do not always grow, mature, decline and die in an orderly and immutable fashion. Some products live seemingly forever. They gain what Ponce de Leon could not discover—immortality. Other products live short lives indeed. When it comes to products, life cycles come in a variety of patterns—your products can grow up quickly or slowly, adolescent products can arise from mature products and elderly products can sometimes be turned young again.

Dhalla and Yuspeh (1976) speak out strongly against the PLC. They find no evidence at all to support the proposition that products follow life-cycle patterns of any kind. Instead, they argue, there are no patterns in product series. The future path of product sales histories is determined by marketing variables, such as advertising expenditures. Marketers, in other words, can influence the cycle rather than just observe it.

The Control Versus Predetermination Issue

Criticisms of the life cycle have led some authors to espouse the opposite opinion, that patterns can be managed. In the parlance of regression analysis, they argue that the PLC is a "dependent variable," which is the result of marketing actions. Marketing controls the life-cycle pattern, not the other way around. According to Dhalla and Yuspeh, one of the most insidious misfortunes of the PLC is that it might lead management to consider abandoning a product rather than redoubling its efforts to turn things around. The PLC might mistakenly signal the inevitable end of a product's life. As the chapter on the BCG Growth-Share Matrix illustrates, problems have arisen when firms inadvertently milk their bread-and-butter products on the assumption that they have no future.

Are life cycles really controllable? Or, are they determined by outside forces? The answer, as with most issues, lies between those two extreme positions. Clearly, the life cycle is not predetermined. But neither is it totally controllable. The best sales and marketing efforts could not reclaim the 8mm movie camera and projector market. Their worlds were forever altered by forces beyond marketers' control.

But in other, less severe, situations marketers have considerable powers to influence. The important issue is not which pattern a product will follow, but which "drivers" will influence the evolutionary path. Some of those drivers can be controlled or influenced by marketers, others cannot.

A Random Walk Down Madison Avenue?

Arguments that there are no inherent patterns in sales series—that sales are determined by external forces—are similar to the financial theory of random walks in efficient markets. In finance, it has long been recognized that short-term stock price movements follow a random walk (Fama 1965). Searching for trends and patterns in those series has been shown to be a fruitless exercise. Past patterns in individual series, or similarities among different series, are of little use in predicting or explaining future movements. Maybe there is an analogous situation in marketing.

In essence, the random-walk hypothesis is the opposite of the PLC hypothesis. It holds that there are no generalizable patterns or trends. Financial series appear to wander aimlessly and randomly. What determines their future is not repeating patterns but future events. Stock prices, for example, move in response to "news" events, which, by definition, have not yet occurred. Consequently, like marketing series, they appear to evolve uniquely. The justification for the random-walk hypothesis lies in the theory of efficient capital markets.

Unlike marketing, most financial theorists sneer at the prospect of forecasting or explaining short-term stock price movements by trying to identify trends and patterns. Numerous patterns have been proposed by technical analysts (e.g., "head-and-shouders" formations). Critics contend that such patterns are merely the result of post-hoc curve fitting. To PLC critics the approach sounds remarkably similar to that used by PLC advocates to identify generalizable patterns of product growth. Maybe the random-walk hypothesis has merits for marketing series as well.

Random Walks in Marketing

Like financial series, the evolution of marketing data series may also be largely determined by external factors that swamp any trends or patterns in a series. Albeit, the time span may be longer, and the factors may be different, but the consequence may be the same—an evolutionary sequence whose course is determined largely by future events rather than repeating patterns that are common to all products.

Furthermore, the presence of a random walk in marketing is not nearly as negative a statement as it is in finance. That makes the concept more palatable. In finance, it means that, with the exception of insider trading, traders cannot profit from the study of available information. Financial markets are uncontrollable. Product markets are far more controllable. Marketing actions clearly influence product evolution. And, unlike financial markets, it is neither illegal nor unethical to do so. It is, in fact, the job of marketing strategy.

A random walk also answers many of the criticisms of the PLC. It is more consistent with the empirical evidence on the shape and timing of the cycle. Finally, it suggests that the focus should be placed on the potential forces that might cause perturbations in a series, rather than fitting the appropriate growth curve. It is a focus on drivers rather than patterns.

The random-walk hypothesis may offer a better model of product evolution than the PLC's pattern-based approach. In implicit recognition of this view, marketing theorists have, in recent years, switched tracks. Few marketers now search for patterns in sales histories. Instead, marketers now look at the forces that drive sales histories.

Generic Drivers of Product Evolution

At the beginning of the 1980s, Day (1981) succinctly summarized the status of PLC research: "Past attempts to validate the existence of the life cycle have uncovered many shapes, durations and sequences. These efforts have not been matched by systematic research into the reasons for the differences between shapes'' (p. 61). Since that time, the focus has clearly shifted from pattern or trend-based approaches to the recognition that strategic, environmental, and competitive factors drive product evolution.

Numerous drivers can affect the evolution of a product. Some are specific to a particular product. Others are generalizable to many different kinds of products. Some of the more common drivers are discussed below.

CONSUMER TRENDS

The evolution of many products is boosted or hindered by underlying consumer trends, which include demographic, social, and market characteristics.

Demographic Trends

Demographics have a strong effect on many product categories. One aspect of demographics is the aging process. Clearly, as consumers progress from birth to decline their needs for products change. Those changes can greatly affect life cycles. Two clear trends in today's markets are the baby boom and the elderly.

The largest bulk of the U.S. population was born between 1946 and 1962. Known as the baby boom, as this group ages, they create extraordinary demand for some products and less demand for others. Likewise, the elderly segment of the population has also caused many markets to grow rapidly. Soda, beer, toys, housing, medical care, and many other product categories have strong connections to demographics.

Most important, aging is predictable. While products follow quite variable patterns, consumers age in predictable ways. Obviously, demographics are not controllable by marketers; but they can be tracked.

Changes in Segment Served

Another trend related to demographics is changes in the segments served by a new product as it progresses from introduction to widespread market acceptance. New products usually offer poor performance and high prices. Often, products begin their commercial lives in market segments where those disadvantages are least important. For example, the military—

where costs are less important—has been the initial market for many technologies. As prices fall and performance increases business-to-business markets become feasible. Finally, sales to individual consumers open up. Computers, for example, found their first applications among government and large business users. Sales to individuals followed when prices declined. Likewise, copiers sold to smaller businesses and individuals soared as prices fell and the market for large business copiers became saturated.

Extent of Buyer Learning

Radically new products, with which consumers are unfamiliar, require a great deal of primary demand advertising. Marketers must teach, explain, and inform consumers of the products' benefits. It is a controllable driver. It is also most important for radically new products, with which consumers have little experience.

Pressure to Adopt

Part of the theoretical reason for the growth stage of the product life cycle is the contagious appeal many products hold for consumers once they start to "catch on." After an initial group of consumers has adopted a new product, large numbers of consumers recognize their desire for the product. Growth accelerates as large numbers of consumers enter the market. At this point, growth seems to take on a life of its own.

Social Trends

Social trends also drive product evolution. The trend towards health and fitness, and the trend away from indulgent behavior, has both created and destroyed demand for certain product categories. Athletic footwear, for example, has grown greatly, while alcoholic beverages have declined slowly in recent years.

Social trends are oftentimes, but not always, related to demographics. Trends toward conservative politics, health and fitness, and other dominant trends often match underlying demographics. Like demographics, social trends are usually external factors that are usually not controllable.

TECHNOLOGICAL TRENDS

Technological trends, and decisions made about the marketing of new technologies, also drive product evolution.

Product Substitution

Growth is driven by technological substitution. The emergence of new technologies sends existing products into decline. CD players, for example, drove LP turntables into decline; VHS recorders made the Betamax obsolete. Technological substitution is driven by numerous factors.

Perceived Attributes of Innovation

In marketing, Ostlund (1974) studied perceived attributes of innovations. He found that growth is driven by:

1. *Relative advantage* over existing products—Products that perform the task better or are less expensive are more likely to grow quickly.
2. *Compatibility*—Products that are consistent with existing practices, and do not require major changes in consumers lives to use the new product (products that are incompatible require greater buyer learning), promote growth.
3. *Design simplicity*—Products that do not require consumers to obtain a graduate degree to operate or understand the product are likely to grow quickly.
4. *Use on a trial basis*—Products that do not require a large and nonrefundable payment to test the product before using promote growth.
5. *Clearly observable benefits*—Products which consumers can see the advantage of using the product grow more quickly.

Changes in perceived attributes from one product to the next, or over time for a single product, can speed or slow the evolution of a new product. To some extent, those changes are controllable by marketers. Through product design, promotion, and other manipulations of marketing-mix variables, marketers can affect the speed of product evolution.

Cost-Benefit Comparisons

The most important attribute of a new technology is the extent to which it performs the task (1) better, and (2) at an acceptable price. Products in favorable cost-benefit positions possess a greater relative advantage. The extent to which they possess those advantages affects the speed of product substitution, causing growth for a new product and decline for an existing product.

Complementary Products

Technological substitution is also affected by the extent to which products are connected to other products. Some new products "stand alone."

Others rely heavily on complementary products. CD players, for example, require the disks themselves. The requirement of complementary products hinders growth. Consumers are reluctant to purchase until a strong supply of complementary products are available. Suppliers of complementary products are reluctant to produce those products until a sufficiently large installed base of customers exists. Often, extensive coordination is required among buyers, suppliers, and firms in allied industries. Products that stand alone have no such hindrances.

Saturation Rate

Growth slows with the onset of saturation. At some point just about all the consumers that will purchase have already done so. Growth then slows. Durable goods—goods that are not consumed during use—saturate more quickly than nondurables. They are then forced to rely on replacement sales. Nondurables—such as soda and cigarettes—have a pattern of many smaller purchases. Their purchase is also less likely to be postponed in times of recession.

Barriers to Adoption

Competitive actions can also affect product substitution. Switching costs and other barriers to adoption can slow growth for new products and maintain sales for existing products.

Marketing Innovations

Innovations in marketing, as well as technology, can affect product growth. The evolution of many products—such as Timex, nylon, Kevlar, Nike and Perrier—have been greatly influenced by creative marketing efforts. Changes in distribution channels, positioning, product design, and variations in just about every variable available for marketing manipulation have been used at one time or another to influence the evolution of products. Clearly, marketing innovations are controllable influences of growth.

ECONOMIC TRENDS

Economics clearly affects product evolution. Product growth is likely to be strongest in times of economic expansion. CD players, for example, were introduced in the early 1980s right at the beginning of the greatest economic expansion in U.S. postwar history. The product's fortunes reversed a downward trend—driven mostly by demographics—towards less interest in music. Similarly, good economic times is attributed by many as a primary cause for the unexpected decline in generic products—those products with the white labels found less frequently these days in supermarkets.

LEGAL/POLITICAL TRENDS

Technological substitutions are affected by legal and political trends. In recent years, trends in those areas have driven growth and decline in many markets.

Standardization

Government policy used to frown on firms within an industry cooperating to set product standards. It was viewed as a variant of collusion. No more. In recent years there has been a trend towards standardization.

Foreign competitors routinely engage in standardization. After the debacle in VCRs, where Sony's Betamax lost out to VHS, manufacturers of CD players cooperated to set standards. Since then standardization has interested many industries in the United States.

Standardization promotes product growth. It avoids consumer confusion over which type of product will dominate. It also allows manufacturers to concentrate on promoting growth rather than competing as to which standard will emerge as the dominant one.

Two Theories of Biological Evolution

At its very heart, the PLC is deficient because it adopts the perspective of an individual organism rather than a species. It assumes that products, like individuals, age gracefully and orderly. They are born, grow, mature, and eventually die.

The empirical evidence suggest a less orderly and less predictable process. Biological theories of evolution, which focus on the adaptation of species to external events (drivers), may offer a more appropriate framework for the study of product sales than the biological aging process (i.e., the PLC). Theories of evolution do not presuppose inevitable patterns. The future path of evolution for a species is as unknowable as the future pattern for a radically new product. In both cases the pattern is not fixed. Responses to environmental changes determine the course of evolution of both species and products. Consider the following two evolutionary theories, and assess their applicability to marketing.

DARWIN'S GRADUALISM

In 1859 Charles Darwin published his *Origin of Species,* which argued that gradual changes in species occur in response to gradual changes in the environment. Darwin viewed evolution as a slow-moving process of change. Species adapt slowly over millions of years to changes in their environment. Those that adapt successfully thrive, those that remain the same decline. Darwin's theory is called gradualism because it proposes slow, adaptive changes.

Gradualism in Marketing

Some marketers argue that products evolve in a similar manner. Markets are in a state of perpetual evolution. There are changes in buyers' needs, shifts in the importance of product attributes, and myriad other changes. Products, like species, adapt to fit that changing environment. Products that adapt thrive. Products that do not, decline, or face extinction.

Tellis and Crawford (1981) apply gradualism to product change. Their application proposes slow, gradual, and continuous changes in markets, which captures three key points:

First, *change is cumulative.* That is, new products and species build on existing products and species. Much of what we know about the innovation process supports that view. Innovation builds on an existing base of knowledge. New products derive from existing products. Innovation is largely a process of "accretion," the slow, gradual build-up of technical knowledge over time.

Second, *change is directed.* In new products, as in biology, there are three dominant trends towards: (1) greater diversity, (2) greater efficiency, and (3) increasing complexity. As evolution progresses, the diversity or selection of products usually increases. Similarly, products move from crude early models—such as the first VCRs, which recorded for only an hour—to more efficient models. Finally, products become more complex, relying on new and more elaborate technologies, and incorporating more advanced features.

Third, evolutionary *change is motivated* by three distinct forces: (1) the generative force, whereby new products are generated by entrepreneurs, (2) the selective force, where the market itself selects the "fittest" products for survival, and (3) the mediative force, where the government often mediates or regulates the progress.

Like Darwin in biology, Tellis and Crawford argue that products, like species, evolve gradually over time in response to pressures from environmental changes. Products, like species, adapt to random events. It is the adaptation to unfolding events, and survival of the fittest, that best describes product evolution.

De Bresson (1987) also draws analogies between technological and biological change, but he observes many differences as well. For one, he notes that technological change is much more rapid than biological change. And it may be accelerating, he contends. Second, technological change is reversible. If the new product proves to be a fad, it is possible to step back to the product that preceded. Biological evolution is irreversible. Third, there is interbreeding in technology, but not biology. Many major technological innovations occur from the creative combination of existing ideas that had never before been combined. In biology it is impossible for a horse to breed with a mouse. Even given those differences, however, it is clear that Darwin's view of gradual evolution has many applications to marketing.

PUNCTUATED EQUILIBRIA

As a student, Charles Darwin was greatly influenced by the work of Charles Lyell, a noted nineteenth century geologist. At the time, there was a great debate in geology between proponents of gradual versus catastrophic change. Lyell argued that geologic change was gradual; and Darwin followed the same line of reasoning in biology.

In recent years, gradualism has been challenged by Stephen Gould, the noted Harvard geology professor, and Niles Eldredge, curator of the American Museum of Natural History. They argue that instead of gradual environmental change in the evolution of biological species, there are long periods where species hardly change at all. Those periods are interspersed with short periods of very rapid change. Their evolutionary theory is called punctuated equilibria. It contains two key features: (1) *stasis*—those long periods where no change is observable, and (2) *sudden appearance*—the rapid rise of new life forms.

The break in stasis comes from two sources: (1) catastrophic events, which appear suddenly, and (2) the break with the past that results from the steady accumulation of stresses.

A central feature of punctuated equilibria is the slow accumulation of stresses that build up in a system. At some point those stresses cause a break with the past, to which species must adapt quickly. It is a process like boiling water. The water gets progressively hotter, and when it reaches 212 degrees Fahrenheit it quickly turns to stream. Gould (1980) draws an analogy with the military in quoting the British geologist Derek Ager: "The history of any one part of the earth, like the life of a soldier, consists of long periods of boredom and short periods of terror" (p. 185).

The interested reader is referred to a short, and highly readable, article by Gould (1980), a book by Eldredge (1985), or a weighty treatise on the subject of punctuated equilibria by both Gould and Eldredge (1977).

Punctuated equilibria is supported by empirical research in biology. The fossil record shows no evidence of gradual change. Instead, there are long periods where species change little along with the sudden appearance of major variations. Gradualists contend, however, that is because the fossil record is incomplete. The data are poor. Proponents of punctuated equilibria argue that it is the theory of gradualism that is incomplete, not the data.

Punctuated Equilibria in Marketing

There are many examples of sudden changes in marketing. Many products exhibit remarkably stable sales patterns for long periods of time, only to be throw into brief periods of rapid change by catastrophic events.

Technical "leaps" sometimes cause rapid changes in competition. Slide rules and electromechanical adding machines, for example, were viable and stable product lines, until the sudden appearance of the calculator. Technical "leaps" occur in two ways. First, and less common, is the emergence of radically new discoveries which result in "breakthrough" innovations. They break onto the scene changing markets rapidly and forever.

More common is product growth due to an "accumulation of stresses." After a discovery is made, and a product is placed on the market, prices are high and performance is usually limited. But, there is usually an increase in the performance of the product and a corresponding decrease in price as the product evolves. At some point, as those trends accumulate, there is a surge in growth. In VCRs, microwave ovens, and more recently, facsimile machines, it is those steady improvements in price and performance that eventually cause rapid changes.

Marketing innovations can also disrupt markets suddenly. Perrier in bottled waters, BIC in inexpensive pens, and Timex in watches each caused rapid changes in the markets they serve.

Government actions, in the form of deregulation, new laws and rules, and huge purchasing power, can change markets. Trucking and the airlines suffered major dislocations after deregulation. Currently, cable television operators are concerned that government approval, which would allow the regional Bell operating companies to enter cable markets, will change their markets.

Finally, new entrants can disrupt markets suddenly. When Coca-Cola entered the wine industry, for example, it raised the level of advertising in what had been a gentlemanly industry. Sudden appearance creates opportunities for some firms but havoc for others. Responses must be quick and effective. If they are not, the firm's product may become extinct.

Elements of Market Evolution

Mostly, the world is gray. Marketing is no exception. Most evolutionary processes in marketing represent a mixture of the theories presented above. As Exhibit 12.3 illustrates, changes can be gradual or sudden. Changes can also be directed or controlled by firms, or uncontrollable, foisted on the firm by the external environment or the actions of competitors.

GRADUAL AND SUDDEN CHANGES

Product sales, as they progress from introduction to decline, are beset by gradual and catastrophic market changes. In each instance, firms must adapt to those changes, or face the fate of the dinosaurs.

In marketing applications, gradual change is probably more common than catastrophic change. The history of innovation is characterized by the slow accumulation of incremental changes more than the sudden appearance of radically new products. There is general agreement on this point. Basalla (1988), in tracing the evolution of emerging technologies over the centuries, reports that "continuity" is a more dominant pattern than discontinuous change. Almost every invention has an antecedent. Basalla explodes the "myth of the genius inventor," who creates new products through sheer genius. Clearly, the evolution of new technologies is an "unfolding" of ideas over time. Even Basalla's ideas have their roots in history. Jewkes, Sawers, and Stillerman (1958) came to similar conclusions. So did S. C. Gilfillan (1935), who credits many of his ideas to authors from the nineteenth century.

Exhibit 12.3 *Types of Change*

		CONTROL OF CHANGE	
		Controllable	Uncontrollable
SPEED OF CHANGE	Slow Gradual	Incremental Innovation by the Firm Standardization Cost-Benefit Comparisons Segments Served Adaptation	Accretion, Continuity Technical Progress Consumer Trends Demographics Social Trends
	Sudden Appearance	Marketing Innovations Market Redefinition Channel Changes Strategy Changes	Technical Leaps Breakthrough Innovations New Entrants Deregulation Changes in Competitor Strategies

Radical changes in product evolution do occur, however. Movements into markets by aggressive competitors with new ways of marketing products (e.g., Perrier), ''breakthrough'' inventions—such as the calculator—and combinations of marketing prowess and the creative application of technology to meet existing problems can radically alter the evolutionary path of existing products. Radical changes are not rare, they are simply less common than incremental changes.

CONTROLLABLE AND UNCONTROLLABLE DRIVERS

Product evolution is influenced by both controllable and uncontrollable drivers, which is an interesting mixture. Marketers have the power to influence, but it is not absolute. External trends often overpower marketers' actions. But, often, marketers are not impotent to moderate the environmental effects of the markets in which they compete. Clearly, marketers do more than merely respond to the external environment.

Controllable drivers are synonymous with the actions of creative marketers. They arise from the manipulation of the marketing-mix variables. Marketers routinely spur demand for product categories with increased promotion, lower prices, product modifications, and channel changes, to name but a few controllable factors.

Many changes in product sales are caused by external events. In recent years, for example, the trend towards healthful living has forced a decline in the use of cigarettes and hard liquors. Throughout the 1970s, astute marketers at the tobacco firms—noted for marketing excellence—were able to moderate the decline. Now, however, external events have over-powered their efforts. In most markets, the interplay between controllables and uncontrollables operates as a series of downward pushes and upward pulls, whose forces change over time.

Consider the case of Gatorade. Sales are growing at 30 percent per year and it owns 90 percent of the sports drink market. Gatorade—named after the university of Florida Gators, where it was first formu-lated—is riding the trend towards amateur sports and exercise. Even Gatorade's vice-president admits that the scientific benefits of the beverage are dubious. It is the intangible benefits of product image that matter most to the weekend athlete. Gatorade has made the most of the market it serves. Spending heavily on marketing, it keeps competitors at bay. Gatorade has the best of all worlds—uncontrollable market trends that are pulling sales upward at the same time that superb marketing is pulling sales still higher. No wonder Gatorade, not oatmeal, is Quaker Oats' number one brand (Levine 1989).

Concepts of Market Evolution

The PLC (Product Life Cycle) continues to dominate discussions of product and market evolution, even though alternative concepts hold greater promise. Consider some of the alternative concepts of product and market evolution that have been offered.

STRATEGIC WINDOWS

Abell (1978) offers the concept of strategic windows, which best captures the combined effects of gradualism and punctuated equilibria while avoid-ing the pitfalls of the PLC. It also captures the power of marketers to influence changes, as well as the power of external events.

The essence of strategic windows is that there are limited periods of time when the "fit" between market requirements and company strengths match. In those instances, the market values what the firm does well. In Abell's terms, the window is open when the fit is good; the window is closed when the fit is bad. Strategic windows are constantly opening and closing, creating new-found opportunities for some firms, and destroying opportunities for others. The essential points of the strategic windows concept are:

Markets Evolve Constantly

Markets are in a constant state of change. Those changes can be slow and evolutionary or abrupt and disruptive. There are four types of change:

1. The creation of new primary demand is a gradual change. The trend towards healthful exercise has, over the years, opened the strategic window for the makers of athletic shoes, such as Nike. At the same time it has slowly and steadily closed the strategic window on cigarettes and most distilled spirits products. The environment changes, while those firms' strengths remain the same.

2. Technological innovation is a more rapid form of change, and can also negate the strategic advantage of incumbent firms. Sunk costs in old technology, and a fear of cannibalizing existing bread-and-butter products, often ensure a late response to rapid and disruptive changes.

Company Strengths Remain Constant

Company strengths change much slower than markets. A distinctive competence—what a company does well—changes much slower than the external environment. A firm that has a distinctive product image, for example, tends to continue with that strength. That firm does not easily change that image radically. It tends to persist in the minds of consumers.

As the market changes the value of those strengths also changes. A strong brand name with an image for selling a popular whiskey, for example, diminishes in value as distilled spirits fall out of favor. At the same time, sales of Gatorade soar.

The Match

The concept of strategic windows runs a middle course between the lack of control implied by the early product life cycle and the subsequent assertions that marketers can control the life-cycle pattern. It recognizes the power of marketing to influence product sales as they progress from birth to decline, but also recognizes that many changes are uncontrollable.

3. Marketers can creatively redefine markets. They can create demand for their products and influence life cycles by redefining how customers perceive the product. Bottled water, for example, which was initially sold as an alternative to polluted water, was repositioned by Perrier in the mid-1970s as an alternative to soft drinks. Sales soared.

Similarly, early sellers of automatic teller machines (ATMs) lost share as larger competitors, such as IBM, sold entire lines of automated financial equipment rather than just a single item.

4. *Marketers can also change channels.* This, too, is a controllable type of change. Timex watches, for example, were unable to find distribution through jewelry stores, the primary means of watch distribution in past decades. In response, Timex went to mass market distribution.

The strategic windows concept embraces both the powers and limits of marketing. It implies serendipity as well as skill, and emphasizes observation and reaction as well as intervention. A central part of this hypothesis is that the window opens and closes on firms. The environment creates the opportunities.

THE HONDA EFFECT

Strategic windows is consistent with the "Honda Effect" hypothesized by Pascale (1984). He studied Honda's successful entry into the American motorcycle market in the mid-1960s and concluded that its entry was replete with miscalculations, strategic mistakes, and success through serendipitous events. Rather than the orderly strategic planning implied by the PLC, Pascale found that Honda executives really had no plan. Instead, they responded to the market as it emerged with no real idea as to where sales would ultimately lead.

Pascale contrasts the actions of Honda with the beliefs of formal theories of strategic planning. He calls the contrast the "Honda Effect." It holds that while many executives, academics, and business consultants prefer theories that stress a rational and orderly progression of events—such as the PLC—the reality is much different. The actual way in which most markets evolve is through a series of fits-and-starts, responses to unforeseen developments, and creative solutions to unexpected problems. Marketing strategy, in short, is a much messier process than presupposed by orderly concepts such as the PLC.

STRATEGIC IMPLICATIONS

The strategic implications of evolutionary theories of market change are many. But, most important, they suggest that a firm should: (1)

look outside its own industry, (2) engage in extensive experimentation, (3) embrace adaptive learning, and (4) adopt a change orientation. Consider each in turn.

Peripheral Vision

Major innovations often come from outside the industry most likely to be affected by those innovations. Even when the innovation does come from within the industry, it usually comes from small firms, not market leaders. Large market leaders tend not to be very innovative. Not only are they not the source of major innovations but they also tend to ignore major developments once they occur. Only when forced by fate do market leaders pick up on emerging trends.

Bennett and Cooper (1984) contend that large firms with many mature products forget how to innovate. The skills required for new product innovation are so different than those of their current product line. As a result, those firms focus on the old and miss the new.

Both Pascale's "Honda Effect" and Abell's "Strategic Windows" deal with the importance of peripheral vision. It is essential that firms focus their attention on the world that lies outside the company gates. It is where most innovations will come from. The concepts of market evolution hold that early recognition can benefit the firm greatly.

Extensive Experimentation

Market evolution also presupposes that a firm should engage in extensive experimentation when it comes to innovation and new product policy. Since the ultimate course of events is unknown, following many paths is a preferable strategy to doggedly pursuing a single course. If markets evolve in unexpected ways, then the best way to ensure that a firm will not be caught off guard is to experiment with myriad potential opportunities. One of those opportunities is likely to lead to success. It is a superior strategy than one that "bets-the-farm" on a single innovation.

Adaptation

An essential part of evolutionary theories in both biology and marketing is the idea of adaptation. It is a concept that is intimately tied to the previous two. A firm, like species, must adapt to changes in the market in which it competes. There must be a willingness to change with markets.

A Change Orientation

The most important element of evolutionary concepts is the focus on continual changes in markets rather than static analysis. One of the pitfalls of formula planning was its reliance on lengthy analysis which moved more slowly than the markets it sought to exploit. The focus on impending change allows the firm to better fit the market it seeks to serve. Whichever theory of evolution is most applicable to marketing, one thing is certain—an evolutionary model is preferable to one that presupposes inevitable trends and patterns. Gould (1983) sums it up best when he notes: "Adaptation, be it biological or cultural, represents a better fit to specific, local environments, not an inevitable stage in a ladder of progress" (p. 159). In marketing strategy, as in biology, it is adaptation rather than predetermination that governs the ultimate course of product sales.

References

Abell, Derek. "Strategic Windows." *Journal of Marketing,* July 1978, pp. 21–26.

Basalla, George. *The Evolution of Technology.* Cambridge, England: Cambridge University Press, 1988.

Bennett, Roger, and Robert Cooper. "The Product Life Cycle Trap." *Business Horizons,* September–October 1984, pp. 7–16.

Cox, William. "Product Life Cycles as Marketing Models." *Journal of Business,* October 1967, pp. 375–384.

Day, George. "The Product Life Cycle: Analysis and Applications Issues." *Journal of Marketing,* Fall 1981, pp. 60–67.

De Bresson, Chris. "The Evolutionary Paradigm and the Economics of Technological Change." *Journal of Economic Issues,* June 1987, pp. 751–72.

Dhalla, Nariman, and Sonia Yuspeh. "Forget the Product Life Cycle Concept." *Harvard Business Review,* January–February 1976, pp. 102–112.

Eldredge, Niles. *Time Frames.* New York: Simon & Schuster, 1985.

Fama, Eugene. "The Behavior of Stock Market Prices." *Journal of Business,* January 1965, pp. 34–105.

Gilfillan, S. C. *The Sociology of Invention.* Chicago: Follett, 1935.

Gould, Stephen. "The Episodic Nature of Evolutionary Change." In *The Panda's Thumb,* pp. 179–185. New York: W. W. Norton, 1980.

Gould, Stephen. "Kingdoms Without Wheels." In *Hen's Teeth and Horse's Toes*, pp. 158–165. New York: W. W. Norton, 1983.

Gould, Stephen, and Niles Eldredge. "Punctuated Equilibria: The Tempo and Mode of Evolution Reconsidered." *Paleobiology*, vol. 3, 1977, pp. 115–151.

Hunt, Shelby D. *Marketing Theory*. Columbus, OH: Grid Publications, 1976.

Jewkes, John, David Sawers, and Richard Stillerman. *The Sources of Invention*. New York: St. Martin's Press, 1958.

Levine, Joshua. "Locking Up the Weekend Warriors." *Forbes*, October 2, 1989, pp. 234–235.

Ostlund, Lyman. "Perceived Innovation Attributes as Predictors of Innovativeness." *Journal of Consumer Research*, September 1974, pp. 23–29.

Pascale, Richard. "Perspectives on Strategy: The Real Story Behind Honda's Success." *California Management Review*, Spring 1984, pp. 47–72.

Polli, Rolando, and Victor Cook. "Validity of the Product Life Cycle." *Journal of Business*, October 1969, pp. 385–400.

Rink, David, and John Swan. "Product Life Cycle Research: A Literature Review." *Journal of Business Research*, September 1979, pp. 219–242.

Tellis, Gerard J., and C. Merle Crawford. "An Evolutionary Approach to Product Growth Theory." *Journal of Marketing*, Fall 1981, pp. 125–132.

Chapter *13*

Speed as Strategy

R ecently, strategy has turned to speed as a way to gain competitive
advantage. It is a belief based on the proposition that responding
quickly to market changes and competitor challenges is a superior strategy
to drawing elegant, but time-dependent plans. It is a strategy that substitutes speed for lengthy deliberation.

Speed as strategy values action over analysis. It is also a strategy
wherein American firms have an inherent competitive advantage. As
Schaffer (1989) notes: "Our greatest strength is the 'let's do it,' 'lets
try it' attitude" (p. 2). According to that view, strategy emerges from
a series of small steps rather than from a grand design.

Speed as strategy also sidesteps the problem of sustainable competitive
advantage, which has proved to be an elusive goal, as well as a common
criticism of strategic formulations. Bhide (1986) sums it up best. He
notes: "Opportunities to gain lasting advantage through blockbuster strategic moves are rare in business. What mostly counts are vigor and nimble-
ness" (p. 59). Speed as strategy replaces sustainable advantage with
an advantage based on quick response. This chapter examines those
issues.

Why Speed Is More Important

Speed as a source of competitive advantage is motivated by a number
of environmental and competitive factors that characterize today's markets.

SHORTER PRODUCT LIFE CYCLES

Speed has become more important because product life cycles seem to
be shortening. Whereas products used to last for decades they now some-

times last only months. The long-term market seems to have been replaced with a series of short-lived fads. If you blink you miss the market.

Firms must get their new products to market before the peak of popularity passes. Otherwise, they miss the majority of profits. There is little time for detailed market research. Firms have to move, and move fast. Uttal (1987) estimates that in some fast-moving industries like electronics "coming to market nine to twelve months late can cost a new product half of its potential revenues" (p. 62).

Consider the speed with which other products have moved from fast growth to rapid decline. In the mid-1970s, CB radios were the rage. After the oil embargo, and the 55-mph speed limit that was imposed to conserve gasoline, CB radios became a means of evading police radar traps. By 1975, sales soared to $400 million. Small firms like Hygrade Electronics dominated the market. Major manufacturers entered later. By 1977 sales were trending decidely downward. Seemingly overnight, consumers become infatuated with other products.

Wine coolers followed a similar path. Sales turned sharply downward after a few years of rapid growth. By the time Miller Brewing entered with its "Matilda Bay" brand, convinced that the market did indeed have the potential for long-term growth, decline had set in.

The experience of those products is by no means unique. Today, many products today seem to act more like hula-hoops than long-lived sources of market opportunity.

PROFITS FROM NEW PRODUCTS

Increasingly, profits come from new products. A 1981 survey of the new product development practices of 700 firms by Booz, Allen & Hamilton found that companies "expected that nearly one-third of their profits in the 1980s would come from new products, compared with slightly over one-fifth in the 1970s" (Fraker 1984). In light of such findings, firms have been introducing more new products in search of more new profits. A firm that does otherwise is likely to find itself facing imminent decline a few years down the road. Firms have to keep a steady flow of new products coming to market.

MORE COMPETITION IN GROWTH MARKETS

It used to be believed that competition was less intense in high-growth markets. No more. Firms fight vigorously for share in high-growth markets. As a result, most growth markets exhibit the classic characteristics of mature markets. There is rampant price competition, products are widely distributed, and the degree of rivalry is more like that found in slow-growth markets. What was once a strategy to avoid competition is now an invitation to intense rivalry.

Severe competition in growth markets contradicts the traditional advice of the product life cycle and the Boston Consulting Group's Growth-Share Matrix, which adopts the life-cycle theory. In theory, there are few reasons to cut prices in growth markets. Demand exceeds supply. It is the growth stage where profits are highest.

Unfortunately, recent experiences have turned past theories topsy-turvy. Today, competition is so severe in most growth markets that profits are hurt rather than helped by this supposedly benevolent stage of product growth.

RAMPANT COPYING

In the past there was more time for extensive market testing. When Procter and Gamble introduced Pampers disposable diapers in the mid-1960s, it had tested the product for nearly a decade. In the present, such luxuries are rare. Competitors routinely steal new product ideas that are in test market. Copying is rampant. While one firm is analyzing, another is acting. It is not unusual to find one firm conducting a market test while another speeds a copy of the product to market. Sara Lee Corp. often eschews market testing. As a product manager noted: "While we were busy testing in a few cities, someone could have taken our idea and run with it" (Alsop 1986).

GAINING SHELF SPACE EARLY

More new products and limited retail shelf space mean that a firm must gain shelf space early or face the prospect of getting no distribution later on. In disposable diapers, for example, the product is bulky, and there is usually room for only a few brands. In the late 1960s and early 1970s later entrants had a tough time finding shelf space for their products. Smaller, later entrants into personal computers faced the same dilemma, even though some products had performance advantages.

LESS RELIANCE ON FORECASTING

Finally, and possibly the most important reason why speed is a superior approach to strategy, is that it reduces the necessity to forecast long-term trends. In the past, marketing strategy—especially long-range planning—relied heavily on forecasts of sales, market growth, competitor reactions, and economic growth. Frequent errors in those forecasts ruined many strategies. Those forecasts prepared firms for a future that never came. Speed sidesteps forecasting. It moves quickly with markets rather than trying to guess the direction in which they will move. Speed replaces an uncontrollable weakness with a controllable strength. It replaces forecasting with speed of response.

Superfast Innovation

One way that speed finds its way into strategy is through faster innovation. Speeding new products to market is an active strategy that embraces innovation. "Superfast innovators," as Dumaine (1989) calls them, move products quickly from the drawing board to the retailer's shelf. Doing so requires that firms replace traditional modes of new product planning with approaches that embrace fast response.

NEW NEW PRODUCT PLANNING

In recent years there has been a revolution in new product planning. Procedures for bringing new products to market have been overhauled to promote speed. Many of the new procedures are copies of those used by Japanese firms with a well-earned reputation for fast response. Reiner (1989), for example, describes the procedure whereby Panasonic brings new products to market.

Speeding new products to market requires three distinct steps. Each is described below.

Technology Development

The first step in a speed strategy focuses on scientific and engineering research. The goal of this research is to make discoveries and perfect new technologies. Researchers might, for example, investigate how lasers can be used to store data.

It is rarely clear where basic research will lead. Discoveries are impossible to predict. It is usually not even apparent where a new technology will find application in useful products. But, that is not the goal of technology development. Uncertainty pervades basic research. Technology development is not concerned with producing marketable products. That comes later. At this stage, the technology itself is the focus of all actions.

Consider the case of CD players. Akio Morita, the chairman of Sony, notes that his firm did not set out to discover the CD player. Instead, developments in laser technology were the goal. They, in turn, led to a useful product. It would have been impossible, he claims, to have so perfectly predicted the course of events that unfolded as research progressed from the lab to the marketplace. Flexibility, and an openness to new ideas, is a characteristic of this phase of research.

The result of successful technology development is what Reiner (1989) calls "technology platforms." Those are workable technologies that can be incorporated rapidly into new and existing products.

Product Development

Once a technology is workable, the second stage—product development—proceeds. At this stage the firm seeks to incorporate the technology platform into marketable products. It might use laser technology to store data on computers, to store snapshots from cameras, and for CD players. The product development stage seeks to apply what was discovered in the first stage. Product development is concerned with the application of technology to marketable products.

The focus is on getting the technology into products quickly. No new technological advances are sought. Revisions and product reformulations to incorporate the latest developments are postponed until a later model is introduced. The goal is to move quickly to market.

Likewise, the focus is on large numbers of products. Product development seeks to apply the "technology platform" into as many products as possible. If it is not possible to predict which products will be successful, many products should be tried. Finally, extensive market research is eschewed. There is no time for careful study in this form of product development. The call is to "try it" rather than "study it."

Market Development

Speed is a strategy that substitutes strength in numbers of new products for accurate long-term forecasts. The idea is to pepper the market with products that incorporate the new technology. It is understood that some products will be successful while many others will fail.

Speed as strategy lets the market decide which products are best.

Extensive market studies and long-term sales projections are avoided. In essence, the market itself is the test market.

A firm must be able to move quickly to produce and sell those products that prove successful. Flexible factories are part of the process. Production is expanded for products that are successful, while unsuccessful products are discontinued. The goal is to concentrate on the products that hit, and quickly withdraw the products that fail to attract customers.

Tonka Corp., the toy maker, follows a speed strategy in an industry where new products come and go quickly and the customer is fickle. Tonka enters fast with a barrage of new toy products. As chairman Stephen Shank notes: "We don't need home runs, we just need reasonable success, but we also need a logical candidate to hit a home run" (Weiner 1989, p. 221). Tonka is equally fast at yanking the losers. Poor sellers are withdrawn from the market in as little as three months. Before moving to a speed strategy such products would have lingered in product lines much longer.

Contrast the speed approach to new product planning to that offered by more traditional new product planning formulations.

Traditional New Product Planning

In the past, the most widely used new product planning formulation was that proposed by Booz, Allen & Hamilton—the consulting firm. It is the opposite of speed as strategy, and embraces careful market studies, long lead times, and a set sequence of events. The basic philosophy is to slowly but surely whittle a large number of product ideas down to a small number of successful products. The goal is to avoid product failure and concentrate spending on products that will ultimately turn into successes. The fundamental idea of traditional new product planning is to focus funds on the successes. There are many steps to follow.

Idea Generation

Before the new product process can proceed, new product ideas are required. Ideas are generated with brainstorming, making unlikely product connections, and other creative approaches.

Idea Screening

The first stage of traditional new product planning is idea screening or the "rough screen." The goal is to quickly and inexpensively eliminate the ridiculous product ideas that serve no market, can never make a profit, or are a poor fit for the firm.

Concept Development and Testing

Concept development and testing follows. At this stage, crude ideas are refined into product concepts, which describe actual versions of the product. Consumer reactions are sought. Losers are dropped from further consideration.

Marketing Strategy

A marketing strategy is designed for products that pass the previous steps. It sets long-term goals for sales, profits, and market share. It also decides pricing, distribution, and promotional strategy, as well as how the product will be positioned.

Business Analysis

Given that strategy, a business analysis is conducted which indicates whether the proposal is worthwhile. At this stage, forecasts of sales, costs, and profits are made. If prediction points to a product that will earn profits, the process moves to the next step.

Product Development

Product development follows for attractive proposals. At this stage the actual product is developed.

Market Testing

Market testing is then conducted to estimate actual sales. This includes small-scale consumer tests to large-scale test markets. Expenses begin to escalate quickly.

Commercialization

Market testing is actually the first part of commercialization. Successful tests are "rolled out" to new markets. As production expands, the product moves into the larger market.

COMPARISON OF APPROACHES

Exhibit 13.1 show a side-by-side comparison of new versus traditional new product planning. This section shows how the new approach to

Exhibit 13.1   *Approach to New Product Planning*

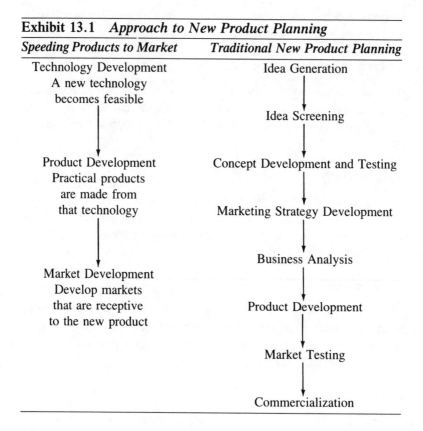

Speeding Products to Market	*Traditional New Product Planning*
Technology Development	Idea Generation
A new technology	
becomes feasible	Idea Screening
Product Development	Concept Development and Testing
Practical products	
are made from	Marketing Strategy Development
that technology	
	Business Analysis
Market Development	
Develop markets	Product Development
that are receptive	
to the new product	Market Testing
	Commercialization

new product development overcomes many of the shortcomings of traditional new product planning paradigms.

Speed Versus Long Lead Times

Traditional product planning is slow, requires long lead times, and avoids errors but at great cost in terms of time. It trades time for precision. By analogy with riflery, traditional planning spends much time aiming the rifle. Speeding new products to market aims quickly but fires many shots at the target.

In strategy, the reduction of risk that theoretically arises from longer lead times is frittered away by disadvantages associated with moving slowly. Changes in the market, and the actions of competitors, often result in a product that is perfectly fitted to a world that no longer exists. The long lead time increases rather than reduces the risk of failure.

Quick Response Versus Accurate Forecasts

Traditional product planning requires accurate forecasts to avoid product failures and focus on the successes. Unfortunately, such forecasts are notoriously inaccurate. This is especially true with "new-to-the-world" products, with which consumers have little experience. Imagine Sony asking consumers of their need or desire for a CD laser-disk player. Would the results of that survey be indicative of the true potential of that market?

Many Versus One New Product

Traditional new product planning focuses efforts on getting to that one best product idea. It puts all eggs in one basket. Speed, in contrast, recognizes the impossibility of such foresight. It acknowledges the inherent inability to predict what the market will want. The assumption of speed is more in tune with today's markets.

Action Versus Analysis Paralysis

Speed as strategy is really part of that larger issue of embracing action over analysis paralysis. It is a recognition that the weighty analysis of past planning formulations has been a hindrance rather than a help. Speed, by definition, is action oriented. Traditional new product planning, in contrast, embraces comprehensive study. Moving quickly is largely a reaction to the criticism that planning is encumbered by analysis paralysis.

Competitor Response Versus Careful Planning

The emphasis of traditional new product planning on careful study precludes fast response to competitors' actions. Most markets today do not allow for the careful study proposed by traditional planning. Competitors will quickly copy good ideas. Careful study carries a penalty that speed overcomes.

REQUIREMENTS FOR FASTER PRODUCT DEVELOPMENT

Speeding up the new product development process requires special skills, which include the following:

Collaboration Within the Firm

Quickening the rate at which new products are introduced requires coordination among those who design, make, and sell the products. Marketing, product design, engineering, and manufacturing must all coordinate their efforts. Specifically, the following aspects of new product design are important.

Parallel Product Development

Takeuchi and Nonaka (1986) argue that traditional new product planning is like a relay race. When the team that designed the product was finished with its work it passed it—like the baton in a relay—to the engineers, who then passed it to manufacturing. Finally, marketing ended up with a product to sell. There was coordination to be sure but events progressed one after another. Exhibit 13.2 illustrates the practice.

Speed as strategy requires parallel processing, which is "a holistic or rugby approach—where a team tries to go the distance as a unit, passing the ball back and forth" (p. 137). As Exhibit 13.2 illustrates, parallel product development speeds the process by overlapping the tasks

Exhibit 13.2   *Sequential Versus Parallel Product Development*

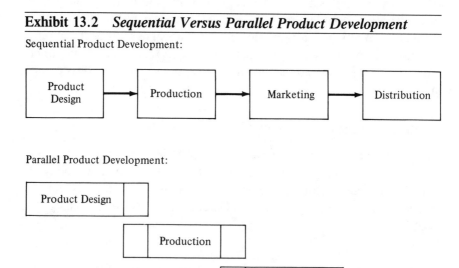

Sequential Product Development:

Parallel Product Development:

of different departments. Marketing, for example, is working on a plan to sell the product, while designers are still designing the product.

Some firms take the sports analogy seriously. Domino's Pizza, for example, is modeled after a sports team. Delivery persons mimic a football player running for a touchdown. As CEO Tom Monaghan states: "Our whole business is based on speed" (Dumaine 1989, p. 59).

Design for Assembly

Superfast innovation requires that products be designed so that they can be manufactured quickly. It is called design for assembly (DFA). IBM's Proprinter is a prime example. Until 1985, IBM imported its printers from Japan's Epson, part of Seiko Corp., the watch seller. In 1985 IBM began making its own printers after designing them for easy assembly. The result, assembly time declined from thirty minutes to three minutes (Port 1989). Likewise, Compaq can design a computer twice as fast as IBM. Honda can bring a car to market five times faster than GM.

DFA cuts assembly time by designing products that have fewer parts. Consequently, fewer assembly steps are needed. Fewer parts also lead to the benefits of higher reliability—there are fewer parts to break down—and lower costs.

Benetton, the Italian apparel firm, moves new designs quickly to market. Clothing is designed on computers, which then send the new product designs electronically to the factory floor, where computer-controlled equipment cuts the patterns automatically in a predetermined set of customer sizes. Goods are sent to retailers shelves in an astounding fifteen days (Bower and Hout 1988, p. 115). Not only are costs lower—due to more efficient cutting of the material—but customers are more satisfied by the quick response to new fashions.

Willingness to Engage in Creative Destruction

Speeding products to market requires a different mindset, as it requires firms to risk destroying their current product line. It is similar to advice offered more than twenty years ago. In 1960, Ted Levitt advised that firms should engage in creative destruction. That is, they should "destroy their own highly profitable assets" (p. 160). Those assets are replaced by new assets. Superfast innovation proceeds on a similar track. It holds that a firm should cannibalize its own successful products, and replace them with new products. It is a job that must be done. If a firm fails to cannibalize its own products, competitors will do it for them. Better a firm does to itself what others will inexorably do to it.

Staying One Step Ahead of the Competition

Introducing many new products to markets can be used to earn competitive advantage by constantly having unique products that are not available elsewhere. When slower firms copy, faster firms move on to new products.

Consider the case of Patagonia. The mail order clothing seller stays one step ahead of much larger competitors, such as L. L. Bean, through a policy of superfast innovation. When competitors copy its innovations, Patagonia comes out with newer products still. For example, it dropped its second best-selling line of polypropylene underwear, which accounted for 25 percent of the firm's revenues when other firms began selling the same product at a lower price. Patagonia switched to capilene, a space-age fabric used by space shuttle astronauts. As Patagonia's founder von Chouinard noted: "As soon as we get stuck competing on price, competing on distribution, I'm out of there" (Meeks 1989).

Put Speed into the Culture

Putting speed into an organization is not an easy task. Firms that move slowly tend to resist changes, no matter how elegant their stated strategy. All employees in a firm must embrace a philosophy of speeding products to market for it to be truly successful. That requires extensive training. It also requires that firms inculcate employees with the belief that speed is of the utmost importance.

Quicker Decision Making

Bureaucracy is one of the worst enemies of speed. Moving quickly requires fast decision making. Therefore, speed as strategy, if it is to work correctly, must have an organization where lower-level employees can make decisions on their own. Along with increased responsibility, speed requires that employees be given increased authority.

Try Teams

Speed requires a corporate culture that values action over analysis. "Try teams" are groups of six to twelve employees that are given the authority and responsibility to bring a new product from design to market (Dumaine 1987). They are given strict deadlines. Their small size, and increased authority, has speeded up development time in many firms.

Worship the Schedule

Companies that have successfully implemented speed as strategy pay strict attention to production and order-filling schedules. By placing the schedule first, decisions get made faster and the customers' needs for quick delivery become the overriding goal.

Killing the Competition with Variety

One strategic consequence of superfast innovation is the sheer number of new products. Not only do products come to market quickly but they come to market in larger numbers. The result is a barrage of new products that can bury the competition with variety. While competitors use traditional new product planning to find that single right product that will be a success in the marketplace, the superfast innovator introduces many new products.

Variety can serve as a strategic weapon. Consider the competitive battle between Honda and Yamaha motorcycles. Yamaha started the war in 1981 when it increased its capacity to make motorcycles. Honda, it assumed, was more interested in automobiles. Maybe, just maybe, it would not fight back. Yamaha was mistaken. Honda changed models 113 times! It changed the style and technology of its bikes. The speed and number of new product introductions overwhelmed Yamaha. As Stalk (1988) notes: "Next to a Honda, Yamaha products looked old, unattractive, and out of date" (p. 45). Honda buried Yamaha's challenge by offering consumers greater product variety. (Also, see Stalk 1990 for a thorough discussion of speed as strategy.)

Variety itself often leads to market changes. The sheer number of different products on the market can serve to heighten the importance of design in areas where fashion did not previously play an important role. In appliances, stereo equipment, and motorcycles superiority in design can result from quickening the pace of product innovation.

Quick Response

Quick response is a different concept than superfast innovation. Quick response concentrates on lessening the time it takes to get *existing* goods to consumers. It speeds up the transmission of marketing information, improves communication between those who make the product and those who sell it, speeds the manufacturing process, and quickens the distribution of goods. The goal is to make sure that the seller has the right product at the right time. If, for example, Benetton's customers suddenly demand red sweaters, the firm wants to be able to have more red sweaters available for sale quickly, not in eight months. To do so requires a quick response system.

Red Lobster, the successful seafood chain owned by General Mills, relies on a quick response system to satisfy changing market needs. As cajun food became more popular in the 1980s the restaurant quickly increased the number of spicy items on the menu.

Firms can respond quickly to one of two aspects of their environment: (1) changes in consumers' needs, or (2) competitors' challenges. Competitors' moves can force firms to respond quickly. The introduction of a successful new product by a competitor necessitates as quick a response as a change in consumer needs.

There are four parts to any quick response system: (1) getting close to customers, (2) improving communication among channel members, (3) superfast production, and (4) speedier distribution.

Getting Close to Customers

Staying close to customers is the basis of quick response. Before a firm can respond quickly to changing consumer preferences it needs to know what those needs are. That requires that firms listen to customers. Quick response systems rely on electronic data collection, rather than lengthy marketing research questionnaires. A typical system records consumer purchases with scanners. That data is fed back to a central location either instantaneously or at the end of each day. It is then analyzed to see which items are selling briskly and which are not. The quick response system often has the added benefit of speeding customers through checkout lines.

The textile and apparel industries, which have been heavily battered by imports, have been among the strongest proponents of quick response systems. Levi Strauss, the blue jeans manufacturer, has one of the most innovative systems. Its "LeviLink," allows the firm to respond quickly to consumer demand.

The Levi Strauss system requires close contact with retailers, the primary customer for Levi products. Levi affixes barcodes to goods at the factory and provides elaborate software services to track the flow of jeans through the retail channel. The experience of Designs Inc., a Levi-only retailer, is typical of the way the LeviLink system moves with customer preferences. At Designs, based in Massachusetts, information on items sold during the day is accumulated in each of the firm's forty-four branch-store computers. At night, each store sends its sales data to a mainframe computer at Design's headquarters. At the end of each week headquarters sends a replacement order to Levi electronically. The retailer's computer communicates directly with Levi's computer. Levi ships the order to Designs within four days. By the end of 1987, 25 percent of all Levi orders came from electronic purchase orders. Larger retailers, such as Sears, J. C. Penney, and Wal-Mart, have moved quickly to install similar quick response systems. On the trend towards quick response systems in apparel, one industry expert contends: "Anybody who doesn't do it will be at a real competitive disadvantage" (Hamilton 1987, p. 92).

The benefits of staying close to customers have been clear. The time between the order of a Levi garment and receipt of shipment has fallen from forty days in 1985 to twelve days in 1987 as a result of the quick response system.

The competitive advantage of the quick response system arises from the inherent disadvantage held by lower-cost imports. Imports cannot respond as quickly to changing consumer needs. Production in distant lands precludes the type of fast delivery offered by systems such as Levi's LeviLink.

Communication Among Channel Members

Quick response requires extensive communication among firms in the channel of distribution. Buyers and sellers must coordinate their efforts to serve customers faster. Many industries have formed voluntary organizations that promote such coordination. The textile and apparel industry is linked as shown in Exhibit 13.3. There are four key linkages which allow the firms in allied industries to work together on speeding orders to customers. It is an example of cooperation being used to fight imports.

The first link in the chain is VICS—the Voluntary Interindustry Communication Standards, which connects the apparel manufacturer and the retailer. VICS sets communication standards between computers so that those two market players can capture information concerning consumer purchases.

The second link in the chain is TALC—the Textile and Apparel Linkage Council, which promotes cooperation between textile manufacturers and

Exhibit 13.3   *Communication in Textile and Apparel Industry*

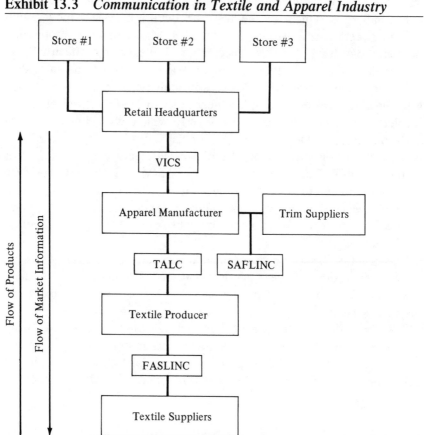

apparel makers. TALC promotes electronic standards for transmitting orders and labeling rolls of fabrics with barcodes between buyers and sellers to speed customer service. TALC also sets standards for product quality, and that speeds the movement of fabrics to garment makers.

The third link is FASLINC—the Fabric and Suppliers Linkage Council, which promotes cooperation further up the channel of distribution—between textile suppliers and textile producers. Its aim is to facilitate faster, more accurate information flow between producers and suppliers of textiles. FASLINC is also concerned with eliminating the cost, time, and need for duplicate quality tests. It also sets uniform quality ratings.

Those uniform quality ratings speed the flow of goods through the channel of distribution. In the past, each buyer up and down the channel had to carefully check goods to see if they met that firm's definition of quality. The multiplicity of quality checks slowed the process of getting goods to market. Firms in the industry spent more time checking up on each other than they did on serving customers. Agreement on what constitutes quality means less need for multiple checking and grading. The result is better customer service.

The final link in the industry chain is SAFLINC—the Sundries and Apparel Findings Council, which promotes cooperation between apparel manufacturers and makers of trim for apparel. The goal is to get the industry to respond quicker to fashion changes and become more competitive against lower-cost imports.

Those four linkage organizations work closely together to coordinate the sending of orders throughout the chain of distribution, forecasting demand at various stages within the chain, and tracing inventory and shipments along the way. The ties are meant to promote quick response, and, as well, to take maximum advantage of the competitive edge of American textile and apparel firms against imports. As products flow up the diagram in Exhibit 13.3, information flows down, back towards the source of those products.

Haggar is a pioneer of quick response. More than 1,000 retailers transmit sales information and purchase orders electronically via Haggar's "HOT" (Haggar Order Transmission) system. Retailers claim that sales have risen 20 to 45 percent as a result of fewer out-of-stock situations, faster inventory turns, and smaller inventories.

Haggar attributes the improved service to computer linkages with its own textile suppliers. Whereas in the past each roll of fabric had to be swatched, shaded, and measured as it arrived at the loading dock, the information now arrives electronically from the supplier, and the product itself is barcoded for quick checking. Quality standards have made suppliers' data more credible.

Toyota, also noted as a fast producer, relies heavily on communications throughout its organization. Dealers in Japan are directly connected to the Toyota factory computer. Once a car has been ordered by a customer, it is entered directly into the scheduling cycle at the plant. Suppliers are likewise connected, and are notified immediately of the needed parts. Customers receive immediate confirmation of the delivery data. Dealers, customers, suppliers, and the production of goods is tied by computer in the Toyota operation.

Superfast Production

The third step in a quick response system is superfast production. Once customer needs have been ascertained, and communications sent back through the channel of distribution, firms must be able to switch production rapidly to the models now in demand. This requires flexible factories, a strong point of many fast-moving Japanese companies. Dumaine (1989) refers to firms that speed up their manufacturing processes as superfast producers.

Superfast production requires an emphasis on time, rather than low costs. It is a different emphasis than that held by Asian competitors. Low-cost labor requires long production runs, and long lead times, to gain production efficiencies. Speed as strategy thrives on short runs tailored to specific consumer demands.

Fast production also requires efficient scheduling. Production is organized by product rather than process to minimize the transport of goods around the shop floor. Likewise, employees are given wide leeway in deciding how to handle production problems.

Superfast Distribution

The final step in a quick response system is superfast distribution. This entails setting up the organization to move products to customers quickly once they have been produced. Advances in logistics have helped in that regard.

Benefits of Quick Response

There are numerous benefits that arise from a quick response.

Lower Costs

Quick response leads to lower costs in at least three areas: (1) fewer markdowns, (2) fewer stockouts, and (3) smaller inventories. The savings can be substantial. A 1986 study by Du Pont analyzed the savings gained from a quick response system in the textile industry. It found savings in the millions of dollars throughout the entire channel of distribution—from textile mills, to apparel manufacturers, to retailers. Quick response yielded tangible results.

Fewer Markdowns

A key advantage of a quick response system is that the seller is forced to take fewer markdowns. Markdowns result from errors in forecasting consumer demand. Orders for fashion clothing, for example, must be made a year in advance. If the fashion proves less popular than expected, markdowns are required to move the merchandise off retailers' racks. Quick response makes it possible to reduce initial order time from one year to two or three months. That, in turn, reduces the time horizon of the forecasts, which allows firms to better gauge consumer demand.

Fewer Stockouts

Stockouts occur when a consumer wants an item that is not available in the store. It too is a forecasting error, but it is an error of conservatism. Quick response systems allow stores to reorder in smaller quantities, and receive their orders quickly, avoiding stockouts. A pilot study with Wal-Mart found that stockouts were reduced from 29 to 17 percent with quick response.

Smaller Inventories

Quick response systems mimic just-in-time inventory systems. Smaller orders, which are sent more frequently, mean that goods move quickly through the channel of distribution. Materials and products are put into action rather than remaining in inventory. The result is that smaller inventories are needed. That, in turn, reduces costs.

In previous decades in the textile industry, it was not unusual for a fabric to take sixty-five weeks to move from the manufacturer's plant to the customer. During that time the material was actually being processed for only fifteen of those weeks. The goods languished in inventory for the other fifty weeks. Inventory costs ran at 6.4 percent of sales. Quick response systems—such as LeviLink—have lowered inventory costs substantially.

BETTER SERVICE

Speeding orders to customers inevitably results in better service. Customers are served more promptly, delays in delivery are minimized, and merchandise in demand is readily available.

Consider how speed improves service in the rental car business. Time is of the essence in getting a business customer from an airport rental car counter to the highway. Business customers equate long lines with poor service. Hertz offers the ultimate in speedier service. Business customers go directly to a car, where the trunk is open awaiting their luggage. The customer drives away after waiting in no lines, and filling out no forms. Speed leads to better service.

HIGHER PRODUCT QUALITY

Advocates claim that speed leads to higher product quality. Superior quality is a by-product of improved communications among channel members. Channel members often agree on uniform standards of quality to speed products to market. Uniform standards define quality similarly throughout the industry. The industry then works to improve the level of product quality as defined by that standard. Rather than checking the quality of goods at each step of the manufacturing and selling process, the entire industry can work to increase quality. In effect, haste does not make waste, it makes for better quality.

BROADER PRODUCT LINES

A greater variety of new products has the result of filling out sparsely populated product lines. As a result, firms that pursue speed as strategy often end up with broader product lines. They compete across a broader front.

COVER MANY SEGMENTS

More new products also lead to greater coverage of segments. A firm that rapidly introduces new products to the market often ends up with a variety of differentiated goods, each of which serves a different segment of the market. Speed as strategy tends to lead to multiple products sold to multiple market segments.

BINDING BUYERS TO SELLERS

A strategic benefit of quick response systems is that they tie buyers to sellers. Computer linkages aid communication among channel members, but they also ensure that the buyer remains loyal to that seller. A buyer who has installed expensive computer linkages has increased switching costs. That buyer is almost forced to remain loyal to that seller's product. Airline reservation systems, electronic ordering systems, and numerous other links result in speedier service to customers. They also build a binding relationship between buyers and sellers.

SUPERIOR CUSTOMER SATISFACTION

The ultimate benefit of a quick response system is that it creates superior customer satisfaction. That satisfaction is the result of the other benefits of speedier service, namely, lower costs, better service, and higher quality. The final chapter covers the issue of customer satisfaction in greater detail.

Questions Raised by Speed as Strategy

Speed as strategy leaves many questions unanswered.

IS SPEED A SHORT-TERM PERSPECTIVE?

In recent decades, American managers have been castigated for focusing too intently on next quarter's results. While foreign competitors take the long view, American firms pursue short-term goals. A way must be found, critics of American business argue, to shift the emphasis from a short-term to a long-term perspective.

Advocates of speed as strategy argue the opposite. Moving quickly, they contend, strongly implies a short-term perspective. Schaffer (1989), for example, writes: "American managers should reject the barrage of criticism they receive for focusing so much on short-term results. . . . Why fight the reality when we can take advantage of it?" (p. 2). It is an interesting, but troubling, proposition. Should American firms take an even shorter-term perspective? Or, will they run faster down the wrong path? Is speed as strategy a mistake?

Critics of marketing would argue that it is. Recall from the first chapter the admonitions of Bennett and Cooper. They argue that American marketers and the marketing concept have led to many minor product modifications, but have missed major product innovations. Those criticisms apply verbatim to speed as strategy. Rushing to market with many new products that contain only incremental changes in hope of fast, short-term profits is a strategy that is subject to the same criticisms as the marketing concept. Speed may concentrate a firm's attention on fads at the expense of more long-lived opportunities. Firms that follow superfast innovation may be forced to switch from one fad to another as growth advances then recedes. They may lack the patience and persistence necessary to succeed with more lasting opportunities. It must be asked whether speed reinforces that mistaken view? To date, that question has not been answered.

ARE THERE BENEFITS TO MOVING SLOWLY?

While speed as strategy has received much acclaim, some benefits are gained by moving slowly and deliberately. McDonald's, for example, moves slowly into new food products. It is known for exhaustive product testing. Salads, which now contribute substantially to store sales and profits, took twelve years to reach their 1987 premiere. McDonald's is moving equally slow with it pizza entry (Schwartz 1989).

Burger King, in contrast, moved too quickly, speeding new products and new ad campaigns to market. Its menu changed so often that consumers were confused and unsure of which products would be for sale when they next visited. Quality and service also suffered. While Burger King embraced innovation, McDonalds' kept a steady course. The clear winner did not use speed as strategy.

Some marketers contend that the trend towards more new products has gone too far. Peter Rogers, a Nabisco vice-president, contends that the pace of new food product introductions should be slowed. He estimates that 10,000 new food products were introduced in 1987, even though each typically costs between $15 million and $20 million to launch. Furthermore, less than 1 percent of the 45,000 new products introduced during the last sixteen years has achieved annual sales of $15 million or more. He contends that much of that money could be spent more wisely (*Marketing News* 1988).

Finally, Royal Dutch Shell, an energy firm known for taking the long-term perspective, avoided the rash moves of its faster moving competitors during the late 1970s and early 1980s. As a result it has profited handsomely. Mack (1989) notes: "They have positioned themselves in such a way that their momentum is going to carry them for five or ten years." Apparently, speed is not the best strategy for all firms in all industries.

DOES SPEED WORK FOR ALL PRODUCTS?

The advantages of speed as strategy may be limited to certain kinds of products. Many of the examples used by proponents focus on computers, and other high-technology businesses, where change is fast and competition is fierce. Developments in computers happen quickly, and the argument for shorter product life cycles is especially applicable. Entering later carries a particularly onerous penalty. Whether that penalty is as severe in other industries is unclear.

Other examples of speed as strategy focus on products where minor product modifications or fashion changes are common—for example, supermarket products and clothing. In such instances, a steady stream of "new and improved" products is crucial.

To date, it is unclear whether moving quickly is superior to moving more cautiously in all product categories, or even most. Do the generalizations presented in this chapter apply to many products? Or, do they apply only to a limited number of businesses? To date, the limits of speed as strategy have not been delineated.

SPEED, CONSUMERS, AND COMPETITION

Whatever its limits, speed as strategy forces a firm to consider both its customers and its competitors. Speed gives customers better service, a goal in keeping with the basic tenets of the marketing concept. It also improves customer satisfaction. Speed focuses on competitors as well, using time to gain competitive advantage. Overall, speed as strategy reinforces the merger between a consumer and competitor perspective of markets. No wonder it has attracted the attention of marketers and strategists alike.

References

Alsop, Ronald. "Companies Get on the Fast Track to Roll Out Hot New Products." *Wall Street Journal,* July 10, 1986, p. 27.

Bhide, Amar. "Hustle as Strategy." *Harvard Business Review,* September–October 1986, pp. 59–65.

Bower, Joseph and Thomas Hout. "Fast-Cycle Capability for Competitive Power." *Harvard Business Review,* November–December 1988, pp. 110–118.

Dumaine, Brian. "How Managers Can Succeed Through Speed." *Fortune,* February 13, 1989, pp. 54–66.

"Food Marketer: Slow the Frenetic Pace of New Product Introductions." *Marketing News,* March 28, 1988, p. 17.

Fraker, Susan. "High-Speed Management for the High-Tech Age." *Fortune,* March 5, 1984, pp. 62–68.

Hamilton, Joan. "How Levi Strauss Is Getting the Lead Out of Its Pipeline." *Business Week,* December 21, 1987, p. 92.

Levitt, Theodore. "Marketing Myopia." In *The Marketing Imagination,* pp. 141–172. New York: Free Press, 1986.

Mack, Toni. "Time, Money and Patience." *Forbes,* August 21, 1989, pp. 60–62.

Meeks, Fleming. "The Man Is the Message." *Forbes,* April 17, 1989, pp. 148–152.

Port, Otis. "Pssst! Want a Secret for Making Superproducts." *Business Week,* October 2, 1989, pp. 106, 110.

Reiner, Gary. "Getting There First: It Takes Planning to Put Plans into Action." *New York Times,* March 12, 1989, p. D3.

Schaffer, Robert. "Don't Waste Time Planning—Act." *New York Times,* October 29, 1989, sect. 3, p. 2.

Schwartz, John. "You Deserve a Pizza Today?" *Newsweek,* September 11, 1989, p. 46.

Stalk, George. "Time—The Next Source of Competitive Advantage." *Harvard Business Review,* July–August 1988, pp. 41–51.

Stalk, George, Jr., and Thomas M. Hout. *Competing Against Time: How Time-Based Competition Is Reshaping Global Markets.* New York: Free Press, 1990.

Takeuchi, Hirotaka, and Ikujiro Nonaka. "The 'New' New Product Development Game." *Harvard Business Review,* January–February 1986, pp. 137–146.

Uttal, Bro. "Speeding New Ideas to Market." *Fortune,* March 2, 1987, pp. 62–66.

Weiner, Steve. "Keep on Truckin'." *Forbes,* October 16, 1989, pp. 220–221.

Chapter 14

Long-Term
Customer Satisfaction

W e have come full circle, back to the fundamental precepts of the marketing concept, as presented in Chapter 1. This book ends where it began—with a focus on consumers. Today, more than ever before, strategy must be customer-driven if it is to be successful. As Ford chairman Donald Petersen notes: "If we aren't customer-driven, our cars won't be either" (Phillips and Dunkin 1990, p. 90).

Today, more and more firms are seeking competitive advantage through long-term customer satisfaction. It is a strategy based on placing customers first. Consistent with the advisements of marketers in the 1950s, firms today are organizing their entire operations in order to better serve customers. They are listening more attentively to their customers and responding more quickly to changes in their needs. The intent is to work closely with customers rather than taking them for granted. The current popularity of that strategy is best captured by a quote from James Anderson of Northwestern University: "There's almost a craze now of people feeling that close, strong working relationships is the way to do business" (Flint and Heuslein 1989, p. 172). This chapter is about that craze.

Consumer Satisfaction: A Long-Term Strategy

Consumer satisfaction is a long-term strategy. Just as it is difficult to radically alter perceptions of product quality over a short time horizon, so too is it difficult to quickly cultivate a reputation for superior customer service. Consequently, customer satisfaction is a competitive advantage that is sustainable over the long term. That, more than anything, is the reason why customer satisfaction has become so popular among American business in recent years.

CURRENT SPENDING

Building long-term customer satisfaction requires that a firm invest heavily in a wide range of activities meant to please present and future customers. It is an expensive proposition. Towle (1989) reports that marketing programs aimed at building consumer loyalty are not something to be rushed into. The start-up cost for such programs is between $1 million and $5 million. The money is spent on providing better service and building long-term relationships with consumers. A strategy of customer satisfaction requires a commitment of both money and people.

Investments in customer satisfaction add nothing to the immediate "bottom line." They are long-term investments aimed at building customer loyalty; they are present investments made to gain future payoffs.

FUTURE PAYOFF

The payoff from investments in consumer satisfaction comes long after the expenditures themselves are made. As such, long-term consumer satisfaction is a forward-looking indicator of business success. It is a measure of how well consumers *will* respond to the company. Other measures of market performance, such as sales and market share, are backward-looking measures of success. They tell how well the firm has done in the past, not how well it will do in the future.

Paths to Consumer Satisfaction

There are many ways to improve customer satisfaction. What they all have in common is a customer focus and a belief in the basic tenets of the marketing concept. This section examines four common practices: (1) building relationships with customers, (2) superior customer service, (3) unconditional guarantees, and (4) efficient complaint handling.

BUILDING RELATIONSHIPS WITH CUSTOMERS

A strategy of consumer satisfaction often takes the form of building long-term relationships with customers that build repeat business and promote customer loyalty. Relationships with customers are everywhere. Selling season tickets promotes multiple attendance in consumer markets.

Computer tie-ins can do the same with industrial customers. The trend towards building long-term relationships is strong and growing. As Levitt (1983) observes: "More and more of the world's economic work gets done through long-term relationships between buyers and sellers" (p. 114).

Discrete Versus Relationship Transactions

Not all sales situations are identical. Dwyer, Schurr, and Oh (1987) distinguish between discrete and relationship sales transactions. Discrete sales transactions focus on an individual sale, where the relationship between buyers and sellers ends with the sale. Relationship transactions, in contrast, assume a continuation of the sales transaction. The relationship between the buyer and the seller does not end after the sale is over.

There are three key differences between discrete and relationship sales transactions.

First, is the issue of time. Discrete transactions are short-term, one-time actions. Relationship transactions are longer-term sales situations where after-sales support continues.

Second, discrete transactions focus on price and other economic criteria. Building longer-term relationships with the customer tends to shift the focus to noneconomic satisfactions—such as service and strength of the relationship.

Third, in discrete sales situations, the buyer and seller have different goals. The buyer wants a good price; the seller wants a profit. In relationship transactions there is a greater tendency for shared benefits; the seller and the buyer both work towards the same goal. A successful relationship improves the buyer's business as well as the seller's business.

Many marketers have de facto assumed that most sales situations are discrete events. They assume, as Dwyer, Schurr, and Oh humorously note, that most sales transactions are similar to "a one-time purchase of unbranded gasoline out of town at an independent station paid for with cash" (p. 12). In fact, sales situations offer an opportunity to gain competitive advantage by building long-term relationships with customers.

Single Transaction Versus 'Relationship Marketing'

Marketers have the choice of pursuing a strategy based on discrete transactions or long-term relationships. In recent years, much work has been done on improving "relationship marketing" in industrial markets. Jackson (1985) makes a distinction between the two types of marketing practices:

Relationship Marketing—where a firm attempts to build a lasting partnership with its customers; and

Single Transaction Marketing—where a firm focuses on a discrete, individual sale.

Given the new-found interest among firms in consumer satisfaction, it is no surprise that many firms are attempting to build long-term relationships with the customers they serve.

Relationships in Industrial Markets

Most of the work in relationship marketing focuses on industrial markets in which Japanese firms have been consummate practitioners. Consider the case of how firms recently competed to build a telecommunications system in Japan.

It has often been said that the rules of business are different in Japan. They are. The real question is are they also unfair? Neff (1989) reports on Fujitsu, which bid one yen—less than one penny—to design an entire telecommunications system for a Japanese city. Did it bid unfairly? By western standards the costs certainly do not reflect the value of the work proposed. Had the bid been a product, and the country been the United States, Fujitsu would surely have been accused of "dumping" goods on U.S. markets—selling at below costs. But, from the perspective of building a long-term relationship, it is a fair bid and a good strategic move. Japanese firms believe that once they have established the opportunity to build a long-term relationship with the customers they serve, profitable orders will follow for many years. The firm may lose money on the initial design, but make it up on future purchases. As the example illustrates, consumer satisfaction is a long-term strategy that requires initial expenditures in search of long-term profit flows.

In the United States, firms that compete in many industrial markets have been quick to adopt relationship marketing. In May 1989 Monsanto, which sells nylon fibers to firms that make carpets, instituted an "Adopt a Customer for Quality" program. The program has Monsanto technicians visit carpet plants to solve customers' problems and give better service. As one manager noted: "The wave of the future is going to be strong relationships, good products and quick response. When customers become dependent on your expertise, then you begin to build not on problems but on opportunities" (Flint and Heuslein 1989, p. 172). In other words, closer relationships with customers, combined with higher product quality and faster service, can be used to gain competitive advantage.

DuPont's relationship with Reebok helped Reebok recognize new product opportunities. In response to Nike's air-filled midsoles, DuPont suggested that Reebok put plastic tubes in its shoes. The result was Reebok's ERS shoes, which return energy upon compression.

Some firms build relationships with suppliers to better serve customers. Consider the case of the Detroit automakers as told by Treece (1989). Traditionally, American automakers selected the suppliers of parts that went into their automobiles primarily on the basis of price. In contrast, Japanese automakers selected vendors on the basis of long-term relationships. While American automakers viewed the transactions as discrete, Japanese makers pursued relationship marketing. Suppliers and buyers worked together to produce a higher quality product. Their product, in turn, led to higher levels of consumer satisfaction.

Risks of Relationship Marketing

A firm that builds a relationship with its customers usually charges a premium price for the increased service. As a result, the firm is vulnerable to price competition from low-price sellers, who offer less service but charge lower prices. Customers that are not tied into the seller's product may switch large orders to lower-priced competitors leaving the smaller, less profitable orders, which the buyer deems worthy of the premium price, to the high-service firm. The seller who worked so hard to build a relationship with the buyer may find that its efficiency has turned into a disadvantage.

Attempts to build relationships with customers may fail for other reasons as well. First, some customers may not want to build a relationship with a supplier. Those buyers may simply refuse to become dependent on a single supplier. In other cases, buyers may not benefit from a long-term relationship with those who sell them products. There may be no motivation for them to pursue a close relationship. Third, some customers may have a short-term focus, and be unwilling to change that focus. Building relationships with customers is often, but not always, successful. Gross (1989) and Jackson (1985) examine the pitfalls of relationship marketing.

Building relationships with customers is not always the best strategy. In some situations, transaction marketing may be more appropriate. When brand switching is frequent, for example, and there is a propensity to spread sales among many sellers, it is difficult for a firm to benefit from building relationships with customers. In those instances, the marketer must make changes in the buying task, or move to more receptive market segments.

Targeting Relationships

In recent years there has been a clear trend towards targeting opportunities for relationship marketing. It entails two aspects of the problem: (1) identifying situations where relationship marketing is most likely to pay off, and (2) attempting to engineer relationships so that buyers will be less likely to switch business to other sellers.

It is possible to envision a continuum of marketing situations ranging from sales situations where it is easy for the buyer to switch to other sellers to a situation where strong relationships can be engineered.

The importance of time to the buyer is one indicator that relationship marketing is feasible. When time is important, there is an opportunity for long-term relationships. The buyer may be willing to favor one seller when quick service is essential and price is of secondary importance.

The presence of switching costs is also a factor that moves a marketing situation towards long-term relationships. Buyers that incur costs for switching suppliers are less likely to do so. Similarly, markets where buyers fear a disruption in the supply of goods promotes the value of long-term relationships. A buyer that values continuity of service over price is more likely to be receptive to a seller offering a long-term commitment.

The seller can also initiate changes that promote long-term relationships. One approach is to get the buyer to invest in equipment that ties the buyer to the seller. This might entail the installation of a computer-ordering system similar to those used in textiles and presented in the previous chapter on quick response systems. Such purchases raise switching costs and induce commitment from the buyer. Long-term contracts offer another opportunity to tie buyers to a particular supplier.

Buyers often evaluate a seller's product on the basis of price of the product alone, not including service and other components of total costs. Marketers can promote the value of long-term relationships by stressing total versus acquisition costs. A supplier that offers better total service may be able to overcome a slight price disadvantage in the product alone. A package deal that offers the product and service may, in the long run, be less expensive than the product alone.

Relationship marketing usually costs more than discrete transaction marketing, but it usually offers more to the buyer as well. Overall, building relationships with customers can be worthwhile if it is targeted to segments and customers where the interdependency and benefits are likely to pay off.

Recent work by Anderson and Narus (1989) suggests six steps for targeting relationship marketing:

1. segment the market by product application
2. assess the value of the product offering to the customer
3. target segments and firms for relationship or transaction
4. develop relationship or discrete transaction offering
5. evaluate outcome
6. update

By following those steps, the marketer can benefit from relationship marketing in industrial sales situations.

Frequency Marketing

In recent years, marketers of consumer products have also embraced the idea of building relationships. The practice is called frequency marketing. Frequency marketing gives special treatment to heavy or frequent users of a product. It focuses marketing efforts on that 20 percent of the market that, in many markets, routinely consumes 80 percent of the products sold in a particular category.

Frequency marketing depends on two key tasks: (1) identifying the firm's best customers, and (2) finding a way to keep them loyal to the firm's products.

The airline industry was the first to employ frequency marketing on a grand scale. In the cutthroat competition of the early 1980s carriers began to reward frequent fliers with free trips if they used a particular airline. The frequent business traveler was then, and remains, the most coveted airline customer. That customer is less price conscious and generates the bulk of airline profits. To gain the loyalty of this most profitable segment is to gain a competitive advantage in the airline industry. In recent years, other industries have followed the example of the airline industry. Today, marketers in many fields are attempting to build loyalty among their best customers.

Supermarkets have been among the marketers that have adopted frequency marketing. They have instituted numerous programs that reward customers for large purchases. They offer merchandise discounts and other incentives aimed at building consumer loyalty.

To be successful, frequency and relationship marketing must offer something special to valued customers. Short-term gimmicks will be recognized for what they are, and will not generate customer loyalty.

Partnerships are also common in frequency marketing. A hotel may team up with an airline, a rental car company may join with an airline, or two firms in totally unrelated businesses may offer each others' products as incentives to their most valued customers.

SUPERIOR CUSTOMER SERVICE

A strategy of customer satisfaction is nearly synonymous with providing higher levels of service. Firms offering better customer service usually charge higher prices for their products. According to PIMS, they usually benefit from the greater service they offer. High-service firms tend to have greater share gains, and grow at a faster rate than lower-service competitors. They are also more profitable.

Service can even be more important than innovation. Consider the case of United Technologies, whose Pratt and Whitney division makes jet engines. The firm spent $2 billion on a new generation of commercial aircraft engines, which were introduced in 1986. Although the engines were marvels of engineering excellence, there were few customers interested in the new product. GE and Rolls Royce gained share from Pratt and Whitney. The reason was poor service. As Vogel (1989) noted: "Spare parts arrived months late. Engineering advice took forever to obtain. And when customers suggested minor changes in service or design they got such icy retorts as: You don't know what you're talking about" (p. 96).

Until recently, customers seemed to come last at United Technologies. That is, until CEO Robert Daniell made the customer king. Now, decisions are made faster, the number of service representatives has been increased by 70 percent, training has been increased, and the firm has embraced the team concept. As a result, market share increased from 29 percent in 1988 to 40 percent in 1989. At United Technologies, customer satisfaction has resulted in improved financial performance.

Firms often have the choice of selling on the basis of lower price or higher service. In many markets, even those dominated by low-price sellers, there is ample opportunity for the higher service option. Consider the case of W. W. Grainger Inc., a $1.5 billion wholesaler of hardware items. Grainger charges much higher prices than low-price, low-service, do-it-yourself competitors like Builders Square. But, it trades time for price, a valuable commodity for many of the contractors and repairmen it serves.

Grainger offers same-day delivery on all purchases, and the option of three-hour emergency delivery. Almost all pick-up orders are ready in thirty minutes. At one branch, the average customer spends a mere seven minutes in the store. Phone orders are handled with a similar level of service. On a given day only 1.6 percent of callers had to listen to music before speaking to a real person who would take their order, an impressive goal by any measure. But one Grainger manager was not satisfied with even that level of customer service: "The goal is 0%" (Siler 1989). Grainger's goal is to serve customers with speed of service rather than price. As a result, sales have increased by 16 percent and earnings are up 20 percent.

UNCONDITIONAL GUARANTEES

A guarantee presents another opportunity to create customer satisfaction. It reduces the risk of consumer purchase and implies that product quality is high, so high that the consumer will not have to act on the guarantee. The value of a guarantee is often in the image it conveys.

Consider the case of large appliances, a product category where Maytag holds a well-earned reputation for quality. In recent years, competitors such as GE and Whirlpool have embraced extensive guarantee programs as a way to compete against a superior image. The risk of performance for consumers is lowered significantly by the presence of those guarantees. Whirlpool offered customers a one-year, free-replacement guarantee on all of its major appliances. GE offered consumers a 90-day, no-questions-asked return policy.

A guarantee must go hand in hand with product quality. Otherwise, customer satisfaction will be lowered, and the cost to the firm of making good on guarantees will be substantial. A well-designed guarantee produces many benefits for the firm that offers it. A guarantee increases customer loyalty, which leads to repeat purchases. It also creates positive word of mouth, which brings in new customers.

A recent article by Hart (1988) presents the characteristics of a good guarantee. First, a guarantee must be unconditional. It should not be loaded with caveats or conditions that the consumer must meet to collect on the guarantee. Second, a guarantee must be specific. It is not enough to state that service will be fast. It is necessary to state that the customer's muffler will be installed in one hour or less, or the job is free. Domino's Pizza offers a specific guarantee. It promises delivery in thirty minutes or the pie is discounted by $3. Likewise, Federal Express promises delivery by 10:30 A.M. the next day, not sometime the next morning.

A guarantee that offers too much may seem unreal, and smack of gimmickry. Before the advent of the ball point pen, for example, many fountain pen manufacturers offered lifetime guarantees. Waterman even introduced the one-hundred-year guarantee for pens it produced in the 1940s. The length of the guarantees brought government requests to moderate the promotions. A gimmick will be recognized for what it is—an attempt to promote products rather than truly satisfy consumers.

Third, a guarantee must be stated in simple and understandable language, not the language of lawyers. It must clearly state the terms of the offer. Finally, a guarantee must be easy to collect on. It must not require that consumers obtain advance clearances, send the product insured to distant places, or retain extensive documentation. Imagine invoking the guarantee on the one-hundred-year pen, only to be told that proof of purchase was necessary.

One of the fears firms have with liberal, unconditional guarantees is that fraud will be pervasive. Consumers will take advantage of the return policy. Most consumers have heard stories of a friend, relative, or neighbor who obtained a refund unfairly. That consumer may have returned a dress that was worn to a party, or a gift that was bought from a different merchant. Such ripoffs are inevitable. But, fortunately for the firms, they are also rare. The vast majority of consumers who invoke guarantees do so only when they are truly dissatisfied with the product. More important, the goodwill and positive word of mouth that is created by the guarantee usually far outweigh the small number of inevitable ripoffs.

Guarantees have other benefits as well. Since shoddy products will be returned for refunds, guarantees make the firm concentrate on product quality. Guarantees can have the effect of promoting an emphasis on customer satisfaction. Refunds and complaints are indicative of how well the firm is doing.

EFFICIENT COMPLAINT HANDLING

Complaint handling offers an opportunity to turn a dissatisfied customer quickly back into a satisfied patron of the firm's products. Recently, firms have begun to focus on improvement in handling consumer complaints. Four aspects of complaint handling are most important: (1) empathy with irate customers, (2) the speed with which the complaint is handled, (3) the equity or fairness with which it is resolved, and (4) the ease with which the consumer can contact the firm.

Empathy with Consumers

Empathy with irate customers is of the utmost importance. If, for example, consumers are angry because a plane was delayed because of bad weather it is not enough to simply state the facts—that bad weather is beyond the company's control. That will only make the customer more angry. Instead, the firm must put itself in the customer's situation. Contrast the response of Pan Am and British Airways. A Pan Am flight delayed by bad weather made customers angry, and Pan Am compounded the problem by giving complaining consumers the wrong information on who to complain to. Eventually, however, it told the dissatisfied consumers that it was not Pan Am's fault: it is not responsible for the weather. The passengers spread the word about the poor service.

British Airways responded differently when a mechanical problem grounded its Concorde. Angry customers were given a full refund, a letter of apology, and planes were chartered specifically to fly them to their destinations. As one executive noted: "We'd rather spend money and keep customers satisfied than initiate five or six complaints" (Sellers 1988, p. 92). British Airways, a firm that exemplifies good customer service, made an investment in long-term customer satisfaction.

Management can gain empathy with consumers by spending more time listening to customer complaints. Xerox, for example, requires that its managers spend at least one day a month listening to customer complaints.

Speed of Response

Speed is a crucial part of complaint handling. If a consumer's complaint is not answered quickly that consumer may become permanently and unchangeably dissatisfied with the sponsor. A complaint that is handled quickly has a better chance of restoring the customer to a state of satisfaction.

Equity of Response

A firm can respond to a consumer's complaint in three ways: it can (1) ignore, (2) overcompensate, or (3) fairly compensate the dissatisfied consumer. Those responses balance current costs and long-term perfor-

Exhibit 14.1   *Equity in Consumer Complaint Handling*

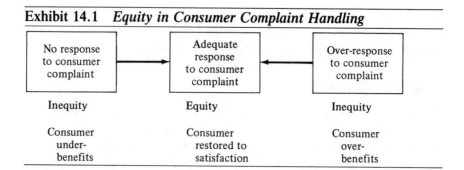

mance in different ways. The firm can either minimize current costs or maximize long-term performance.

Gilly and Hansen (1985) frame those responses in terms of Equity Theory. Exhibit 14.1 illustrates the equity of the three approaches to handling complaints.

First, the firm can ignore the complaint, the worst possible choice, but often a common response. Ignoring the complaint compounds the problem. It infuriates customers, and risks losing that customer and generating negative word of mouth. In terms of Equity Theory, the consumer "underbenefits" from such a response. Ignoring consumer complaints keeps costs low but risks long-term loss of customers.

Second, a firm can respond to complaints by providing overgenerous reimbursements—double your money back, for example. In such instances the consumer "overbenefits" from the complaint. It, too, is a poor choice. It burdens the customer with the feeling of ill-gotten gains. Like receiving no response at all from the firm, receiving an overgenerous response is inequitable. It is also expensive for the sponsoring firm. It flaunts costs.

The best response to consumer complaints is to restore consumers to the same level of satisfaction that they had before the purchase. That response balances long-term profits and current costs. It is the most equitable response. A quick response, with a full-price refund, is most likely to restore the consumer to a state of satisfaction with the firm's products.

Ease in Contacting the Firm

In recent years, many firms have installed 800 numbers, which allow consumers to contact a company with comments, questions, and complaints. Those lines are expensive, but they are widely used by consumers. They create good-will over the long term.

A firm that promotes communication with customers lies in stark contrast to the firm that has no distinct department or procedures for listening to consumer complaints. One of the quickest ways to build consumer dissatisfaction is to pass a consumer from one person to another in the organization until he gives up and shops elsewhere. Often, just the act of complaining can create dissatisfaction. Thus, making it easy to complain is an essential feature of efficient complaint handling.

Consumer Satisfaction and Orientations Toward Markets

A focus on customer satisfaction is motivated by an orientation toward both consumers and competitors.

CONSUMER ORIENTATION

According to the marketing concept, consumers stand at the center of any organization. The firm must orient all of its activities so that it can satisfy the customers for its products and services. More than any other topic covered in this book, the emphasis on customer satisfaction is driven by the marketing concept. It is a strategy driven by consumers. Customer satisfaction, and the marketing concept, both hold that consumers are the end all and be all of a business.

COMPETITOR ORIENTATION

Competition also plays an important role in customer satisfaction. The sheer choice of products available in most markets means that firms must keep customers happy in order to remain competitive. Many firms are being forced to pay more attention to customers. To do otherwise is to be put at a competitive disadvantage.

Consider, once again, the experience of sellers of large home appliances. In recent years, manufacturers have begun to offer guarantees on their products. Other firms have been forced to follow. Not to do so would place them at a severe competitive disadvantage. The level of consumer satisfaction in that industry is increasing. Competition is forcing sellers of large appliances to increase their service and commitment to customers.

Risks of Customer Dissatisfaction

Customer satisfaction provides benefits to both consumers and the firm. Making consumers angry and dissatisfied creates horrendous problems.

Long-Term Customer Loss

The damage done by dissatisfied customers is severe and oftentimes irreparable. Clearly, dissatisfied customers are likely to take their business elsewhere. The permanence of that loss, however, is where the real problem lies. The key lesson of creating satisfied customers is that, while it is easy to lose customers, it is difficult to woo them back after a bad experience.

In the 1960s Frederick Herzberg proposed two factors to explain job satisfaction—hygiene factors and motivators. Hygiene factors are aspects of the work environment—such as working conditions, job status, and compensation—that produce dissatisfied workers if they are deficient. But, they do not motivate employees. Instead, Herzberg proposed "motivators," which are factors based on human relations.

Gelb (1987) argues that an analogous situation exists in marketing. Consumer satisfaction is akin to Herzberg's hygiene factors. If the peripheral aspects of the product—what Levitt calls the augmented product are missing or deficient—consumer dissatisfaction results. Poor service, the absence of guarantees, and other deficiencies quickly and lastingly create dissatisfied customers. The presence of those factors, in contrast, promotes continued patronage of the firm's products. In short, the presence of product intangibles promotes a continued relationship, while their absence hurts the firm badly.

Clearly, consumer satisfaction is most important when repeat purchase is an important part of the business. It is less important in those rare situations where a steady stream of new customers makes loyalty less important. Some consumer electronics retailers in New York City, for example, prey on tourists and commuters. They are frequently accused of "bait-and-switch" practices. Their goal is not to satisfy consumers over the long-term, but to make a continuous series of discrete purchases.

Negative 'Word of Mouth'

The power of opinion leadership is well known. Negative 'word of mouth' can be as devastating as positive word of mouth can be beneficial.

A dissatisfied consumer can spread dissatisfaction. That consumer can infect others with a strong predisposition towards dissatisfaction with a firm's products even though those consumers have no direct experience with the firm. In fact, Sellers (1988) contends that dissatisfied consumers are more likely to tell others about their bad experiences than satisfied consumers are likely to relate their experiences. Like a virus, bad experiences can spread quickly and widely through a population of consumers. No wonder that Jagdish Sheth, a noted marketing scholar, has referred to dissatisfied consumers as terrorists. It is an appropriate analogy. Such consumers can wreck havoc on a firm's products and its reputation. If for no other reason, firms must engage in customer satisfaction to avoid negative word of mouth.

Consumer Satisfaction and Competitive Advantage

A strategy of long-term consumer satisfaction blends together many of the concepts previously examined in this book. This section looks at how customer satisfaction leads to competitive advantage in the marketplace.

DIFFERENTIATION

Many firms are using superior consumer satisfaction to differentiate their products and services. They rely on superior service, unconditional guarantees, more efficient complaint handling, and many other consumer-based practices to set themselves apart from the crowd of competitors. As an executive of Whirlpool noted in regard to the firm's offer of a money-back guarantee to consumers of its large appliances, a product category where many products are physically similar: "The key to our offer is to differentiate the Whirlpool brand from the competition" (Stern 1987, p. 104).

Superior consumer satisfaction also avoids price competition. Foreign competitors often have lower cost structures and sell at lower prices than American sellers. Consequently, many American firms have been moving to the premium segment of many markets. While low-cost producers sell on the basis of price, firms that pursue a strategy of consumer satisfaction charge higher prices for superior service. They differentiate their product by offering better value. There is a widespread belief that firms with a reputation for superior customer satisfaction can charge a significant price premium.

Building long-term relationships with customers can also serve as a point of differentiation. It is especially important when most products are physically similar, and it is difficult to differentiate the product itself. When products are similar, social bonds often decide consumer brand choice.

PRODUCT QUALITY

There is a great deal of overlap between product quality and long-term consumer satisfaction. The two strategies often lead to the same goal. Improving consumer satisfaction many times entails raising product quality. Likewise, increasing product quality often results in superior levels of consumer satisfaction. The concepts are similar but not interchangeable.

SPEED

Speed also plays an important role in consumer satisfaction. Firms that are customer-focused deliver faster, rush new products to market, and respond quickly to changing consumer needs. Increasing the speed of an organization's reaction is often the way to improve customer satisfaction.

Rapid response is especially important when a firm is responding to consumer complaints. Flint and Heuslein (1989) argue that it is important to identify a customer's problem immediately, before the customer gets mad and takes the business elsewhere.

Computer linkups tie customers to a single supplier. The benefits of speeding orders from customer to supplier was covered in depth in the previous chapter. But computer linkage between buyers and sellers serves another purpose as well. It satisfies customers and, as well, induces switching costs. Furthermore, American firms are ahead in this area, whereas Japanese competitors lag behind.

UNIFIED CORPORATE PURPOSE

Long-term consumer satisfaction provides a unified purpose for the firm. It inculcates employees with a clear mission—that consumers, and the services and support they require, are the central focus of the firm's activities. It forces employees to focus on the firm's customers.

It also recognizes that workers on the line or in the field best understand the reasons for consumer satisfaction. In a marketing situation, it is the salespersons that have the greatest contact with customers.

Some firms have built an enviable reputation for superior consumer satisfaction. Disney is a company noted for its emphasis on customer service. In fact, its stated mission is "to make people happy." That, of course, is why customers flock to Disney theme parks. A family that travels a long distance to visit a Disney park and returns home dissatisfied would wreck havoc on Disney's product. Disney is aware of that potential outcome and trains its employees heavily so that it is an unlikely outcome. Disney's corporate culture strives to keep employees happy, requires them to smile to theme park visitors, and conveys the Disney image. The firm's reputation for superior consumer satisfaction is so well known that it offers courses for other firms at Disney U (McGill 1989).

DISADVANTAGE OF HEAVY DEBT

It is difficult for a firm burdened with heavy debt to concentrate on satisfying its customers. Usually that firm must focus its attention on servicing debt rather than customers. Debt leaves little money for programs that satisfy long-term goals. Immediate payments take precedence over distant goals like consumer satisfaction. Firms in that unfortunate position end up serving banks rather than their consumers. Often, financial strategies force a focus away from customers of the firm's products. Rarely is there mention of customer satisfaction, and how it will be impacted, by leveraged buyouts and debt-laden takeovers.

Theories of Consumer Satisfaction

Most of the marketing effort on consumer satisfaction has focused on how individual consumers become satisfied with products and services. It is a psychological rather than a strategic perspective of satisfaction.

Many theoretical frameworks have been applied to explain customer satisfaction. The most prominent paradigm is the "expectancy disconfirmation paradigm" from social psychology. That paradigm holds that consumers form expectations of products or services prior to their purchase. Those expectations are then either confirmed or disconfirmed after the product or service is purchased and used.

FOUR CONSTRUCTS

Four constructs are central to the model of consumer confirmation and disconfirmation. Those constructs are related as shown in Exhibit 14.2.

Expectations

Expectations are formed prior to purchase. They are anticipations about how brands or products will perform. Consumers may expect products to be easy to use, reliable, stylish, inexpensive, indicative of good taste to their friends and neighbors, or laden with features. Consumers form expectations from previous experience with similar products, word-of-mouth communications with friends, relatives and neighbors, and marketing efforts. Marketing efforts can make claims that overstate, understate, or realistically portray the product's benefits.

As Exhibit 14.2 illustrates, expectations influence perceptions of product performance. Two explanations have been offered based on two prominant theories: (1) consistency theory and (2) assimilation contrast. Consistency theory implies that expectations are more important than

Exhibit 14.2   *Factors Affecting Consumer Satisfaction*

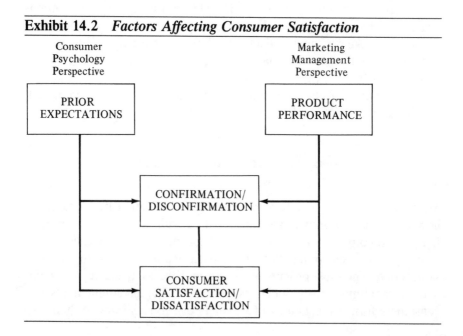

actual product performance. It predicts that consumers will avoid inconsistencies in their beliefs at all cost, and will bend their perceptions of product performance to match their prior expectations for that product. Consumers with high expectations for a product will be more satisfied with a product than consumers with low expectations (Olshavsky and Miller 1972). It is, in essence, an argument for marketers to overstate the claims they make for their products. Doing so will result in higher expectations and higher levels of customer satisfaction.

Consider, for example, product evaluations of automobiles. Consistency theory predicts that consumers with low expectations for American-made cars will, in fact, judge those cars to be of low quality, even if actual product quality has been improved. Likewise, high expectations for Japanese cars will result in judgments of higher quality, even if the products' actual performance is less than expected. Consistency theory argues that consumers will maintain psychological consistency at all costs. Their expectations will color their judgments of product performance, and their ultimate satisfaction with the product.

Assimilation contrast theory argues otherwise. It contends that if expectations are set unrealistically high, and actual performance falls short, consumers will experience a contrast effect with their prior expectations. Consumers will end up perceiving the product as worse than it actually is. If, on the other hand, the original claim sets up an expectation that stretches the truth just a little, consumers will assimilate the difference and perceive the product to be better than it actually is. Involvement with the product category determines their latitude of their acceptance. High involvement leads to a narrower latitude of acceptance and a greater likelihood of a contrast effect.

Consider, again, consumers' evaluations of automobiles. Assimilation contrast predicts that if consumer expectations are set unrealistically high, and the product performed poorly, consumers will contrast the difference between the product's performance and their prior expectations. They would judge the product's performance to be especially poor, and be dissatisfied with their purchase.

Which theory is right? Over the years, studies into the relative importance of prior expectations, product performance, and confirmation/disconfirmation on customer satisfaction have produced different results. Some studies have found that prior expectations are more important than actual product performance, while others have found product performance to be more important. Still others have found that both constructs are important. It seems that both theories offer a partial, but incomplete, explanation of how expectations influence customer satisfaction.

Product Performance

The second component of customer satisfaction looks at actual product performance, i.e., how well a product works. Performance is more strategic, and less psychological, in its outlook than expectations. Unlike expectations, product performance is something that can be engineered into the product. When measured objectively, some products simply offer higher levels of performance than others. That is, independent of expectations, products offer consumers different levels of performance. It is a more tangible and a more controllable component of customer satisfaction than expectation, although performance can also possess a strong perceived dimension—such as in the notion of perceived product quality.

Actual product performance is a key component in building customer satisfaction. Churchill and Surprenant (1982) found that for a major new technological product, actual product performance directly affected perceptions of satisfaction. Higher product quality led to higher consumer satisfaction. Most important, this study found that the actual performance of the product was a more important predictor of customer satisfaction than the other psychological constructs. Clearly, and more recently, actual product performance has proved to be an especially important component of customer satisfaction. Improvements in actual product quality may constitute better strategy than attempts to manipulate expectations.

Confirmation/Disconfirmation

The third construct in theoretical examinations of consumer satisfaction results from a comparison of prior expectations and actual product performance. That comparison constitutes the central concept in satisfaction theory. Consumer expectations are either confirmed or disconfirmed when compared with actual product performance. Three outcomes are possible, two of which are disconfirmations of prior expectations and one of which is a confirmation.

Confirmation of Expectations

First, the product can perform as expected—expectations are confirmed. What consumers thought the product would do, it did do. A product that is expected to perform well does; a product that is expected to perform poorly does that too.

Positive Disconfirmation

Second, the product may work better than expected—a pleasant disconfirmation of prior expectations. Expectations may have been too low or product performance exceptionally high.

Negative Disconfirmation

Finally, and least fortunate for the seller, the product may turn out to perform worse than expected. Expectations may have been set too high, or product performance may have been allowed to deteriorate.

Just as prior expectations and actual product performance directly affect customer satisfaction, so to do they affect confirmation/disconfirmation. Negative disconfirmation leads to lower customer satisfaction.

Consumer Satisfaction/Dissatisfaction

The final construct in the theory of customer satisfaction is customer satisfaction, or dissatisfaction, itself. Exhibit 14.3 shows how the relationship between confirmation/disconfirmation and satisfaction/dissatisfaction. There are two paths to consumer satisfaction and one path to dissatisfaction.

According to the theory, a product that meets or exceeds expectations produces a satisfied customer. The product that meets expectations produces a confirmation of prior expectations, which results in customer satisfaction. Likewise, a product that exceeds expectations produces satisfaction, but disconfirms prior expectations. A product that performs worse than expected produces consumer dissatisfaction. It disconfirms prior expectations.

The most recent studies have found that expectations, disconfirmation,

Exhibit 14.3 *Confirmation of Expectations and Satisfaction*

	Confirmation	Disconfirmation
Satisfaction	1 product meets expectations	2 product exceeds expectations
Dissatisfaction	3	4 product falls below expectations

and product performance all combine to influence customer satisfaction (Oliver and DeSarbo 1988).

SATISFACTION-BUILDING STRATEGIES

Three strategies arise from the theoretical framework presented above.

Increase Expectations

One possibility is to overstate claims for a product in the hope that increased expectations lead to greater judgments of product performance. It is the argument made by proponents of consistency theory. Consumers that expect products to perform better often conclude that those products do perform better, independent of actual product performance. Social psychologists argue that consumers have a need for consistency—their perceptions of how well a product performs must be made consistent with their prior expectations regarding that product.

It is, however, a dangerous strategy. It implies that poor product performance can be overcome by favorable expectation. It stresses the psychological aspects of the process rather than the effect of actual product quality.

Overstated product claims are likely to fail in the long-run, no matter what the theoretical constructs suggest. A strategy based on raising expectations in the absence of real improvements of product quality is a strategy in search of disaster. The quality advantage of many imports is real and successful, as well as expected. Imports have produced satisfied customers by focusing on superior product performance, not superior expectations. As a result, calls for a strategy of inflated product claims appear dated. Today, customer satisfaction is more likely to embrace improvements in actual product performance rather than expectations.

Minimize Negative Disconfirmation

Another strategy that arises from a review of the customer satisfaction literature is to focus on confirmation of expectations. That strategy seeks to minimize the extent to which consumers will experience the psychological state of negative disconfirmation. That strategy accounts for the importance of the quality of product performance in the disconfirmation process. But, it too places most of its emphasis on the disconfirmation process rather than real product quality improvements.

Increase Product Performance

The best strategic choice is to improve customer satisfaction by focusing directly on improving product performance. It is a product quality perspective, which argues that superior product performance can overcome abstract psychological tendencies.

Trends in Consumer Satisfaction

The trend in creating customer satisfaction is clearly towards the managerial perspective, and away from the psychological. Past research has stressed the psychological perspective and downplayed the importance of actual product quality. As Churchill and Surprenant (1982) note: "Most satisfaction research has ignored variations in product performance except as it affects disconfirmation. The major variables of interest have been expectations and disconfirmation" (p. 503). As a result, marketers focused their attention on the wrong variables. While they manipulated expectations, and tried to minimize disconfirmation, others made better products, which better satisfied consumers.

The trend in customer satisfaction is akin to the trends sweeping other areas of marketing. As marketers move from the more micro, psychological perspective of consumer satisfaction to the more macro, strategic view of product performance and product quality, they take a different view of consumers. Consumers are still the key focus of marketers. But today it is a more strategic view of customer satisfaction that dominates. That trend can be expected to continue.

References

Anderson, James, and James Narus. "Value-Based Segmentation, Targeting, and Relationship Building in Business Markets." *ISBM Report 12–1989*, Penn State University, College of Business Administration.

Churchill, Gilbert, and Carol Surprenant. "An Investigation into the Determinants of Customer Satisfaction." *Journal of Marketing Research*, November–December 1982, pp. 491–504.

Dwyer, F. Robert, Paul Schurr, and Sejo Oh. "Developing Buyer-Seller Relationships." *Journal of Marketing*, April 1987, pp. 11–27.

Flint, Jerry, and William Heuslein. "An Urge to Service." *Forbes*, September 18, 1989, pp. 172, 176.

Gelb, Betsy. "How Marketers of Intangibles Can Raise the Odds for Consumer Satisfaction." *Journal of Services Marketing,* Summer 1987, pp. 11–17.

Gilly, Mary, and Richard Hansen. "Consumer Complaint Handling as a Strategic Marketing Tool." *Journal of Consumer Marketing,* Fall 1985, pp. 5–16.

Gross, Irwin. "Partnering: Games Businesses Play." *Marketplace: ISBM Review,* Spring 1989, pp. 1–4.

Hart, Christopher. "The Power of Unconditional Service Guarantees." *Harvard Business Review,* July–August 1988, pp. 54–62.

Jackson, Barbara Bund. *Winning and Keeping Industrial Customers.* Lexington, MA: Lexington Books, 1985.

Levitt, Theodore. "Relationship Management." In *The Marketing Imagination,* pp. 111–126. New York: Free Press, 1983.

McGill, Douglas. "A Mickey Mouse Class—For Real." *New York Times,* August 27, 1989, Section 3, p. 4.

Neff, Robert. "And Now Another Form of Japanese Hardball: Lowball Pricing." *Business Week,* November 20, 1989, p. 50.

Oliver, Richard, and Wayne DeSarbo. "Response Determinants in Satisfaction Judgments." *Journal of Consumer Research,* March 1988, pp. 495–507.

Olshavsky, Richard, and John Miller. "Consumer Expectations, Product Performance, and Perceived Product Quality." *Journal of Marketing Research,* February 1972, pp. 19–21.

Phillips, Stephen, and Amy Dunkin. "King Customer." *Business Week,* March 12, 1990, p. 88–94.

Sellers, Patricia. "How to Handle Customers' Gripes." *Fortune,* October 24, 1988, pp. 88–100.

Siler, Charles. "The Goal is 0%." *Forbes,* October 30, 1989, pp. 95, 98.

Stern, Sara. "Guarantees at a Fever Pitch." *Advertising Age,* October 26, 1987, pp. 3, 104.

Towle, Lisa. "A Race to Woo the Most Loyal Customers." *New York Times,* December 3, 1989, p. F13.

Treece, James. "Shaping Up Detroit." *Business Week,* August 14, 1989, pp. 74–80.

Vogel, Todd. "Where 1990s-Style Management is Already Hard at Work." *Business Week,* October 23, 1989, pp. 92–100.

Author Index

Subject Index